The United States and the Great Powers

To Ole Wæver

The United States and the Great Powers

World Politics in the
Twenty-First Century

Barry Buzan

polity

First published in 2004 by Polity Press Ltd.

Polity Press
65 Bridge Street
Cambridge CB2 1UR, UK

Polity Press
350 Main Street
Malden, MA 02148, USA

ISBN: 0-7456 3374-9
ISBN: 0-7456 3375-7 (pb)

A catalogue record for this book is available from the British Library and has been applied for from the Library of Congress.

Typeset in 10 on 12 pt Times
by Graphicraft Limited, Hong Kong
Printed and bound in Great Britain by MPG Books, Bodmin Cornwall

For further information on Polity, visit our website: www.polity.co.uk

Contents

Foreword

This book grew out of my work with Ole Wæver on the book that became *Regions and Powers* – the last of our Copenhagen school projects to be undertaken under the auspices of COPRI before it was summarily closed by the Danish government at the end of 2002. Earlier versions of chapters 3 to 5 were originally part of that book, but got taken out when it became too long. The two books can in some ways be seen as complementary treatments – this one focusing on the global political structure, *Regions and Powers* concentrating on the regional level – though in this volume I have departed somewhat from the joint framework of the co-authored work. In bidding for an ESRC grant I undertook to look at the concepts of polarity and world society, and to apply these to thinking about the US. While this book started as the former project, the three strands quickly became entangled. My interest in polarity is longstanding. It was the idea that first inspired me to take a big interest in international relations (IR) as far back as 1965, when I first encountered it as a second-year undergraduate student in Kal Holsti's Introduction to International Relations course. I have followed it through my engagements with neo-realism and strategic studies and, while I have moved on from there, I still find it interesting and challenging, though it has been a long time, if ever, since I was convinced that polarity could provide some sort of master variable for understanding world politics. An early version of part II can be found in Buzan (2004b). The interest in identity comes partly out of my work with Ole Wæver on security, partly out of my work on English school theory, particularly the concept of world society, and partly from engagement with Alex Wendt's ideas in trying to reformulate English school theory (see Buzan 2004a). In one sense, this book is written as a kind of counterpoint to the US debate about grand strategy. It runs parallel to it at many points, but it uses polarity theory to build a top-down system-level perspective rather than one looking out from the US, formulates polarity in a somewhat different way, and does not take polarity to be the determining factor.

I make no apology for combining material and social theory. My stance is one of basic theoretical pluralism. I am not wedded to any one approach as containing 'the truth', and I am attracted by any approach that seems to offer disciplined and systematic insight into how the international system works. I see no reason why one cannot examine the interplay of different approaches in a disciplined manner.

I am grateful to the following for comments on earlier drafts: Chris Browning, Mick Cox, Thomas Diez, Stefano Guzzini, Lene Hansen, Pertti Joenniemi, Anna Leander, Richard Little, Noel Parker, Vibeke Pedersen, Gearoid O Tuathail, Ole Wæver, Jaap de Wilde and two anonymous referees for Polity. I am also grateful to Rashmi Singh, who provided me with invaluable and efficient research assistance. Particular thanks to Ole Wæver, who, in the course of our work on *Regions and Powers*, made several substantial contributions to the argument. I am grateful to the ESRC for funding this work (Award no. R000239415-A), and to both the Centre for the Study of Democracy at the University of Westminster and the Department of International Relations at the LSE for allowing me the time off to complete it.

I dedicate this book to Ole Wæver, both for his friendship over the years, and for all that he has taught me during our many collaborations. It was he who first invited me to join COPRI, thereby opening an extremely fruitful and pleasurable encounter that lasted for fifteen years and generated the Copenhagen school along the way. His influence on my thinking has been huge, and collaboration with him and other colleagues at COPRI has enabled me to make contact across generations, cultures and epistemologies in ways that would otherwise have been much more difficult to achieve.

Barry Buzan
London, February 2004

Abbreviations

ABM	anti-ballistic missile
AIDS	Acquired Immune Deficiency Syndrome
APEC	Asia-Pacific Economic Cooperation
ARF	ASEAN Regional Forum
ASEAN	Association of Southeast Asian Nations
ASEAN + 3	ASEAN plus China, Japan and South Korea
BWC	Biological Weapons Convention
CFSP	common foreign and security policy (for the EU)
CIS	Commonwealth of Independent States
COPRI	Copenhagen Peace Research Institute
CTBT	Comprehensive Test-Ban Treaty
CWC	Chemical Weapons Convention
EC	European Community
ESRC	Economic and Social Research Council (UK)
EU	European Union
G8	Group (of) Eight (USA, Canada, UK, France, Italy, Germany, Russia, Japan)
GATT	General Agreement on Tariffs and Trade
GDP	gross domestic product
GNP	gross national product
HST	hegemonic stability theory
ICC	International Criminal Court
ICJ	International Court of Justice
IGO	intergovernmental organization
IMF	International Monetary Fund
INGO	international non-governmental organization
IPE	international political economy

IR	international relations (as a subject discipline)
JSDF	Japan Self-Defence Force
NAFTA	North American Free Trade Association
NATO	North Atlantic Treaty Organization
NMD	national missile defence (US)
NPT	Nonproliferation Treaty
OAS	Organization of American States
RSC	regional security complex
SADC	Southern African Development Community
TNA	transnational actor
UN	United Nations
UNESCO	United Nations Educational Scientific and Cultural Organization
UNSC	United Nations Security Council
US	United States
USSR	Union of Soviet Socialist Republics
WMD	weapons of mass destruction
WTO	World Trade Organization

1

Introduction

1.1 Identity and polarity

To understand the subject of this book ask yourself: what would world politics have been like between 1945 and 1989 if the US and the Soviet Union had both been democracies? What difference would it have made if the two superpowers that emerged to dominate international relations after the Second World War had shared a liberal ideology rather than being at opposite ends of the political spectrum? If you think there would have been little difference, then you accept the logic that the distribution of power – in that case bipolarity – is the overriding determinant of how great powers relate to each other. You assume that *any* two great powers facing each other in the international arena will necessarily fall into rivalry and seek at least to balance, and perhaps to destroy, the power of the other. You will discount the arguments of believers in democratic peace theory that liberal democracies relate to each other in a less security-driven way, and that condominium might have been an alternative outcome to rivalry. You will also have to reject much of Huntington's (1996) argument about the clash of civilizations, the logic of which rests on differences of identity much more than on the distribution of power. If, on the other hand, you think that a bipolar world composed of two liberal democracies would have generated a very different history from that of the Cold War, then you accept that identity matters, and that by itself the distribution of power cannot predict how the major states in the international system will relate to each other. The first view offers a compellingly simple way of understanding world politics, but only at the price of the heroic assumption that identity doesn't matter. The second view is inevitably more complicated because it introduces another set of factors into what one needs to know in order to think coherently about world politics. Some of the flavour of this complexity can be exposed by asking yourself what the 1945–89 history would have been like if both superpowers had been communist ruled? Given the actual record of rivalry among communist states during the Cold War it is not unreasonable to speculate that, in such a case, ideological closeness of that particular kind might have produced an outcome not all that dissimilar from the Cold War. Indeed, taking into account the narcissism of small differences, an inter-communist rivalry might well have been worse than that between the champions of communism and capitalism. If identity makes a difference, it does so in ways that depend heavily on the particular characteristics of the identities in play, and not just whether they are similar or different. The aim of this book is to explore what a combination of polarity and identity can tell us about the structure and character both of the world politics we have been in since the ending of the Cold War, and of the world politics that lie ahead post-September 11.

The question of how polarity and identity play into each other matters for two reasons, one broad, one narrow. The broad reason is that the idea of polarity has been, and continues to be, enormously influential in the media and public policy discussions about world politics. During the Cold War, bipolarity framed the entire understanding of what was going on. Because there was nearly complete harmony between the polarity assumption that two superpowers must be rivals, and because of the ideological clash between totalitarian communism and democratic capitalism, the identity issue got largely absorbed into the debates about the distribution of power, only re-emerging when the Soviet Union began to abandon its ideological position. Bipolarity defined Africa, Asia and Latin America as the third world, and supported a logic of balancing that legitimized not only huge accumulations of weaponry, but also many interventions, some large and deeply destructive to the societies concerned. With the ending of the Cold War a period of confusion developed in which there were competing claims about whether the world was (or was shortly going to be) multipolar or unipolar. There was also a strong challenge to the whole idea of polarity in the rhetoric of globalization, which put forward a quite different, much less state-based, way of understanding the general structure of world politics. But by the late 1990s, and particularly after the events of 11 September 2001, the idea that world politics was unipolar had achieved dominance in the public debates. The narrow reason why the question of polarity and identity matters is that polarity theory is a lively and influential force in academic theories about how to understand the operation of the international system. So although it is contested, polarity plays a big role in how large numbers of people, both expert and lay, understand the world in which they live. Since in the social world how we understand things conditions how we behave, the prominence of polarity as a concept is itself part of the political reality it purports to explain. And since polarity is important because it is believed, it is vital to make explicit the limits to the understanding of identity that are built into polarity theory.

In this book I do four things:

- I set out the idea of identity, survey the problems of using this idea to think about world politics, and look specifically at how identity and polarity interact with each other. This is the subject of chapter 2 and the conclusions to part I;
- I investigate the concept of polarity and the theory attached to it in their own right, identify some core problems with the basic ideas, and propose solutions to them. This is the subject of chapters 3 to 5;
- combining these two approaches, I develop three scenarios for thinking about the future of world politics in terms of the most likely combinations of polarity and identity. This is the subject of part II;
- finally, I offer some reflections on the policy opportunities and constraints that affect how both the US and the other great powers can affect which of the scenarios becomes dominant.

The book is thus a conscious attempt to combine material and social approaches to understanding world politics. Polarity is a materialist concept. It assumes that the distribution of capabilities largely determines what the behaviour of the actors in the system will be. Identity is a constructivist concept. It assumes that who the actors think they are, and how they construct their identities in relation to each other, shapes behaviour independently from the distribution of capabilities. In a materialist view, the basic relational dynamics of the world never change: power politics is always the game, and the only key variable is the distribution of capabilities. In a social view, a whole spectrum of games is possible, ranging from conflictual power politics on one end, through coexistence and cooperation in the middle, to convergence and confederation on the other end. My approach will be to locate polarity within a social context. I take as given that there is a society of states which has its own rules, norms and institutions (Buzan 2004a). The character of this society is itself open to change as some institutions die out (e.g. colonialism), others rise to prominence (e.g. nationalism during the nineteenth century, the market and multilateralism during the nineteenth and twentieth centuries) and yet others remain in place but get reinterpreted in ways that alter the practices that they legitimate (e.g. sovereignty and non-intervention, war and balance of power during the second half of the twentieth century). The society of states is the container within which the distribution of capabilities and the logic of power politics operate. Sometimes the social structure will line up with, and reinforce, the logic of power politics, as was the case during the Cold War. Sometimes the social structure will undercut the logic of power politics, as might have been the case if both the Soviet Union and the US had been liberal democracies after the Second World War, and as many thought was the case in the decade after the end of the Cold War.

A discussion of this sort inevitably hinges to a considerable extent on definitions. I will have more to say on definitions in subsequent chapters, but let me set down some general markers now. Under the influence of Waltz (1979) the usage of polarity has become more disciplined. Polarity refers to the number of great powers in the international system. It does not mean the coalition structure among the powers, which is (somewhat confusingly) called *polarization*. Thus a multipolar system like that in 1914, which had as many as nine great powers, was bipolarized because most of the powers were members of either the Triple Alliance or the Triple Entente. Polarization may or may not follow the pattern of polarity, but in this book I intend to observe the distinction between these two concepts. Identity has many facets, and I will explore these briefly in chapter 2. Because this is a book about international relations generally, and relations among great powers in particular, my main focus is on how identity, and the interplay between Self and Other, works for collective actors (mostly, but not only, states). I concentrate specifically on political identity, particularly the ideologies that political actors use to constitute themselves, legitimate their political structures and processes, and differentiate themselves from each other.

1.2 Outline of the book

The four chapters in part I set out the ideas of identity and polarity on which this way of understanding world politics rests. Chapter 2 focuses on the question of collective identity in international relations as a way of understanding how the major powers relate to each other. The inherently relational quality of the linkage between Self and Other means that identity is an inescapable part of whether the major powers interact as enemies, rivals or friends. Indeed, the status of great power is itself an element of identity which shapes how certain states see themselves. The particular character of specific collective ideological identities also matters, with some forms and combinations particularly likely to generate conflict, and others more open to possibilities of coexistence or friendship. The problems of (in)stability in identity are investigated and found to be neither more nor less difficult than those associated with changes in material power. I adopt a Wendtian scheme of enemies, rivals and friends for looking at the social structure of interstate society as composed by the major powers, and link this into neorealist, liberal and English school models for understanding interstate society. The conclusion is that polarity structures can only be understood and interpreted on the basis of knowing what sort of international social structure contains them.

Chapters 3 to 5 take a close look at both the concept of polarity and the concept of great power, which underpins polarity and establishes why the domestic character of such power matters. The reason that polarity gets three chapters while identity gets only one is that my use of identity is fairly straightforward, whereas I need to argue for some significant changes to the conventional understanding of polarity. The central concern is that neorealism's commitment to what Hansen (2000: 18) calls a single stratification of states into great powers and other states is flawed, and this flaw is crucial to how polarity is understood. The argument is that the approach more common among practitioners of distinguishing between great powers and superpowers is both more descriptively accurate and more theoretically rewarding. This discussion is focused primarily on the internal logic of polarity theory, largely leaving aside the question of how polarity and identity relate.

In chapter 3 I sketch out what polarity means, what role it has played in academic and public policy debates over the past half century, and what its strengths and weaknesses are as an analytical device for understanding international relations. I raise the question as to whether it is polarity in general that is interesting, or only bipolarity, and note that, while unipolarity has become a mainstream way of characterizing the present international power structure, the theoretical and analytical implications of this have only begun to be addressed. In the chapters that follow, I argue that polarity remains a valuable way of understanding international relations, and particularly international security, but not in the excessively narrow and rigid form that has followed on from Waltz's formulation of neorealism. The aim is to combine in a single argument the insights of policy debates and academic theory, and to bring these two worlds into stronger contact.

Chapter 4 presents a critical survey of how the concepts of great power, and more recently superpower, are used to understand the structure of international power politics during three historical periods. The period before 1945 is generally thought of as multipolar, and is talked about in terms of between four and nine great powers. The Cold War period is almost always characterized as bipolar, and is talked about in terms of two superpowers. The period since 1991 has proved more difficult to pin down in polarity terms. Some talk of unipolarity and a single superpower, others of re-emergent multipolarity, and others of some kind of mix containing one superpower and several other significant powers. The argument is that most of these usages represent a flawed conception of great power. The source of this flaw is traced to the transfer of the concept from a European to a global context, and I argue that here, as elsewhere, size matters. What serves on one scale does not necessarily work on other scales. Some of the confusion about the present era arises from failure to recognize that the distinction between great powers and superpowers also operated during the Cold War and pre-1945 periods. Understanding that, and following through its implications, makes the present era look less unusual than it does if seen as following from a strict bipolar structure.

Chapter 5 turns to the problem of definition on which these confusions rest. It looks first at the classical definitions of great power, and at the two contending traditions – material capability and standing in international society – underpinning these. It also looks at the longstanding problem of inability to devise objective material measures with which to underpin a ranked classification of states in terms of power. The argument builds on the understanding from chapter 4 that there are reasonably clear and systematic criteria by which great powers and superpowers can and should be differentiated from each other. It goes on from that both to propose new all-purpose definitions for *great powers* and *superpowers*, and to set up *regional powers* as the most useful way of designating the next rank down. The chapter concludes by examining two main consequences of these redefinitions for polarity theory, and for the public policy discourse that rests implicitly or explicitly on the idea of polarity. The first consequence of a framework based on distinguishing among superpowers, great powers and regional powers is to render almost unworkable the idea that simple characterizations such as bipolarity can be used as a basis for general cause–effect statements about world politics. In a world in which both superpowers and great powers are recognized as coexisting, simple polarities will be the exception rather than the rule. But since much effort over the last decades to find firm relationships between polarity and a variety of aspects of war and peace has anyway proved fruitless, this loss is not as serious as might at first appear. The second consequence of the differentiation among superpowers, great powers and regional powers is to highlight the need to investigate structural questions about how different combinations of superpowers, great powers and regional powers relate to each other. This turns out to be the basis for some very useful scenarios (the subject of part II) with which one can capture the essential dynamics, dilemmas and directions of the post-Cold War international system. The essential idea of polarity theory – that one can understand a few big and important things about world politics by looking at the international power structure – turns out to be sound. What gets opened up is both a more accurate conceptualization of the global power structure and a set of hypotheses with which one can explore the structural logics both of power politics within any given configuration of power, and of the potential transformations from one configuration to another. What may be lost in the ability to represent the international system in terms of simple numbers is made up for by the ability to explore the interplay between superpowers and great powers, and between both and regions. In this case, bringing the academic and practitioner conversations about polarity more into line may not only facilitate communication between them, but also make theorizing more relevant to policy.

The conclusions to part I draw together the arguments about polarity and identity by showing how they fit into (neo)realist, neoliberal and solidarist assumptions about the social structure of international politics in terms of Wendt's scheme of enemies, rivals and friends.

The three chapters in part II focus on the interplay of polarity and identity, or material and social structure, in the contemporary world. Each takes on one of the main scenarios suggested by differentiating great powers and superpowers. The current system is presented as one superpower plus four great powers (China, the EU, Japan, Russia), and if that is accepted then there are three main scenarios that define its most probable future. The key to these scenarios is possible change (or not) in the number of superpowers.

Chapter 6 explores the first and most likely scenario, which is for relative continuity with one superpower plus several (e.g. three, four or five) great powers. In this scenario, the US remains the sole superpower, and the number of great powers either stays the same or rises or falls slightly (perhaps India makes it into the great power ranks, perhaps Russia drops out). The scenario starts by deriving some basic neorealist-type rules for how the superpower and the great powers relate to each other under these structural conditions, and widens out from this narrow assumption of enemies and rivals to consider social structures of rivals and friends. The argument is that, while the US is substantially conforming to neorealist expectations, the great powers are doing so only in a limited way. The chapter then turns to the interplay between powers and regions, looking at the role that regions play in sustaining, and even defining, the US position as the sole superpower. The US has adopted a *swing-power* strategy in which it positions itself as a member of three macro-regions (Asia-Pacific, North Atlantic, Western hemisphere) as a way of legitimizing its actual presence as an outside power in Europe, East Asia and Latin America. The chapter concludes that continuity of the existing structure is more possible than is suggested by strict neorealist rules, and that the major potential for disrupting the present structure lies in how the US conducts its foreign policy.

Chapter 7 sets out the scenarios where, in a reversal of the historical trend towards decline in the number of superpowers, their number increases. What would a world politics with two or possibly three super-powers plus several great powers look like (e.g. where there are three or four great powers, and either China or the EU, or both, achieve promo-tion to superpower status)? These scenarios are the least likely ones for the near future because neither the EU nor China is convincingly posi-tioned to achieve superpower status for at least a couple of decades. A two-superpower scenario would return us to the polarity structure of the Cold War, but I argue that, whether the second superpower was either China or the EU, the social structure, and therefore the whole character of relations among the superpowers, would be sharply different from what happened between 1945 and 1989. With the EU, and even with China twenty years down the line, there would be much less of an iden-tity clash with the US than there was with the Soviet Union, and much more possibility for relationships of rivals and/or friends. The three-superpower scenario would create a polarity structure similar to that of the interwar years, yet again with a radically different and much less ideologically divided social structure. In each case the same approach is used as in chapter 6, starting out with rules for superpowers and great powers, and looking at the consequences for and from regions. Among other things, the development of this scenario would sharply undercut the swing strategy that is a core feature of present-day US superpower status.

Chapter 8 opens with discussion of a scenario that has so far been largely hidden by the rigidities of neorealist definitions of polarity, but which comes into clear view when the distinction between superpowers and great powers is introduced. This is the case in which the historical decline in the number of superpowers continues, leaving a system with no superpowers and a number of great powers. I argue that this is the most likely alternative to the present structure of one superpower and no great powers. The necessary condition is that the US either loses, or steps down from, its superpower status, leaving a system composed only of great powers. As far as I am aware, nobody has explored the idea of an international system which has *no* truly global powers in it, but only a collection of super-regional great powers. For the all-great-power scenario the key question is whether or not one or more of the powers would bid for superpower status. Neorealist reasoning would suggest that such a bid, or possibly more than one, should be the expected out-come. This idea and the possible alternatives to it are given close exam-ination, as is the argument that any expectation of such an outcome would be a constraint on US options to abandon the sole superpower slot. Both scenarios are examined in terms of how the present behaviour of the powers lines up with or against the expectations of the rules of power politics. In addition, I extend the discussion of the significance of and for regions in such a global power structure, and also for international society and the international political economy.

The two chapters in part III focus on US foreign policy and what can be done about it. In chapter 9 the key questions are why the US has moved into a more imperial mode, and how durable that shift might be. Because the US plays such a central role in all three scenarios, the intertwined questions of how its domestic character plays into its foreign policy, and how international relations play into US domestic affairs, become absolutely crucial. I look at the sources of US foreign policy in American exceptionalism, and at the impact on these traditions first of unipolarity, and then of September 11. The argument is that unipolarity and September 11 have greatly amplified predispositions towards unilateralism, Manicheanism and hypersecuritization, and that while this shift could be durable it creates tensions with other powerful strands within American exceptionalism.

Chapter 10 provides a summary of the main arguments, and then examines the options and responsibilities of the great powers in relation to the US and the structure of international society. Because a substantial part of the structure of unipolarity is social, what the great powers do matters both to the stability and the character of the sole superpower system, and to which of the alternative scenarios becomes its most likely successor. The great powers have some ability to shape US behaviour, and have to face hard and complicated decisions about whether the new imperial tendencies in US policy are best countered by opposition to, detachment from, or seeking to remain in partnership with, a sole superpower displaying rogue tendencies. I argue that the great powers need to accept US leadership, but to reject its imperial project. They have to reassert the role of loyal opposition and friendly critic, and reject emphatically the 'with us or against us' choice offered after September 11 by President Bush.

Throughout the argument I adopt a strategy of deliberate theoretical pluralism. My argument rests on the conclusion that, while a strict neorealist approach is an interesting and powerful place to start, it is by itself too narrowly based to tell us all that much of interest about the condition of unipolarity. The distribution of material power among states is a key foundation on which to build, but the other neorealist assumptions about survivalism and the struggle for power represent an impoverished, and in some ways dangerous (because of the risk of self-fulfilling prophecies), view of the motivations and relationships that comprise

international relations. So also does neorealism's sidelining of the
domestic level, which puts too much weight on systemic determinants of
behaviour and the 'likeness' of units, and largely reads out of the analysis
the effect of the internal structure and ideology of the great powers. To
build on the neorealist foundation, one needs to take into account not
just power and conflict, but also the social and economic structures of the
international system, and the way these are projected by, and play into,
the domestic life of the major powers. To accomplish that I bring in
insights from the English school, IPE, globalism, and constructivism about
international society, as well as from literatures focused mainly on the
domestic character of states, and explain how those elements play into
foreign policy and are affected by inputs from the international system.

My approach retains a neorealist quality in its emphasis on the major
powers. I broadly accept the proposition that this simplification is an
efficient way of capturing many of the core features of international relations. This view is compatible with English school thinking, which alloc-
ates a central managerial role to great powers; with the Wendtian version
of constructivism; and with those branches of IPE that make hegemony
or its absence their focus of concern. Particularly in the context of a
discussion about unipolarity, it can also be interpreted as having some
complementarity with those branches of globalist thinking that highlight
a centre–periphery structure as their way of understanding international
relations. As a corollary, I accept the costs of such a simplification, among
which are that the analysis marginalizes both the smaller players and
issues such as human rights, which have high moral claims but which
rank lower in the practical agenda of the powers. This choice reflects the
theorist's inclination to simplify in order to understand the essentials of
things that are otherwise too complex to grasp in full. It also reflects the
normative view that a better understanding of these big things is a pre-
condition for effective action on a wide range of other agendas. I do not
take up the macro-critiques of neorealism partly on the grounds that my
theoretically pluralist approach covers some of them, and partly on the
grounds that such a move would take the book into the general debates
about the conceptual and normative problems of theorizing international
relations, a subject adequately covered elsewhere in the literature (Hollis
and Smith 1990; Smith et al. 1996; Rengger 2000). To this extent, my
approach is in bed with neorealism, but in several other ways it runs
quite strongly against the neorealist canon. I take the particularities
of history not as an unimportant background above which structural
forces play, but as an important counterforce against pure structural
logic. I depart from a strictly military/political (and, more to the point,
materialist, power political) view of structural theory, and accept the
role of social and economic structures as independent determinants of

behaviour. And I reject (its attractions as another great simplifier not-withstanding) the strict rationalist view that actors and their interests and identities are preconstituted and fixed. The rationalist approach, it seems to me, is only tenable (and perhaps not even then) within a single sector (whether economic or political). When one moves into consideration of multiple sectors, the playoffs among different interests and identities, and the necessity to resolve them in some way, point powerfully to the mutual constitution of actors and structures. Combining insights from these different theoretical layers is a way of building a bridge between the insights of academic theorists and those of the public policy discourse.

PART I

Identity and Polarity

Introduction

Of the four chapters in part I, the first introduces identity, and the next three focus on the concepts of great power and superpower. This imbalance is not intended to imply a difference of weight in the analysis. To the contrary, the argument is that polarity can only be useful if interpreted through the social structure in which it is embedded. Power structure and social structure arguments deliver more if they are taken together than if used separately. Combining them helps to address the distortion of using polarity as a concept isolated from social context, or rather not isolated, but carrying a fixed rather than an open assumption about what the social context is. Indeed, it can be argued (Bull 1977) that concepts such as great power and superpower are not just statements about relative material weight, but for the states concerned are also important aspects of their identity. The work of chapters 3 to 5 is to contest the neorealist claim, central to much academic thinking about polarity, that there is a single, clear distinction to be made between great powers and all other states. In challenging this claim my aim is not to destroy polarity theory but to change how it is understood, and to reposition the sorts of questions it is used to generate. The conclusions to part I show how polarity and identity are combined to generate the scenarios in part II.

2

Identity

It is not my intention in this chapter to offer an exhaustive discussion on the question of identity. Rather, I plan to offer elaborations around a few key ideas about how identity plays into the practice and study of international relations, and to set these up as the social context for thinking about polarity. In particular, I focus on the *political* identity of the actors in the international system. The next section examines the relational logic of Self and Other that underpins much of the discussion about identity. Section 2 surveys the character of collective identity and how this plays into international relations. Section 3 discusses the (in)stability of identity, and section 4 looks briefly at historical variations in the society of states produced by different sorts of identity. The analytical perspective in this chapter is that of Wendt (1999: 309) that 'distributions of ideas are social structures', a position that underpins almost any view of the international system as a society. More specifically, my argument runs close to Wendt's (1999: 314, 249, 262) that: 'materialist theory of structure ... makes invisible what actually determines the logic of anarchy, its culture and role structure' and 'anarchies only acquire logics as a function of the structure of what we put inside them.' Consequently, 'enmity [or indeed rivalry or friendship] gives capabilities a particular *meaning*, which derives neither from their intrinsic properties, nor from anarchy as such.' Wendt's understanding of social structure is strongly linked to identity. 'When states engage in egoistic foreign policies ... more is going on than simply an attempt to realize given selfish ends. They are also instantiating and reproducing a particular conception of who they are' (1999: 340–1). 'Structural change [is] a problem of collective identity formation' ... it 'occurs when actors redefine who they are and what they want' (1999: 338, 336). Wendt links his constructivist approach to

the idea that social interaction is not just about 'the adjustment of behaviour to price', as the rationalist would see it, but also about the reproduction of the agents involved, of their identities and interests (1999:
316). Patterns of identity arising from shared ideas thus constitute social
structures that stand alongside, and give meaning to, the material structures
defined by polarity. Like the material structures alongside which they sit,
these social structures are in continuous flux. Since identity and material
capability both change, both can be seen as ongoing processes. But within
that generalization is the fact that long periods of relative stability may
occur in which a given pattern becomes sufficiently sedimented that it can
be seen as a structure. In order to set the foundations for thinking through
the scenarios in part II one needs to get some sense of the nature of these
international social structures (a subject I have tackled at greater length
in Buzan 2004a).

2.1   The relational logic of Self–Other

The debates about identity display a remarkable degree of agreement
around the idea that any identity of 'Self' can only be defined in relation
to an 'Other'. Huntington (1996: 21) gives a typically robust version of
this proposition: 'we know who we are only when we know who we are
not and often only when we know whom we are against.' The 'against'
part of Huntington's formulation is a typically realist twist. But there are
many others who would position themselves far away from Huntington
both politically and epistemologically, who nevertheless operate with the
same general assumption that any Self requires an Other. Whether this
link is negative, as Huntington suggests, or simply reflects a necessary
sense of difference that could be positive (as among the interdependent
members of a band) or neutral, should be an open question determined
by specific cases. Wendt (1999) makes extensive use of Self and Other in
discussing his three forms of social structure based on relations of enemy,
rival or friend. Among political theorists (WSRG 2000: 12–13; Brown
1995: 100–6) there is a longstanding concern that the idea of a universal
sense of community (i.e. a universal sense of identity) is at the very least
seriously problematic, and at worst an oxymoron, because a sense of
being 'We' requires an 'Other' against which to define itself. Salter (2002:
8–12) notes the popularity of this formulation among postmodernists
such as William Connolly, Stuart Hall, Michael J. Shapiro, David
Campbell and Iver Neumann.
     If this Self-requires-Other logic underpins the identities that constitute
the international social structure, then the implications for international
relations are quite strong. In the international arena, we are talking about

Self not in terms of individual human beings, but in terms of collective actors, whether they be states, nations, religious groups, lobbies or whatever. 'Self' in the context of international relations is about the sense of collective identity as 'We' that constitutes actors on this larger scale – what Anderson (1983) so nicely labelled as 'imagined communities' where large numbers of people feel a collective sense of belonging even though they never directly meet each other. But if the constitution of a collective We requires an Other who is both outside and different, then We cannot be universal. This means that a solidarist collective of humankind is impossible, and that the necessary fragmentation of humankind into a number of identity groups has built into it elements of estrangement that could easily, though not necessarily, tip into the fear and antagonism that Huntington suggests. At least for primitive international systems, as illustrated by much of history, the Self–Other logic of identity points towards a rather realist world in which cooperation at the global level will be difficult (because interdependence is low) and conflict easy. The definition of Self against Other contains a predisposition towards relationships of mutual securitization that can only be offset by the development of sophisticated social systems in which difference can be constructed more positively.

There are some paths out of this Hobbesian trap. For one thing, at least in principle, because Self needs Other to maintain its own existence, the Other cannot be destroyed without destroying the Self. In practice, however, genocides such as the Nazi plan to eliminate the Jews suggest that this might not be much of a constraint. Wæver offers a more sophisticated exit with his idea that, if one factors time into the equation, the Self might serve as its own Other. He observes that 'Europe's "Other" is neither Russia, nor Islamic fundamentalism: Europe's Other is Europe's past' (Buzan and Wæver 2003: 354). In other words, during the second half of the twentieth century the Western European states came to see their own history of rivalry and war (Westphalian Europe) as the Other against which they wanted to define their new Self (European Union Europe). This unique move enabled them to desecuritize their relationships with each other without finding an enemy outside, and is the foundation of the EU. It is not clear how transferable this idea is in practice, but in principle it is easy to see how this kind of interpretation of the Self–Other relationship could transform the politics of places such as the Middle East, South Asia and Northeast Asia. Even more optimistically, as already suggested, there is the argument that difference does not have to inspire fear. Otherness can be accepted, even celebrated, as a key component of what defines Self. Cronin (1999: 17) provides a handle on this thought with his spectrum of degrees of identity from negative to positive, from Other as opposite of Self to Other as extension of Self.

On the negative end, he starts from hostility (Other as anti-Self) and proceeds through rivalry (Other as competitor), indifference, cohesion (some sense of common good and group identity) and altruism (willingness to sacrifice Self for Others) to symbiosis (shared core identity dissolves Self–Other distinction). Cronin's spectrum provides a bridge to Wendt's idea that the social structure of the international system can be described in terms of relationships of enemies, rivals or friends, about which I will have more to say below.

Even the idea that a universal identity is impossible can be questioned. The general position is that convergence should be possible among subsets of the identity units in any system, but not among all of them (because then there would be no Other). Yet the current society of states already has a practice of nearly universal membership with virtually all states recognizing each other as being the same type of political and legal entity, and no principle standing in the way of complete universality on these grounds. Even if one argues that states still have an Other in the form of non-state entities that might challenge them for the role of prime unit, this still does not stand in the way of interstate society as expressing a universal identity among sovereign equals. Furthermore, postmodernists typically take the view that actors can hold more than one identity at the same time. Thus individuals may simultaneously hold some identities that require an Other (family, football supporter, nation, race) and some that do not (member of the human race) – or at least are not prevented from achieving universal scale within the referent group (humankind). There is no reason to think that states or other collective actors are different in this respect. States can retain their sense of difference and uniqueness, while both clustering with subgroups of others sharing key aspects of their identity (democratic, Islamic, communist, great power, Arab, Portuguese speaking) and being members of a global-scale international society based on mutual diplomatic recognition, acceptance of international law, and membership of the UN and other intergovernmental organizations.

The importance of all this is that the Self–Other link establishes the inherent relationality of identity which serves as the foundation for the idea that international systems are socially structured, and that these social structures can range from negative (identities formed against each other) to positive (identities based on difference within an interdependence of shared values). The key to Self and Other is difference, and in the sphere of international political identity this difference is most easily observable in terms both of the various ideologies that states use to legitimize their domestic structures and of the layers of status (superpower, great power, regional power, and suchlike) by which states define their claims and roles in relation to each other.

2.2 The character of collective identity and the implications for international relations

In international systems Self is both collective and relational. Groups of people shape their collective identities as states, nations, religions or whatever by defining themselves in relation to other groups. Identity thus both results from, and in part constitutes, the process of international relations. That said, it still makes a difference what types of identity are in play. If 'anarchy is what states make of it', then it matters whether the states in question are liberal, fascist, communist, monarchical, theocratic, something else, or some mixture, a logic that extends to the character of the non-state actors in the system as well. Some of the ideologies around which international and transnational actors can organize themselves will predispose towards more hostile, securitized and conflictual relations, others towards more tolerant, pluralist and rule-governed relations. In saying this I am fully aware that I am looking down the dangerous path that leads towards attempting a typology of states and/or other international actors as a basis for a theory of foreign policy behaviour. There are many wrecks along this path (Rosenau 1966), and I have argued at length elsewhere as to why it cannot be done (Buzan and Wæver 2003: 20–6). Although states do share some likenesses, there are simply too many variables in play to try to reduce them to some set of formulaic expectations about how they will behave. Every state and every transnational actor (TNA) will have its own exceptionalism, and at the end of the day it is easier to see why such actors are unique than how they are the same. Although this problem does block the way to predictive positivist theory, it does not bar one from more interpretive evaluations of particular cases. Since my focus in this book is on global-level powers, we are talking about small numbers, and as I show in part II it is quite possible to make useful assessments about how the character of the states in play shapes the kind of anarchy they make and inhabit.

We are now back to the question with which I opened chapter 1: would it have made any difference to the history of 1945–89 if the US and the Soviet Union had both been liberal democracies (or communist)? We are also back to Wendt's idea that social structures can be characterized as enemies, rivals or friends, although now with the added question of what it is that disposes actors to relate to each other as enemies, rivals or friends. For neorealists, this 'what' question hardly arises because they assume enemies and rivals, discount the possibility of friendship, and focus on how the distribution of power drives patterns of alignment. For those who take a more open view of what social structures are possible internationally, this 'what' question matters a lot. Do the ideologies around which great powers and superpowers constitute themselves shape the way in which they behave and interact, or does the dumb logic of power politics override all such social considerations? If one assumes that the social does matter, that the Cold War would indeed have played very differently if the Soviet Union had been a liberal democracy, then it draws one's attention to the factors that might predispose the major powers to construct their relationships as enemies, rivals or friends. A key to this enquiry is the extent to which the ideology with which each major power constructs itself is supportive of, neutral to, or antagonistic towards the ideologies with which its contemporaneous major powers construct themselves.

It is not difficult to see how this logic of interplay among identities works in international relations. I have for long used the example of India and Pakistan to illustrate a situation of structural threats where the political constitutions of two neighbouring states are so designed that each stands as a permanent threat to the principles and legitimacy of the other (Buzan 1991a: 121–2). India's organizing principle of secular feder-alism threatens Pakistan with absorption, while Pakistan's organizing principle of Islamic unity threatens India with fragmentation. The mutual exclusivity of their principles of legitimation underpins not only the bitter territorial dispute between them in Kashmir, but also their general stance of hostility and their nuclear arms race. The same point about structural threats could be made about the US and the Soviet Union during the Cold War. Part of their antagonism may indeed have been driven, as neorealists would claim, by simple bipolarity logic in which the superpower identity of each necessarily made them rivals. But it is hard to ignore the powerful synergy between the material fact of bipolarity and the extreme zero-sum character of their political and economic ideo-logies. Wherever totalitarian communism spread, democracy and liberal values were expunged, and vice versa. And wherever command economies were set up, markets were expunged, and vice versa. This meant that a success for either superpower, in terms of a third country converting to one ideology or the other, was a direct blow to the legitimacy of its rival. The claim of both ideologies to embody the future of industrial society amplified the effects of such gains and losses on their legitimacy. There are many other examples of structural threats where identities get constructed in mutually exclusive forms, with or without conflicts over territory: apartheid South Africa and its front-line neighbours; Israel and the Palestinians; many of the conflicts within the former republic of Yugoslavia; and, in earlier times, the relationship between nomadic, pastoralist 'barbarians' and the sedentary farming civilizations of the ancient and classical world. On the other side are all of the arguments about democratic, or liberal, peace, which assume that it is not only the fact of shared ideology that matters, but also the specific character of liberal democracy which allows states sharing that ideology to desecuritize their relationships in many ways, not least by the pursuit of joint gains in an open economy which delinks ownership of territority from access to markets and resources.

In thinking about what it is in their internal makeup that disposes states to define each other as enemies, rivals or friends, one has to go beyond mere similarity or difference of ideology. Difference mattered in the making of the Cold War, and similarity underpins the democratic peace position, but it is the nature of similarity or difference that matters most, not the mere fact of it. In the democratic peace argument it is the fact that the shared values are liberal ones that enables desecuritization of relations to occur. The historical record suggests that some other forms of similarity do not have this effect. The monarchies of eighteenth-century Europe hardly treated each other as friends, and were regularly at war. During the Cold War it was not uncommon for one communist state to attack or occupy another. It is hard to imagine that a world of fascist great powers would be peaceful. This record points to the need to consider the intrinsic qualities of different types of political identity, as well as the way in which they play into each other.

One route into this discussion is to make a distinction between exclusive, or communitarian, forms of identity, and inclusive, or cosmopolitan, ones. Exclusive forms of identity work by emphasizing the difference between the set of people sharing it and all others. Nationalism, particularly where based on blood ethnicity, is a clear example (Smith 1991). Such identities generally emphasize an internal reproductive logic and will be difficult or impossible for outsiders to join. Inclusive identities work by setting up membership criteria that are acquirable as an act of will, and in principle (sometimes less so in practice) are open to anyone who does acquire the necessary characteristics. Universal religions are the clearest example, but some forms of national identity also have this quality. Immigrant countries such as the US and Canada, for example, have identities that can be acquired, in principle, by anyone willing to conform to their requirements. Taking this route could lead to the large debate among political theorists between communitarians and cosmopolitans, and thus back to the Self–Other logics discussed above (see Brown 1995; Rengger 1992; Cochran 1999). But I am not so much interested here in the complicated philosophical issues raised by the communitarian–cosmopolitan distinction as in the relatively simple matter of how these two types of identity might play into international relations through the agency of the major powers.

Exclusive forms of identity can play into international relations in either of two basic ways: coexistence or hierarchy. The coexistence model is captured in Herz's (1969: 82–9) idea of 'self-determining and self-limiting nationalism', in my old idea of 'mature anarchy' (Buzan 1991a: 175–81), and up to a point by pluralist thinking within the English school. Here the identity in question is characterized by a contained and status quo view of Self. It seeks the right to maintain and reproduce itself, and makes no claims against others except that they allow it the necessary degree of self-control to do that. The strongest form of this position is utopian isolationism, where an identity group seeks to minimize its contact with the rest of the system. Nationalism can have this self-limiting quality, especially when the sense of identity it carries is firmly tied to a specific, well-delineated and not contested territory. This is the benign, pluralist form of the nation-state ideal-type, where each nation has its own historic territory, and a society of states based on sovereignty, mutual recognition and non-intervention allows each to pursue its own path of cultural development as it wishes. With culture, territory and politics all in alignment, coexistence becomes feasible. In the contemporary international system countries such as Bhutan, Denmark, Iceland, Japan and Sweden come close to this model, but the problem is that it has never been close to universal, especially among the major powers. Religious identities can also be exclusivist, especially where linked to ethnicity, as in the case of Judaism, or (more loosely) to a specific territory, as, up to a point, is the case with Hinduism.

But exclusive forms of identity can also project themselves in hierarchical mode, where the specifics of difference are interpreted as making the Self superior to Others. The general framing of this is in terms of social Darwinism, where international relations is seen as a ruthless game of survival of the fittest, an interpretation that neatly fits into power politics, where 'fittest' can be understood as 'most powerful'. History is all too replete with examples of imperial exclusivisms. Much of nineteenth-century imperialism rested on racial theories that construed one race (or sometimes nation) as superior to others, thereby justifying unequal treatement in terms of rights and resources. The French and British empires, the US doctrine of manifest destiny, and the Japanese drive for a 'Greater East-Asia Co-Prosperity Sphere' all rested on versions of this reasoning. This logic reached its ghastly peak in Nazi theories of the master race, with its right to expropriate, enslave or exterminate lesser breeds. Extreme claims of this sort are not a necessary feature of hierarchical exclusivism, which can also be driven by survival claims. If a state pursues its own survival needs as the highest priority, then even without an explicit vision of superiority, or an imperial mission, a position can develop in which the needs of the Self override the rights of others. National security and revolutionary and imperial logics all flow easily in this direction, with the need to make the Self secure involving an ever-expanding range and degree of control over others. Germany (or France, or Russia or . . .) could only be secure when they could gain hegemony over Europe; the US can only be secure when the world is safe for its version of democracy and capitalism; Israel can only be secure when it has killed all 'terrorists'; and so forth. The presence in a system of two or more political identities that are exclusive and hierarchical is of course a recipe for enmity and conflict when the different projects of expansion get in each other's way.

Inclusive forms of identity offer the same choice between benign and malign outcomes, though the malign potential is more obvious, and the benign one much narrower and less likely to happen. By definition, inclusive forms of collective identity cannot be self-contained, especially if they tend towards universalism, as most do, and even more so if they are committed to proselytizing. If one or more such identities are loose in an international system they will easily clash both with each other and with exclusive identities. It is easy to read the history of the twentieth century in this light. The First World War was basically about a clash among a set of exclusive hierarchical identities, though it put into play two (the US and the Soviet Union) that were later to become inclusive and universalist. The Second World War featured a mixture of imperial exclusivist identities (Britain, France, Germany, Italy, Japan) with two inclusive universalist ones (American liberalism and Soviet communism). Since the inclusive universalist powers came out on top of that conflict, the Cold War was about the rivalry between them. Almost any mixture of exclusive imperialisms and/or inclusive universalisms points towards a social structure of enmity. The only way in which an inclusive universalist identity can reach stability is if it succeeds in taking over the whole system. Something like this happened in some of the 'universal' empires of ancient and classical times, where a single polity and culture came to dominate a known world (e.g. Rome, China). But nothing like it has happened in modern times, and, given the robust persistence of variety in the patterns of human collective identity, nothing like it is in immediate prospect. The only candidate is the form of liberal market democracy projected as an inclusive universalism by the US in particular and the West in general. Having seen off its communist rival, this has had a quite remarkable success in dominating the industrial core but still remains heavily contested in the Islamic world and Asia. One of the worries about the 'neocon' doctrine dominant in Washington after 11 September 2001 is that it represents precisely such an imperial universalist project bent on using the superiority of US military power to enforce its model across the world.

The distinction between exclusive and inclusive identities provides a useful general frame for assessing the likely social structure among any given set of collective actors. One needs, however, to combine these general considerations about the character of collective identity with the specifics of particular actors. Since the number of major powers in an international system is generally fairly small, this is not an insurmountable task. Indeed, as I show in part II, in the contemporary international system one needs to look into only a handful of states, most obviously the US, which are central to all of the scenarios.

2.3 The (in)stability of identity

Getting a handle on the character of collective identities solves one part of the problem of how to combine polarity and identity for analytical purposes. But it still leaves open the question about how stable (or not) collective identities are as a feature of international relations. This question is similar in form to the traditional one in IR about capabilities versus intentions. The argument went that, since capabilities change relatively slowly, while intentions can change overnight, it was better to base one's analysis of threat, and security policy, on capabilities and assume the worst about intentions. Katzenstein (1996: 17–26) seeks to counter the neorealist view by arguing that identity is what makes states unlike, but that identity and the social contexts that it generates are also in constant evolution. Since there is also a quite widespread belief among postmodernists that identities are in a continuous state of flux and renegotiation, there are grounds for asking whether identity is a useful analytical category for IR. Against this view of permanent fluidity is the idea that, while identities are in principle always open, in practice they can become sufficiently sedimented to constitute reasonably stable features on the international landscape. Ethno-national identities, for example, are remarkably durable. While it was relatively easy (which is not to say easy) to beat fascism out of Germany and Japan in the middle of the twentieth century, it is hard to imagine how the identities of being German and Japanese could have been beaten out of those peoples without more or less exterminating them, although it is equally clear that within the continuity of these identities there were some significant changes in the content of being German or Japanese. Smith (1991: 26–38) offers useful thoughts on the many factors affecting the durability or disappearance of national identities in the international system. Religious identities can also be durable, as suggested by the re-emergence of Orthodox Christianity in Russia after seventy years of vigorous suppression.

That identities can change is not, in itself, a problem. Capabilities also change, and with the availability of outside arms suppliers even military capabilities can change rapidly if one or both sides receive large injections of military equipment. In events such as the famous naval race between

Britain and Germany before the First World War, or the nuclear race between the US and the Soviet Union, the pace of change in the strength of the respective forces was determined by industrial capacities available within the two states which could not be changed overnight. But look at the various wars between Israel and its neighbours, or at the clash between Somalia and Ethiopia during the 1970s, or the long civil war in Angola, and one can see how quickly external suppliers can change a local military balance. And change of identity is not just a problem but also an opportunity. The expectation that identities change, and that such change can in some ways be encouraged or directed, lies at the heart of most of the hopes and fears that drive political life. At its simplest this dynamic can be seen in the hopes and fears that attend changes of political leadership. Whether the US president was to be Kennedy or Nixon, or Bush or Gore, carried expectation of difference about how America's interests and identity would be interpreted. Individuals such as Stalin, Hitler, Churchill, Mao, Nasser and Gorbachev clearly made a substantial difference in what their countries stood for, and because leadership can change quickly for all sorts of reasons (illness, term limits, accident, assassination, coup, revolution, war) there is a certain volatility in the identity of collective actors. Indeed, the fact that identities can change underlies a great deal of foreign policy. At the crude, short-term, end of the spectrum is regime/leadership change of the type that the US and Britain implemented against Afghanistan in 2002 and Iraq in 2003, and which has many precedents in outside sponsored coups in places ranging from Chile, Nicaragua and Panama to Iran, Uganda and Hungary. On the longer-term, more sophisticated, side of the spectrum one finds policies such as the 'civilizing missions' of the type conducted by the EU/NATO in several of the successor states to Yugoslavia and the various attempts to shape the behaviour and identity of third-world states by imposing on them conditionality pressures regarding member-ships and/or access to aid and credit. The attempts by George Soros to use his billions to renovate and Westernize education in the former Soviet Union also rest on such hopes, as does the 'constrainment' game with China, which depends on the idea that, over a couple of generations, the workings of the market should push China towards a more liberal form not just of economy, but also of society and politics, as it has done in Japan, South Korea and Taiwan. Indeed, divided cultures such as Korea and China, and earlier Vietnam, provide a fascinating laborat-ory for the study of identity, where one sees a single national culture pushed in opposing directions by the imposition of different political ideologies.

A more systematic approach to the problem of (in)stability in identity can be found in the idea that it matters how identities, and the behaviours associated with them, are internalized. Wendt (1999: 247–50) offers three possibilities, which he sees as both degrees and modes of internalization: coercion, calculation and belief (see also Kratochwil 1989: 97; Hurd 1999; March and Olsen 1998: 948–54). The shallowest and least stable is coercion, when the social structure is essentially imposed by an outside power. A social structure built on this foundation is hardly internalized at all, and is unlikely to survive the removal of its outside supporter. The underlying fragility of a social system of coercively imposed norms is amply illustrated by the rapid collapse of the Soviet empire, and then the Soviet Union itself, and many similar cases can be found in the histories of empires. In the middle is calculation, when the social structure rests on rational assessments of self-interest. Such a structure is only superficially internalized, and is stable only so long as the ratios of costs and benefits remain favourable to it (Hurd 1999: 387). A concert of powers, for example, will collapse if one power comes to believe that it can and should seek hegemony, and a liberal trading system will collapse if enough of its members begin to think that the costs of exposing their societies and economies to global trade and finance outweigh the benefits. The deepest and most stable mode is belief, where actors support the social structure because they accept it as legitimate, and in so doing incorporate it into their own conception of their identity. Deep internalization of this sort can survive quite major changes of circumstance, as shown by many cases of the persistence of religion long after its sponsoring imperial power has faded away (Christianity after Rome, Islam after the Abbasid dynasty, Buddhism after the Mauryan empire).

This way of thinking suggests that the (in)stability of identity could be dependent on how it is internalized, with the spectrum ranging from rather unstable in the case of coercion (or, at least, stability dependent on being able to maintain coercion at a reasonable cost), through a middle ground, where (in)stability rests on calculation (and therefore on the maintenance of positive outcome from behaviour), to firm stability, where identity rests on belief. This approach raises the problem of whether identity can be thought of only in terms of belief, or whether it should be seen as a sustained pattern of behaviour. Was Soviet identity less real as identity because it was substantially held in place by coercion and calculation, or was it equally real but simply less stable? Continuing down the same line, can coercion sometimes hold an identity in place for long enough to allow elements of calculation and belief to develop? These are issues I have taken up elsewhere (Buzan 2004a). In what follows, I take the position simply that identity and belief are separable, and that identity can be supported as well by coercion and calculation. As I show in part II, doing so offers useful leverage for thinking about the interplay of polarity and identity in the contemporary society of states.

2.4 Historical variations in interstate society

The previous sections of this chapter have focused on the collective identity of individual actors in international society. I have argued three points:

- that such identities are inherently relational and thus an inescapable part of international relations;
- that some types of identity easily fall into conflict with others, but that this is not true for all types – coexistence is also possible; and
- that identity, like material capability, is capable of both long-term stability and rapid change, and that how identity is internalized is one key factor affecting its (in)stability.

In this section I shift the focus from the identity of the units to that of the international society that they compose, particularly the society of states formed by the major powers. More specifically, this section is about the way in which the identities of the major powers both shape and are shaped by interstate society. The argument is that the interplay between the identity of the major powers on the one hand, and how they relate to each other and lesser powers through the society of states on the other, is a key element in how one interprets the configurations of polarity. This argument is a necessary underpinning for the scenarios in part II.

One aim of this section is to show that different interstate societies can take different forms, that any given one can change and evolve, and that such change is a readily observable phenomenon. This may seem too obvious to need demonstrating, yet it is necessary to establish the counter-position to realist and liberal views of state (and indeed human) motivation, both of which offer fixed and unchanging assumptions (respectively the calculated pursuit of relative or absolute gains). It is the realist fixity of assumption about the permanence of power rivalry that underpins orthodox polarity theory. The argument here is fairly simple in form. It is uncontroversial to note how the domestic character of the major powers has changed. Even within the small timespan of the last few hundred years the character of the major powers has evolved dramatically. In eighteenth-century Europe, monarchy, often absolutist, was the dominant form of government, and mercantilism the dominant economic doctrine. During the nineteenth century, nationalism shifted sovereignty from the monarch to the people and some great powers became republics. At the same time, liberalism began to challenge mercantilism as the dominant economic doctrine, a rivalry not finally settled until the collapse of communist mercantilism in 1989. After the First World War various forms of mass government became dominant: the fascist and communist versions of one-party totalitarianism, plus authoritarian dictatorships and democratic states based on universal suffrage. It is worth remembering that, of the seven great powers that entered the Second World War, only three (Britain, France, the US) were democracies, while three (Italy, Japan, Germany) were fascist, and one (the Soviet Union) was communist. And by that time also, all of the major powers had reverted to mercantilist economic policies. During the Cold War a majority of the major powers were democratic and capitalist, and the market economies triumphed over the remaining mercantilist ones. As the domestic constitution and life of the major powers has evolved, so too have the norms and institutions that they project into the society of states. During periods of severely clashing ideologies among the great powers, such as the 1930s and the Cold War, global international society was weakened. When great power political and economic identities were more harmonious, as during parts of the nineteenth century, the 1920s and the 1990s, global international society was stronger. In a longer view, one can see that some of the defining institutions of interstate society underwent significant change: colonialism, and the formal inequality of peoples, for example, disappeared; nationalism and, more slowly, the market became central; and multilateralism steadily developed as a distinctive variation on diplomacy. As already noted, the whole theory of democratic peace, and the idea that post-Cold War there is a security community among (most of) the major powers (not universally within the wider society of states, which is more pluralist) based on (solidarist) shared values of democracy and market economics, hangs on the understanding that the interplay between the domestic identity of states, and the nature of the society they form, matters.

There is an extensive literature available, much of it within the tradition of the English school, but also more recently from constructivists and institutionalists, which addresses the processes of continuity and change in interstate societies. Wight (1977) pioneered the comparative study of different premodern societies of states, work taken forward by Watson (1992), Buzan and Little (2000), Kokaz (2001) and Zhang (2001). English school writers have also conducted historical studies of the development and expansion to global scale of European interstate society (Bull and Watson 1984; Sofka 2001; Keene 2002). The work of institutionalists such as Ikenberry (2001) and Keohane (1988, 1995), who see the development of global governance in terms of intergovernmental agreements and organizations, in some ways runs parallel to this. From the constructivist side, but building on English school ideas, Wendt (1999) has developed a typology of social structures (relationships of enemy, rival, friend, generating Hobbesian, Lockean and Kantian social structures) and has thought hard about the processes of continuity and change in them. Building on the work of Bull (1977), Holsti (2002) and Mayall

(1990), I have elaborated on Wendt's scheme using the English school idea of deep or 'primary' institutions as benchmarks for change. I elaborate a spectrum of interstate societies ranging from *conflictual* (unrestrained power politics, largely antagonistic identities); through *coexistence* (pluralism, in the sense of mutual recognition of status and right to exist, and mutual interests in institutionalizing some rules of the game); and *cooperation* (more overlapping of identities, expressed in the development of joint projects around shared values such as trading and financial systems, or human rights, or big science); to *convergence* (where there is a conscious project to merge identities by making domestic structures more alike) (Buzan 2004a). Pluralism is abandoned when states not only recognize that they are alike in being states, but see that a significant degree of similarity is valuable, and seek to reinforce the security and legitimacy of their own values by consciously linking with others who are like-minded, building a shared identity with them. Convergence in this sense begins to look like a form of community, and in its stronger forms will involve acceptance of some responsibility for other members of the community. The literature on pluralist security communities (Deutsch et al. 1957; Adler and Barnett 1998) explores exactly this type of development, as, in a different way, does the English school's normative debate centring on whether interstate societies are basically stuck in a pluralist mode in which states share little other than a measure of commitment to an orderly coexistence, or whether there is scope for solidarist interstate societies sharing a wider range of values (Bull 1977, 1984; Dunne and Wheeler 1996; Jackson 2000; Mayall 2000).

One can conclude that there is a strong case, both empirically and theoretically supported, that the character of interstate societies changes and evolves along with the character of the states that compose them. In thinking about how any polarity structure will function, it is necessary first to ask what kind of social structure it is located within, and how stable (or not) that structure is. I will return to this in part II. Next it is necessary to set out the concept of polarity, and to ask questions about the way it is used to characterize the structure of international politics.

3

Polarity in Theory
and Practice

This chapter looks at the concept of polarity and its use both in IR theory and public policy debates. Section 1 surveys generally the place of polarity in the analysis of international relations and how its usage has evolved historically. Section 2 focuses specifically on polarity in IR theory, examining the problems posed both by unipolarity and by the idea of a distinction between great powers and superpowers. Section 3 reviews the critiques of polarity theory and assesses the utility of polarity for academics and practitioners.

3.1 Polarity in international relations

How should the US, its allies and opponents, and the rest of the world understand the international power structure within which they now have to operate? There is no significant disagreement, among either academics or those involved in the policy-making process, that understanding the global power structure is an essential starting point for thinking about international relations. Much more disputed is how to characterize this power structure, with options ranging from the traditional focus on great powers, through Marxian-inspired models of a core–periphery structured international political economy, to more postmodern and globalist notions of diffused and disaggregated power operating through a complex tangle of transnational networks. Polarity is the simplest and most traditional of these approaches. The basic propositions underlying it are as follows.

- Power is *the* (in the harder versions) or one of the (in the more moderate versions) key driving force(s) behind international relations.

- The most powerful actors in the system are states, not only because they control most of the military capability and remain the central providers of political authority and law, but also because the society of states remains the principal provider of international order and because states are still a major frame for identity.
- As a matter of historical record, international relations have been dominated by a relatively small number of great powers, varying between one and nine.
- Taken collectively, these great powers control most of the material resources (military capability, production capacity, wealth, technology) in their system. Because of this, their activities, and often their ideas, dominate international systems, and their interests are sufficiently wide ranging to give them a strong interest in international order.
- On this basis, one can understand a great deal about international relations simply by understanding the structure and process of relations among the great powers.
- Numbers matter, especially when they are small. Thus systems with four or five or more great powers can be lumped together as multipolar and treated as a single category, but, as the numbers drop towards one, sharply distinct system dynamics emerge, with tripolar, bipolar and unipolar systems each having their own unique qualities.

This understanding of power structure generates two points of interest: first, what are the effects on the behaviour of states of being inside any particular polarity structure; and second, what are the likely consequences of changes from one degree of polarity to another? It also supports a third, generally less explored point, already raised in chapter 2, which is how the domestic structure and character of the leading powers, particularly their ideology and their identity as great powers, affect the operation of polarity logic.

These propositions are of course similar to those for the realist approach to theorizing about international relations, and it is true that polarity does stem from (neo)realist writings, with Waltz (1964, 1979) being the *locus classicus*. But although polarity has realist roots, its use does not confine one to realist logic. Polarity can be used to move forward into realist assumptions about conflict of interest, balance of power, and war, but it can just as easily fit with international political economy concerns about leadership and the provision of collective goods, Gramscian ones about hegemony, globalist ones about a dominant core, world system ones about world empires and world economies, and English school ones about great power management and international society. Viewing this through Wendt's (1999) idea that international social structures are built around relationships of enemy, rival and friend, neorealists assume that the international system is composed of enemies and rivals, and that polarity therefore matters primarily in relation to military and political security. But as thinking about both hegemonic stability in IPE and the institutions of international society in the English school suggest, polarity can also matter, and in a very different way, in systems composed either of rivals and friends, or just friends. This adaptability arises in part from the chronic ambiguity surrounding the meaning of power. Realists generally start from material capability, but they too allow in the more ideational forms of power typical of post-positivist approaches to IR. Despite the current challenge from globalization, polarity is probably still the most widespread way of capturing in shorthand form the essentials of the global power structure. The terms bipolarity and unipolarity, and to a lesser extent multipolarity, act as a common currency across academic journals, government statements, diplomatic discourse and media reporting and commentary.

Although polarity has been implicit in IR thinking at least as far back as Thucydides, it came into explicit use only during the Cold War. For several hundred years before the Second World War the Europe-centred international system had contained four or more great powers, and thus had the quality that would later be described as multipolar. Changes in the number of great powers did not affect the basic characteristics of the system, and although the concept of polarity can be read back into this period it was little used at the time. Only after 1945, when the number of great powers dropped down to two, did the small number effect kick in, and the concept of polarity arising from the idea of 'the big two' become central to the discourse of IR. Once polarity became an established way of thinking, it was applied retrospectively to the analysis of historical international systems.

During the nearly fifty years of the Cold War most policy-makers and analysts framed their thinking in polarity terms, with argument going back and forth about whether bipolarity was a temporary effect of the outcome of the Second World War or was more durable. The understanding that the international power structure was durably bipolar became dominant during the 1970s, though it remained a focus of contestation and argument (Wagner 1993). For those engaged in public policy debates, bipolarity was a handy simplifier. In one word it seemed to capture all of the main features that made the Cold War period different from what had come before. Instead of several great powers, there were only two relatively huge superpowers whose global economic and political dominance was reinforced by possession of vast arsenals of nuclear weapons. Rather than a multitude of national and ideological divisions among states and peoples, there was an overriding worldwide ideological division between the communist and capitalist worlds. And rather than international security being managed through shifting patterns of alliance, there were two relatively fixed and durable camps. Bipolarity was the guiding star for everything from alliance policy and the theory and practice of deterrence to intervention in the third world and the theory and practice of arms control. The superpowers consciously pursued their rivalry in a bipolar (and bipolarized) framework (first world, second world), and everyone else, whether allies or the 'third world', or even peace activists, took their positions in relation to that idea. The close of the Cold War ended bipolarity in two senses: the breakdown of a material power structure based on two superpowers; and the cessation of an ideational confrontation in which totalitarian communism and democratic capitalism staked rival claims to be the future of industrial society worldwide. The comprehensive collapse of both the Soviet Union and communist ideology raised the question: after bipolarity, what? Would a new version of polarity emerge to define the strategic policy framework for the post-Cold War era, or had the implosion of bipolarity actually destroyed the utility of the polarity idea itself?

The ending of the Cold War and the demise of the Soviet Union brought a decisive close to the era of bipolarity, and in the process generated a challenge to the whole process of thinking in terms of polarity. Bipolarity was clearly over. What remained unclear was how to designate the polarity of the post-Cold War system. Without an explicit answer to this, neorealist theory was in deep trouble, and even the more pragmatic public policy discourse risked hanging on to a concept that distorted more than it explained. Confusion about this question reigned for some time in both academic and public policy circles. Since polarity theory rested on the idea of a single distinction between great powers and other states, there were only three possibilities. The system could be unipolar, in which case the US was the only candidate for sole remaining superpower. It could be multipolar, in which case Russia, China, Japan and the EU had to be elevated to parity with the US as great powers. Or it could be that polarity had somehow become obsolete, as some enthusiasts for globalization maintained, and was no longer a useful way of trying to understand the structure of international politics. For much of the 1990s, opting for unipolarity seemed to give more weight to the US than it deserved, especially in the wake of the then fashionable declinist interpretations of the US position in the world (Kennedy 1989). Opting for multipolarity posed the opposite dilemma of seeming to give Russia, China, Japan and the EU more weight than they deserved. Dismissing polarity as obsolete required not only abandoning a longstanding tradition of thought, but also buying into a globalist conception of international reality that many found suggestive, but less than fully convincing as a replacement. The globalist critique in particular raised the question of whether the Cold War had perhaps been a unique era in which analysis in terms of great power polarity seemed to produce a passing moment of clarity. If that was the case, perhaps polarity theory had little to offer once the bipolar period had closed. Perhaps *bipolarity* was interesting, but polarity theory generally was not.

The most common position in the early years of the post-Cold War era was the idea of a temporary unipolarity that would inevitably and quite quickly evolve into multipolarity (Mastanduno 1997; Kupchan 2002). But as time wore on, the unipolar moment looked more like an era in its own right, and multipolarity looked increasingly to be a long way down the line. The claim of the US to be a unipole was strengthened both by the gloss being taken off Asia by the economic crisis of the later 1990s, and by successive demonstrations of huge US military superiority in the first Gulf War, former Yugoslavia, Afghanistan, and the invasion of Iraq. Those inclined towards a unipolar thesis also drew strength from the increasing unilateralism that began to mark US foreign and defence policy. By the late 1990s a consensus had emerged among both academics and policy-makers that the unipolar 'moment' was going to be prolonged and that unipolarity was therefore the new structure of international security. Although the globalists sustained their critique, much of their analysis of a centre–periphery world, in which a developed capitalist core dominates a less-developed periphery, fitted quite comfortably with unipolarity. September 11, which many pundits pronounced as changing the basic character of the international security environment, has in fact reinforced the idea that we live in a unipolar world. The attacks on the US underlined its unique position, and the war against international terrorism both strengthened US inclinations towards unilateralism and amplified the widening gap in military capability between it and the rest of the world. September 11 and the responses to it can be interpreted as unipolar politics in action, where the lack of a balancer at the state level creates incentives and opportunities for transnational players on the dark side of global (un)civil society.

The post-Cold War crisis of polarity posed less of a problem for practitioners than for academics. The public policy debates could quite easily take a pragmatic view that the system was indeed a mixture of one superpower and some great powers without worrying about the theoretical consequences. As the end of the Cold War has receded into history, most practitioners have remained comfortable talking about a mixed system in these terms. For the more theory-minded in the academic community, however, both unipolarity and a mixture of one superpower and several great powers posed problems.

3.2   Polarity in international relations theory

During the Cold War, academic IR was not far behind the policy community in its enthusiasm for bipolarity, and the term thus successfully
established itself alongside *balance of power* and *deterrence* as one of
those relatively rare concepts used frequently in both the public policy and
academic debates. The leading figure in this development was Kenneth
N. Waltz, who in a series of seminal works laid down the theory that
became known as neorealism (Waltz 1959, 1964, 1969, 1979, 1986, 1990,
1993a, 1993b, 2000; see also Keohane 1986; Buzan et al. 1993; Wagner
1993). One of the many reasons for the ongoing success of the literature
on polarity was that it tapped into older traditions of diplomatic analysis,
international history and realism that also centred themselves on great
powers, power politics and the balance of power. Although neorealism
seemed new, and at least superficially scientific, it was in fact a reworking
of a well-established 'classical' realist perspective on world politics.
Instead of being rooted in human nature, neorealism put the cause of
power politics into the politically divided ('anarchic') structure of the international system. It provided explanations in terms of polarity for both
balance of power behaviour in general and Cold War behaviour in particular. The interest in polarity that followed generated a very substantial
literature not only during the Cold War, but continuing vigorously until
the present day. (Some of the highlights of this literature, which is too big
to list here, are: Bueno de Mesquita 1975; Cederman 1994; Deutsch and
Singer 1964; Gaddis 1992–3; Haas 1970; Hansen 2000; Hopf 1991;
Huntington 1993, 1999; James and Brecher 1988; Jervis 1993; Kaplan
1957; Kapstein and Mastanduno 1999; Kegley and Raymond 1992, 1994;
Kupchan 1998, 2002; Layne 1993, 1997; Mansfield 1993; Mastanduno
1997; Midlarsky and Hopf 1993; Nogee 1974; Rosecrance 1969, 1973;
Rosecrance and Chih-Cheng Lo 1996; Sabrosky 1985; Schweller 1993;
Singer et al. 1972; Wagner 1993; Wayman 1984; Wight 1977.)
    Neorealism was the dominant orthodoxy in IR for much of the 1980s
and 1990s and, although regularly challenged, remains influential as a
way of thinking about IR in general and the contemporary global security order in particular. Many academics shared the policy community's
descriptive assessment of the bipolar nature of the Cold War, and valued
the entry into policy debates created by a shared vocabulary. Beyond
that, many of them were stimulated by the scientific potential that polarity seemed to offer. Here was a relatively clear and simple way of characterizing the structure of international security which, in principle, could
be extended into a general theory for all times and places. Given the
eagerness fashionable at the time in IR and other social sciences to emulate
the methods of the natural sciences, this was an attractive proposition to

many. One could count the number of great powers in any international system to determine its polarity, and then test those numbers for correlations with phenomena such as war, peace, crisis, arms racing, trade and suchlike. Changes in the number of great powers could be used as benchmarks for identifying points of significant change in international systems. Logically, it was relatively easy to move outward from bipolarity to talk about unipolar, tripolar, multipolar and diffuse systems. However, the ending of bipolarity, and the subsequent debate about how to characterize the post-Cold War power structure, posed problems for neorealists in relation both to the idea of unipolarity itself, and to the notion of a mixture of one superpower and several great powers.

Unipolarity was a problem because neorealist theory had never developed a coherent image of it (Hansen 2000: 1), and the very idea seemed to go against the grain of Waltz's theory. In his original formulation, to which he has remained true, Waltz never explicitly discussed unipolarity. The closest he got was a discussion of world government, which suggests that unipolarity collapses the deep structure of anarchy and replaces it with a hierarchical system structure, in other words some form of world government. In a hierarchical structure, polarity would be less interesting than functional differentiation among the unlike units that would compose the system. The logic of his argument in *Theory of International Politics* weighs against unipolarity being a stable or durable form, and Waltz confirmed that view in his writings during the decade following the demise of bipolarity. Waltz's theory suggests that stable unipolarity should be impossible because unipolarity means the end of balance of power, and therefore effectively a drastic political transformation of the international system into some form of hierarchical structure. Realists, both 'classical' and 'neo', are wedded to the view that balance of power is an extremely strong practice deeply embedded in the sovereignty of states and the self-help, survival demands of anarchic structure. On this logic, not only should the balance mechanism operate to prevent the emergence of a unipole, but a unipole, by defying the balance mechanism, would be very close to tipping the system into a deep structure transformation from anarchy to hierarchy. Within Waltz's theory, therefore, the only room for a unipolar structure under anarchy should be a brief, and probably turbulent, period of transition, in which the unipole either succeeds in creating a world empire or federation, or else triggers vigorous balancing efforts by others which restore a system of two or more poles. Waltzian neorealism sees unipolarity as unlikely and unstable (because of balance of power countermoves) and undesirable (because of the danger of imperial world government).

For Waltz, an anarchic system requires a minimum of two great powers in order for balancing to occur. In his reflections the number of great

powers can only ever go up from two, never down (Waltz 1979, 1993a).
He does go so far as to say that it can be inferred from structural theory
that 'Countries that wield overwhelming power will be tempted to misuse
it. And even when their use of power is not an abuse, other states will see
it as being so' (Waltz 1993b: 189). This could certainly be read as suggesting that moves towards unipolarity would trigger vigorous balancing
behaviour against the sole superpower by others. Until the reality on the
ground of the post-Cold War system demanded it, Waltz (1979, 1993a,
1993b) didn't consider unipolarity because, if the system was still anarchic
and no frenzy of balancing was taking place, it could not be unipolar.
More recently Waltz (2000: 5, 24, 27–8) acknowledges the post-Cold War
system as unipolar, and finesses the problem of the absence of balancing
by saying that the balancing mechanism will restore itself, but that his
theory cannot say when. Waltz (2000: 13, 27) has managed to tweak his
theory to deal with the apparent fact of unipolarity within anarchy,
but still argues, contra Hansen (2000: 80), that 'unipolarity appears as
the least durable of international configurations' on the grounds that
'unbalanced power is a danger no matter who wields it', and because
unipoles will be tempted (as he thinks the US has been) into foolish
policies of overextension. The US-led invasion of Iraq in 2003, and the
seeming dominance of the crusading 'neocons' in Washington, did much
to widen the perception that the US was heading down this route.

An alternative, and less negative, view of unipolarity, and one with
significant connections to neorealism, has for long been available within
international political economy (IPE). Hegemonic stability theory (HST)
was de facto about a kind of unipolarity (Gilpin 1981, 1987). Because its
main concerns were about the stability of liberal international economic
orders, it did not really consider balance of power issues, emphasizing
instead the role of hegemonic leader in the world economy, which combined power and elements of consent. Unipolarity in this version had
many positive qualities in underpinning the global economy. It was seen
to have a long historical track record extending back through the US and
Britain to the Netherlands and Portugal. Ironically, its main worry was
that the burdens of hegemonic leadership tended to undermine the power
providing it, therefore periodically destabilizing the system. While HST
and neorealism might agree that unipolarity was unsustainable, HST had
no difficulty imagining that it might last for decades or even a century or
more, while the Waltzian model predicted at best a very short and probably highly turbulent existence. With the notable exceptions of Kapstein
(1999) and Guzzini (1993, 1998), no attempt was ever made to reconcile
the contradiction between HST's assumption of relatively durable unipolarity and mainstream neorealism's rejection of that possibility. Kapstein
(1999) has used HST to explain how unipolarity could in fact be stable,

and Kapstein and Mastanduno (1999) also note the trouble for Waltzian logic in the mounting evidence that the great powers are not balancing against the US. This seeming contradiction between two versions of neorealism can be understood in terms of the different conditions affecting processes of (de)securitization, depending on whether one factors in or leaves out the question of identity, and the existence or not of a strong international society based on shared economic values. The Waltzian model leaves out international society (seeing it as at best an epiphenomenon of power, not having explanatory value in its own right) and pushes economic relations to the margin (because superpowers are largely self-reliant). Put these things back into the theory, add the idea that joint gain might be a significant motive within the international system, and a quite different view of unipolarity becomes possible.

Unipolarity was thus a theoretical problem only for strict Waltzians. Those prepared to think more historically, economically, and in terms of international society had less of a problem with it. Despite being critical of Waltz's theory for its narrow understanding of this question, I intend to keep both of these perspectives in play. The HST view is a more comfortable fit with the immediate reality of the first post-Cold War decade, but Waltz's warnings of the logic of balancing and the likelihood of reactions against an overbearing hegemon still have force.

The second problem for theorists was the mixture of one superpower and several great powers that became prominent in both the practical and the academic discourses about IR during the 1990s. Waltz's theory was strict about *great power* representing a single classification. To accept a mixture of great powers and superpowers would be to undo the whole logic of making a simple calculation of polarity. As Hansen (2000: 18) states uncompromisingly: 'neorealism makes only one stratification of states: into great powers and other states.' Because Cold War bipolarity was defined by superpowers and historical multipolarity by great powers, not much thought had been paid to whether the difference in terminology implied a difference in classification that might matter for polarity theory. Leading polarity theorists such as Waltz treated the two terms as synonyms, with *superpower* simply corresponding to low-number polarities (two or three) where the small number of great powers made them correspondingly large. This reasoning might be extended to cover the label *hyperpower*, sometimes applied (Ash 2002) to the US as the 'sole superpower'. In terms of polarity theory, there was no problem if great power, superpower and hyperpower were just labels reflecting different degrees of polarity (multi-, bi- and uni-). The difficulty arose if these labels represented different types of major power that could coexist within the same international system at the same time. The post-Cold War talk of one superpower and several great powers raised exactly this problem. If there were two or more different levels of 'great power', how did one count polarity?

Practitioners continued to talk about one superpower and several great powers. The logic of HST also seemed open to this formulation inasmuch as the role of hegemonic leader was about a particular role rather than about one power outweighing the other great powers. But neorealist theory required a stricter formulation, and neorealists increasingly formed a consensus on the unipolar interpretation. Among other things, this consensus pushed into the background classification problems about great powers versus superpowers. If the system was designated as unipolar, then the question of great powers did not arise. Hard-core neorealists anyway don't care so much about descriptive accuracy. They aim to capture structural features from which they can derive generalizable laws governing the behaviour of states, especially great powers. In this move they were helped by the questionable standing, in neorealist terms, of some of the supposed post-Cold War great powers. The EU was not a state, Russia was an economic basket case, Japan's power was almost all in its economy, and China, while presenting a balanced profile of power, was still pretty weak and had a lot of internal restructuring still to do (Buzan and Foot 2004). Since great powers were supposed to be states, and to have world-class power in all sectors, all of the post-Cold War candidates for great power status looked problematic in the terms laid down by Waltz (more on this in chapters 4 and 5). The surge in US unilateralism and military spending after September 11 helped to reinforce a unipolarist interpretation that was already pretty well established.

So polarity survived the initial confusion following the collapse of bipolarity, albeit with a conspicuous split between harder and softer versions of unipolarity and some ongoing awkwardness about the existence of great power, or near great power, states and entities (the EU) alongside the sole superpower. But how useful was it as both a theoretical and a political idea?

3.3   The utility of polarity

For both academics and practitioners polarity possesses two strong attractions as a way of thinking about international relations. First, it puts the balance of power, that most venerable concept of diplomatic parlance and realist analysis, into theoretical form, and holds out the prospect that its mechanisms can be explored systematically. By providing a causality rooted in the structure of international politics, it also distances the logic of power politics from conservative assumptions about human nature. Second, polarity offers a stunningly bold way of simplifying the horrendous day-to-day complexities of world politics. The move of reducing inter-national politics to relations among the great powers established a basic set of benchmarks (shifts in polarity) against which to measure change and stability in the system. For academics, thinking in terms of polarity held out the prospect of a more rigorous, scientific approach to understanding international relations. For the public policy discourse it offered a starting point simple enough for almost anyone to grasp, and capable of serving as a foundation for a wide variety of positions on major policy issues ranging from nuclear deterrence and alliance policy to the standing of the third world. But how well has polarity served the aspirations of both social science and public policy?

In terms of social science, the record has been mixed. Like most other attempts to turn IR into a hard science, polarity theory largely failed to fulfil the ambitions of those who tried to correlate it formally with war, peace and system stability. The longstanding inability to quantify power in its international relations sense was one obstacle. Without such a measure, how can one reliably identify which states are, and which are not, great powers? If the classification of great powers is indeterminate, then so is the specification of polarity and the ability to know when or if polarity is undergoing change. But even where acceptable common-sense definitions of polarity were applied, no clear correlations or causal pat-terns emerged on the big questions. By itself polarity proved too simple to act as any kind of general predictor about war, peace and stability in the international system. The polarity of the system was, for example, much the same in 1920 as it was in 1914, but the intervening years of global war had greatly changed the whole prospect for peace or war. The recent literature on 'democratic peace' points to an alternative variable, not linked to polarity, that appears to bear significantly on the question of war or peace (see, for example: Doyle 1986; Oneal and Russett 1999; Chan 1997; Cohen 1994). I have myself argued (Buzan and Little 2000: 333, 391) that, in a macro-historical perspective, polarity is a less import-ant signifier of structural change than a shift from one type of dominant unit or units (empires, city-states, barbarians) to another (sovereign ter-ritorial states). That criticism, however, does not prevent polarity from being interesting within shorter historical timespans.

So the most obvious criticism is that, by itself, polarity does not seem to determine much. If it cannot provide a general explanation for IR even in its own terms, what use is it? Other lines of opposition address not just technical points, but the whole conception, questioning both its accuracy and its ethics. In terms of accuracy, polarity rests on a realist understanding of what the international system is and how it works. It defines the system primarily in terms of states, and the dynamics of international relations primarily in terms of conflict. It assumes that the

driving logic behind state behaviour is the need to accrue power in order
to ensure survival in a more-or-less Darwinistic system whose basic rule
is survival of the fittest. Many argue that this is no longer, if it ever was,
a good way of understanding the international system. Boxing everything
into states pushes hosts of powerful and important non-state actors
such as firms, religions, and the many organizations of global civil (and
uncivil) society into the background. State-centrism also emphasizes a
military–political interpretation of what makes the system tick, too often
at the expense of, for example, interpretations rooted in the world economy and/or international society. Polarity is essentially a material view
of the system, resting on relative accumulations of capability. Such an
approach discounts the whole social side of life. It assumes that the
actors in the system are at best rivals, at worst enemies, and never friends.
It assumes that the drive for power to preserve security always trumps
other, more potentially collaborative, motives, such as desire to increase
wealth, welfare and knowledge. And it discounts the effects of homogen-
ization among states, such as the convergence in domestic values and
structures that underlies the 'democratic peace'. On ethical grounds these
assumptions have long been criticized for the danger they pose of creating self-fulfilling prophecies. Analysing international relations in terms of
power politics risks increasing the possibility that actors will behave in
that way.

   Despite both the descriptive and ethical challenges that can be put to
it, and its failure to fulfil the more extreme ambitions for it, polarity has
still been extremely useful in academic thinking about world politics and
international security. Not least, it stimulated a much higher awareness
throughout the discipline of IR of the advantages of differentiating between structural explanations (where observed behaviour is accounted
for by the principles governing the arrangement of the units in the system) and unit level explanations (where observed behaviour is accounted
for by the internal processes of the actors composing the system and the
interactions between them).

   As with many social science concepts, its strengths are the mirror
image of its shortcomings. While oversimplification is a fault from a
descriptive point of view, it is a necessity for theorizing. Whatever its
weaknesses, polarity captures a basic feature of the international power
structure. So long as humankind remains divided up into political entities
claiming the ultimate right of self-government (states), and so long
as relations among those states are sufficiently competitive in character
to carry a risk of war, the distribution of power among them is going
to matter. Even if the ruthless Darwinistic side of international politics is
substantially overlaid by concerns carrying at least partly cooperative
imperatives, such as sustaining a global economy or managing the

planetary environment, the distribution of power still matters as far as what kind of international orders are possible and how they will function. This is clear from the long agonizing within IPE about the (in)stabilities of liberal international economic orders in relation to the presence or absence of a hegemonic power (Kindleberger 1973, 1981; Buzan 1984; Keohane 1984; Gilpin 1987). Polarity matters so long as war remains a possibility, and so long as major outcomes in international politics have to be achieved by negotiation among politically independent entities. Because it rests on a plausible claim to capture a fundamental feature of international politics, polarity offers a theoretical starting point from which one can build more nuanced analyses by bringing in other variables. By itself, polarity provides insufficient information to construct a reliable basic characterization of international politics. But in combination with just a few other factors it still holds out the prospect of achieving a relatively simple way into the complexities of international relations. For example, polarity can be combined with geography, as it is in the work of those who point out the importance of the fact that one great power, the US, is relatively isolated from the other great powers, which are all co-located in Eurasia. Distance matters to the extent that it affects the ease or difficulty of bringing power to bear, and among other things this was why Soviet power was particularly threatening after the Second World War (Wagner 1993; Layne 1997; Buzan and Wæver 2003). Polarity can be combined with assessments about the foreign policy orientation of the great powers (whether they are revisionist or status quo) (Schweller 1993; Schweller and Wohlforth 2000) and/or with more precise assessments of the nature of the balance of power, such as Wagner's (1993) distinction between 'loose' (no state is close to being able to dominate the system) and 'tight' (one power is close to dominance). It can also be combined with constructivist and/or English school insights into the social structure of international systems (Wendt 1999; Buzan 2004a). Such relatively simple combinations allow analysts to offer plausible general interpretations of the main lines of world politics.

Polarity is attractive as a theoretical starting point because of the immediate way it bears on the relational logic among the players in the game of international politics. As noted, polarity does not always determine outcomes. But it is a very useful guide to understanding the logic of pressures and imperatives that are inherent in many situations, not just in military security, but also in diplomacy, international institutions and economic management. For example, knowing the polarity of a system suggests hypotheses about how power balancing is likely to work. In a bipolar system, most balancing will have to be internal (i.e. by the rivals expanding or mobilizing their domestic resources), whereas in a multipolar system states can balance more economically by seeking other powers as allies (Waltz 1979: 168). Hansen (2000: 53–68) argues that in a unipolar system there will be no balancing against the single great power, but a lot by other states against each other. She also suggests (2000: 14–15, 68–73) that changes in polarity create distinctive transition periods in which the analyst has to look more for effects of the transition than for effects of structure. By extension, polarity also implies quite a lot about the likely patterns of alliance formation: probably durable and fairly rigid under bipolarity, probably opportunistic and flexible in multipolar structures, perhaps irrelevant in unipolar ones. Polarity says a lot about the logic of nuclear deterrence, which is relatively simple between two powers (because there can be only one source of strike and one target for retaliation), but gets extremely complicated when three or more powers are in play (Buzan 1987: 173–7). A similar pattern of polarity logic works in relation to the design and implementation of arms control agreements. Although polarity was conceived as a way of thinking about great powers in the international system as a whole, nothing prevents one from applying it to the analysis of international regions. Walt (1987), Lake and Morgan (1997) and Buzan and Wæver (2003) have done this in the security domain. In the study of the international political economy, some think it crucial to how, or possibly whether, the international economy is managed, with a unipolar hegemon as the favoured option for a liberal economy (Keohane 1984). This type of thinking runs parallel to that in economics, where the character of markets can be understood according to whether their structure is unipolar (monopoly), multipolar (oligopoly) or diffuse (perfect competition), and it is no accident that neorealism drew heavily on this economic model. Underlying much of this insight is a fairly simple general logic of coalitions. Arranging bargains of whatever kind is affected by the number of parties to the negotiation, and the effects are particularly strong when the number of parties is small (Riker 1962). Overall, polarity fitted nicely with the rational choice approach to international relations that was particularly strong in US social science.

One can conclude that, from an academic perspective, while polarity did not fulfil the hopes of some for an economistic grand theory of international politics, it did sharpen up theoretical thinking in a general way, and made a number of specific contributions to thinking about strategic, diplomatic and economic relations among states at both global and regional levels. It might still be argued that most of these contributions centred on the Cold War and bipolarity, leaving open the questions of whether it was bipolarity specifically, rather than polarity in general, that was interesting and useful. Despite the efforts of Kapstein and Mastanduno (1999), Hansen (2000) and others, it is not yet so clear whether unipolarity by itself will be able to provide much structural guidance to the behaviour of states, or what else it will have to be combined with to generate the kind of analytical leverage that bipolarity gave during the Cold War. One of the purposes of this book is to try to push forward on that front.

Whatever problems academics might have with it, polarity has been hugely influential in public debates about international relations. This success is not just confined to the Cold War, when bipolarity framed the bulk of the discourse, but extends right down to the present day. The unipolar interpretation of world politics has steadily gained strength in the public discourse, and has been much reinforced by the surge in US unilateralism following September 11. Unipolarity is now a ubiquitous point of reference in public discussions about international relations, and that fact helps to keep it in play in the academic debates. Those academics engaged in the policy debates can hardly be expected to ignore either the opportunity or the responsibility to make something out of the existence of a shared concept. Bipolarity flattered the US and the Soviet Union by elevating them to special status and legitimating their claims to exceptional rights and roles in international politics. Unipolarity does this even more for the US, and thus has huge attractions within the American debate. Within the US, unipolarity serves as a kind of touchstone around which options for American foreign policy and grand strategy are debated. As with other elements of the analytical apparatus of IR, widespread and sustained use of a term such as unipolarity becomes part of what it purports to describe. Acceptance of unipolarity helps both to make it true and to hold that 'truth' in place, and this works for both those in favour of (or resigned to), and those opposed to, the position of the US as the unipole. Outside the US, unipolarity serves in a general way to define the policy problem for two quite different groups. First are those who oppose the US 'hyperpower', and would prefer a multipolar power structure (and whose voices are loud in China, Russia, France, Iran, India and elsewhere). Second are those friendly to the US, but who worry that unipolarity is somehow fuelling an increasingly unilateralist policy in Washington which is undermining a whole framework of international institutions and multilateral agreements that the US was previously instrumental in supporting. So whatever its flaws, polarity is well established as both a theoretical approach to understanding the international power structure and a social fact in the public debates about world politics. Since it is so firmly embedded in this way, academics have some social responsibility for improving public understanding about what it does and does not signify and explain.

4

Great Powers:
A Troubled Concept?

This chapter takes a historical perspective on understanding the concept of great powers. Its main subject is the practical way in which the concept has been understood in relation to three periods: before 1945, the Cold War and since 1989. The main focus is on the European origins of the modern concept of great power, and the main argument is that insufficient account has been taken of the problems created by expansion from a European-scale international system to a global-scale one. There is of course a story about great powers and polarity to be told before the rise of Europe, and readers interested in exploring this aspect of the ancient and classical world should see, *inter alia*, the works of Raymond Cohen (1995a, 1995b, 1998), Watson (1992), Wight (1977) and Buzan and Little (2000). I do not pursue it here because I want to look mainly forward rather than backward.

4.1   Understanding 'great powers' up to 1945

The modern concept of great power comes out of European diplomatic history, though it has antecedents in thinking about the classical histories of Athens and Sparta, Carthage and Rome, the empires of the ancient Middle East, and China. Over the last 500 years, the very vigorous international politics of the European states system could usefully be simplified by the distinction between great powers and others. Some countries such as France, Britain and Russia were always in the ranks of the great powers. Others, such as Spain, Sweden, Austria and the Ottoman empire, waxed and waned. New great powers could be created, as in the unifications of Italy and Germany during the nineteenth century. In the war-prone European context, the principal criteria for great power standing were military power and victory in war, though there was also a diplomatic element of formal status recognition by the peer group at the top table. The focus of all this was very much within the cockpit of Europe, and in that context the only need was to differentiate between types of great power (and empire) – maritime, such as Britain, based on naval capability; and continental, such as Germany and Austria-Hungary, based on land power. The geographical smallness of Europe, and the close interlinkage of its wars and balance of power from the seventeenth century onwards, meant that what in actuality were quite different types of power could easily be considered as a single set. Although there might be some arguments about who qualified as a great power, the idea that a distinction could be drawn between great powers and all the other states was not controversial. This way of thinking read back easily into the more familiar (i.e. Mediterranean) bits of classical history, seeming thereby to gain a long historical validity.

Difficulties for this classification arose when this compact European regional international system began taking over most of the rest of the world. Between the sixteenth and nineteenth centuries, the European system virtually became the global international system, with most of the planet at one time or another under the direct control, or heavy influence, of European powers. Some of the European states, particularly those on the Western fringe, became major overseas imperial powers, as indeed did some quite small European states such as Portugal, the Netherlands, Denmark and Belgium. On the other side of Europe, Russia expanded overland deep into Central and Northeast Asia, eventually reaching the Pacific coast of North America. The Ottoman empire encompassed much of the Middle East and the Balkans, as well as North Africa, and thus, like Russia, extended well beyond Europe, but it was in decline and increasingly held in place by the balance of competition among the European powers. The expansion of Europe opened up a fundamental difference between European powers with multi-continental empires (initially Spain and Portugal, but later mainly Britain, France and Russia) and those whose power was largely based in, and confined to, Europe (Sweden, Prussia/Germany, Austria-Hungary, Italy). The Ottoman empire, on the fringes of Europe but increasingly part of the European states system, was somewhere in between.

This distinction between powers operating largely within their own region and those operating in two or more regions is different from the standard distinction between maritime and continental powers. It is not just about the nature of military power (navy or army) or whether empires are continental or overseas. It is about the difference between world powers and local ones. Because the main focus of world power was still overwhelmingly centred in Europe, this distinction did not register, and has not registered much since, in thinking about that time. In effect European history *was* world history during this era. By the nineteenth century, none of the major centres of power of the classical world could withstand European might sufficiently to register as a great power in European eyes, not even China. The stone-age empires in the Americas had been quickly eliminated during the sixteenth century. India was largely under European control by the late eighteenth century, and China and Japan had lost their ability to resist European (and American) military pressure by the middle of the nineteenth century. The wars and the balances that really mattered were those in Europe, for it was in that cockpit that all of the great powers resided, where their status in relation to each other was made or lost, and where influence in, or control over, other parts of the world was decided. Because those great powers largely confined to Europe and those with far-flung overseas possessions were all bundled together within the space of Europe, and fought their main wars there, it was easy to see them as being essentially all one class of great power, despite their differences. As a consequence 'great power' was still understood in a European context even though the international system had in some very important ways, and for the first time, become global (Buzan and Little 2000: 241–345).

From the late nineteenth century a new factor entered the picture in the form of non-European great powers. Until quite recently, this was the story of Japan and the US, though in the last few decades China and India have also been knocking on the door. The US was a European offshoot, but for much of the nineteenth century aloof from the European system. Its burst of overseas empire-building in the late nineteenth century, its successful industrialization and its intervention in the First World War established its great power credentials. Japan's story is unique: it was the only non-European country to acquire Western techniques fast enough not only to prevent itself from being colonized but also to enter the great power ranks. Japan set about pursuing the political fashion of the day by carving out an empire in East Asia, and in the process acquired great power status both by allying with Britain and, more decisively, by defeating in war a recognized European great power, Russia. Yet despite their different origins, there are some striking similarities in the rise of the US and Japan to great power status, and not just the fact that each occurred at about the same time. Japan's history in East Asia is not unlike that of the US in relation to Latin America. Both countries developed as major industrial and military powers within regions largely composed of colonial, semi-colonial or ex-colonial states that were relatively weak (politically, economically, militarily) compared to them. During the nineteenth century, both Japan and the US moved decisively out of the global periphery and into the core, while their neighbours (except Canada) did not. Because of their relative economic, political and military strength, both became regional hegemons. They would not have been able to avoid dominating their adjacent international environments even had they wished to exercise such restraint. In fact, both embraced the imperial opportunity. Both became successor threats within their regions to earlier impositions by European colonial powers on the local peoples, and both acquired regional reputations for arrogant military intervention and self-interested economic dominance. For both, the imbalance in power with their regional neighbours resulted in a love–hate relationship: part admiration and emulation, and part envy, fear and dislike. Since 1945, their paths have diverged, though both still have awkward relations with their neighbours. The US has maintained its industrial superiority over its neighbours by a large margin, whereas Japan has had an experience more like Britain's, in which later industrializing neighbours eventually (and sometimes sooner than expected) catch up and overtake the initial leader. A reassertion of the kind of military and political dominance in Asia that Japan enjoyed from 1895 to 1945 is simply impossible. The neighbouring states are now much too strong in both conventional and nuclear military capability, and Japan's postmodern society is no longer inclined to express its power in aggressive military terms.

The arrival of these two new powers broke Europe's monopoly hold on great power status, and opened an era in which great powers could be more geographically remote from each other. But right down to the end of the Second World War, and up to a point even during the Cold War, Europe remained the principal focus of world power, and the place where the decisive world wars were mainly fought. Thus to the middle of the twentieth century the concept of great power remained essentially Eurocentric, with the US and Japan relating primarily to a European-centred balance of power.

The conventional list of great powers given for 1914 is nine, and includes the two newcomers: Austria-Hungary, Britain, France, Germany, Italy, Japan, the Ottoman empire, Russia, the US. For 1939 the list shrinks to seven: Britain, France, Germany, Italy, Japan, Russia/USSR, the US. These lists give an accurate assessment of the location of the main economic and military powers in the international system, and they also accord with diplomatic recognition of this rank, though by 1914 the Ottoman empire was included more out of courtesy than for its capability, and there were some doubts about Italy's standing. If one thinks of these lists in the Eurocentric context of their time, they make pretty good sense. But if one strips away the Eurocentric bias and looks at them purely in the context of the global-scale international system that was by the twentieth century fully established, then different conclusions emerge.

Most obvious is that a standard of entry that allows in the likes of Italy and the Ottoman empire is not all that demanding, and that the range of difference between those two at one end of the scale, and the US at the other, is enormous. Kennedy (1989: 314, 429) notes that in 1914 the national income of the US was already more than three times as great as that of Britain and Germany, nine times that of Italy, twelve times that of Austria-Hungary and eighteen times that of Japan. In 1937 the range is similar, with the US still having seventeen times the national income of Japan and eleven times that of Italy. Equally striking in a global context is that these lists differentiate fairly clearly into what I will for the moment call *superpowers* (possessing and using intercontinental military–political reach) and *regional great powers* (largely confined to their own continental or subcontinental area). Unquestionably in the superpower rank would be Britain, the US and Russia/USSR. Unquestionably in the regional great power rank would be the Austro-Hungarian empire, Italy and Japan.

Schweller (1993: 75), in a study of the run-up to the Second World War, agrees with the need to differentiate classes of great power, but does so on the material basis that, to count as a 'pole' of power, a state must possess 'more than half the resources of the most powerful state'. On his measures, he sees the international system of the 1930s as tripolar, with the Soviet Union, the US and Germany counting as poles, and Britain, Japan, France and Italy counting as 'middle powers'. This approach certainly captures material weight, but it undervalues the reach of power, which counts against Germany and in favour of Britain and France. Wight (1979: 56, 63) toys with a similar distinction to the one I am getting at with his idea of 'world powers', 'with interests in the world at large', and 'regional great powers'.

In my scheme, France and Germany are problematic. Both (but especially Germany) were in the same material capability rank as the superpowers. According to Kennedy (1989: 314) Germany ranked second in national income in 1914, well below the US, but just ahead of third-placed Britain. France ranked fifth, just below Russia. As a latecomer, Germany acquired few overseas colonies, and after the First World War it had none. But, as demonstrated during both the First and the Second World War, Germany did possess intercontinental military reach. By contrast, France had extensive colonies, but because of the threat from Germany had to focus its military capabilities on Europe. Partly because of the threat they posed to each other, these two states were predominantly regional great powers in Wight's sense in terms of their military deployments. Germany clearly had the stronger potential to bid for superpower status but was frustrated in its ambition both by its late start and by its geostrategic position locked into the heart of the European system. France had a better de facto claim for superpower status on the basis of its overseas empire. More on this problem in chapter 5.

A distinction between superpowers and regional great powers based on the operational range of power holds, regardless of changes in the factors that generate power. It works as well before the industrial revolution as after it. Pushing the global perspective harder back into the pre-1945 period than is usually done makes what happened after 1945 much easier to understand. An oversimplified version of the story would be that, in the course of two world wars, the three superpowers (Britain, the US, Russia/USSR) either eliminated (Austria-Hungary, Ottoman empire) or demoted (Japan, France, Germany, Italy) all of the regional great powers. This rendition of course greatly understates the role of Germany. Germany might be said to have played the major part in demoting France, and twice came close to eliminating Russia and Britain. Germany could be held substantially responsible for Britain's inability to hang on to its superpower status for more than a few years after the end of the Second World War. This story reflects the lopsidedly strong position of Europe, and therefore of its regional great powers, in the global international system up to the middle of the twentieth century.

4.2   Understanding 'great powers' during the Cold War

This Eurocentric story leads into the familiar territory of the Cold War. Britain, its resources drained by two world wars, and its empire beginning to crumble away, drops out of 'the big three' during the late 1940s. Germany gets divided and becomes the front line of the Cold War. Japan comes under US suzerainty, as in a less extreme fashion does Western Europe as a whole. Although the UN Security Council designates five great powers, France and China only get there courtesy, respectively, of Britain and the US, and China loses its place de facto between 1949 and 1971 when US-sponsored Taiwan holds the seat. By the mid-1950s, the international system had clearly become bipolar, with each of the remaining two superpowers constructing coalitions of lesser powers around its own ideological, economic and military core.

While bipolarity was in some ways an accurate structural description of the Cold War international system, it also unquestionably served the interests of the two superpowers. It lifted them and their ideological rivalry to the centre of world politics, and helped to justify their assertions of hegemony and/or suzerainty over their respective camps. As Freedman (1999: 23–5) notes, it enabled them to form a kind of diplomatic club from which all others could be excluded. Since polarity is an American theory, this self-serving aspect is important. It perhaps goes some way to explaining why the designation of bipolarity effectively resisted the mounting evidence against it that accumulated from the 1960s onwards, though in seeking an explanation for this durability one would also have to point to academic considerations. First was the need of polarity theory for very clear categorizations without which the whole idea was a non-starter. Second was the failure of most of the academic IR community to think carefully enough about the meaning of polarity in terms of great powers, and particularly about what qualified a state for entry into the great power ranks. Among other things, IR failed to register sufficiently the impact on definitions of great power of the shift from a Europe-centred international system to a more genuinely global-scale one. Talk about 'poles of power' stretched across the past several centuries as if there was no difference except the number of great powers between the seventeenth-century European system and the twentieth-century global one. On the common-sense level, bipolarity was a pleasingly simple way for the press and the person in the street to grasp the complexities of world politics.

There were three problems with bipolarity as a blanket designation of military–political system structure. First was the growing realization from the 1970s onwards that the Soviet Union was an 'incomplete' superpower (Dibb 1988; Kennedy 1989: 554ff). It possessed first-rank military forces and could compete in space and nuclear technology. But it increasingly failed to register as a significant element in the world economy, eventually being surpassed by Japan. Thus, according to Waltzian materialist criteria, the Soviet Union did not really measure up as a full-spectrum great power in the way that the US did, though just as clearly it did meet the criteria of recognition. The superpower club remained operational in terms of summitry and talks about arms control, and the military duopoly was reinforced by what seemed a deeply embedded rivalry between alternative systems defined by radically opposed ideologies. In relational terms it was the Soviet Union that the US had both to worry about and to treat as its sole peer.

Second, and in some ways related, was the marked disaggregation of power that emerged during the Cold War (Buzan et al. 1993: 51–65). This was principally to do with the resurfacing of Japan and West Germany as economic great powers, but prevented by the deep hangover of their behaviour during the Second World War from taking on 'normal' great power roles and functions. More broadly it was also expressed in the rise of the European Community/Union as an economic giant with some actor quality, but not enough by way of political–military institutions to count as a state. Could such an entity be counted as a great power? Did great powers have to have nuclear weapons or could 'civilian powers' count? The problem of disaggregated power was registered even more broadly in the globalization perspective, which saw international power generally as shifting away from the state to other institutions (firms, markets, IGOs, INGOs) and from the military–political sector to the economic one. What kind of bipolarity was it when one of the two poles of power had an economy smaller than some countries outside that inner circle, and where military power seemed increasingly less relevant to understanding the driving forces of international relations?

Third was the re-emergence of regional powers. In some ways this overlapped with the disaggregation problem, in that Germany, Japan and the EC could be seen as old centres of power re-emerging from the catastrophe of the Second World War. But there was more to it than that. In particular, China re-emerged during the 1950s and 1960s from a much more remote past as a great power. The pace of China's real development, as well as its endlessly mooted potential, seemed to cast it in a role in Asia similar in some ways to Germany's role in nineteenth-century Europe: big, centrally located, rapidly industrializing, authoritarian, and perceived as a threat by most of its neighbours (Buzan and Segal 1994). Since China, unlike Germany and Japan, was evidently aiming to be a full-spectrum power, it was a clear potential challenger to bipolarity. Its significance was underlined by the importance attached to the US opening to China during the early 1970s and the subsequent way in which 'the China card' was played in US–Soviet relations. This empirical challenge to bipolarity was never properly addressed by polarity theory. One fudge was to talk of a 'great power triangle' (or sometimes quadrangle) *in Asia*, thereby avoiding the question of China's global standing (Segal 1982; Thomas 1983). Another fudge was to talk of China as a 'half' pole (Hinton 1975), while avoiding the crucial definitional question of what this might mean for the theory. China might have been seen as a regional great power and explicitly differentiated from the two superpowers in that way. But the European historical tradition of thinking about great powers as a single set did not encourage this kind of differentiation. Neither did neorealist conceptions of polarity, which were perhaps even more rigid in their requirement for a single category of great power. A serious differentiation between superpowers and regional great powers would have required a major reformulation of the theory.

Despite these problems, the bipolar designation of the global power structure largely clung on among both academics and practitioners down to the end of the Cold War.

4.3   Problems of the 'great power' concept in the post-Cold War world

The ending of the Cold War and the implosion of the USSR unequivocally brought the period of bipolarity to an end. But in doing so, it amplified the problems posed by regional great powers and the disaggregation of power to such an extent as to prevent the quick and clear designation of an alternative system polarity. In itself, this was perhaps not unusual given that it took quite some time for bipolarity to emerge as the designator of the Cold War structure (though this test is perhaps a little unfair because polarity theory itself was not in place until a couple of decades after 1945). At least initially, common sense failed utterly, focusing on the rather formless idea of 'a new world disorder' (Carpenter 1991). Academic opinion split, with some (Wohlforth 1999) going for the idea of unipolarity (based on the US as 'the last superpower') and others (Kupchan 1998) opting for multipolarity. The main initial position among those who still accepted the utility of polarity, as noted above, was to see a unipolar 'moment' (of unspecified duration) to be followed inevitably by multipolarity (Layne 1993; Waltz 1993a; Haass 1999; Kupchan 2002). Another position was to attempt mixtures, such as Huntington's idea of 'uni-multipolarity' (Huntington 1991). For those opposed to the idea of polarity, the main position was globalization.

During the Cold War, bipolarity had been accepted even by those who opposed it (Kaldor 1990). But post-Cold War, liberal triumphalism produced a globalization school of thought that attacked the state-centric, power politics assumptions on which the core idea of polarity theory rested. Globalists emphasized the diffusion of power away from the state and the military sector to other actors and other sectors. The globalist perspective is generally understood to be the antithesis of realism's (and neorealism's) statist, power-political understanding of international system structure. Globalization is rooted mainly in cultural, transnational and international political economy approaches. Perhaps its clearest guiding theme is the deterritorialization of world politics (Held et al. 1999: 7–9; Woods 2000: 6; Scholte 2000: 2–3; for the arguments against globalization, see Hirst and Thompson 1996). In its stronger versions (whether Marxian or liberal), deterritorialization sweeps all before it, taking the state, and the state system, off the centre stage of world politics (Held et al. 1999: 3–5). Milder versions leave the state and the state system in, but put lots of non-state actors and systems through and alongside them (Held et al. 1999: 7–9; Scholte 2000; Woods 2000: 1–19; Clark 1999). In this context, the motives of 'postmodern' or 'competition' states are driven more by economic than by *Machtpolitik* motives (Cerny 1995; Cooper 1996; Zacher 1992).

In terms of structure, the globalist position is clearer as an attack on neorealism's state-centric approach than it is as a statement of an explicit alternative. The global market, or capitalism, or various forms of world society probably best capture the underlying ideas of system structure in the globalist perspective, and the key point is rejection of the idea that an adequate sense of system structure can be captured by privileging states.

Marxian and liberal versions of globalization differ more in their normative perspectives than in their basic understanding of what globalization means: here, as elsewhere, they are mirror images of the same phenomenon. Both see the macro-structure of the international system as taking a centre–periphery (or 'rich world–poor world', 'developed–developing') form, with a core of societies (or elites) controlling most of the capital, technology, information, organizational and ideological resources in the system and shaping the terms on which the periphery participates. In the Marxian view, this structure is fundamentally exploitative, unequal, unstable and undesirable, whereas in the liberal one it is fundamentally progressive and developmental, and its tendencies towards instability, though serious, are not without institutional solutions. Some versions of globalization, which stressed Americanization, could be read as supporting a unipolar view, albeit not in a classical Westphalian sense. But most took the view that power had become so dispersed and disaggregated that the concept of polarity was neither sustainable nor useful in the post-Cold War world.

The case for unipolarity rested on the unique position of the US. After the demise of the USSR, the US was very clearly the only superpower. It alone had world-class capabilities across a broad spectrum, and its military capabilities in particular were far ahead of those of any other state. Given the disparity of capability, role, global reach and status between the US and the next group of great powers, the system could not simply be described as multipolar, at least not without repeating the same distortion that ranking Italy and the Ottoman empire alongside the US, Germany and Britain created in 1914. Just as obviously, the US was nowhere near powerful enough to have eliminated the possibility of great power balancing, let alone being able to transform the international system from anarchy to hierarchy. Waltz's concerns about 'overwhelming power' notwithstanding, the deeply institutionalized role of the US in so many parts of the system meant that it did not immediately inspire a counter-balancing coalition fearful of its power (Ikenberry 2002a). In some ways the US's will to lead diminished sharply once its great rival was defeated, most notoriously in its sustained assault on the UN and other IGOs and in its acute sensitivity (before September 11) to military casualties. Yet in other ways US leadership, and acceptance of it by others, remained strong. The US was still firmly engaged in four major regions: Europe, East Asia, the Middle East and its traditional backyard in South America (as well as, of course, in its home region of North America) (Buzan 1998). In the first two, it retained the main Cold War arrangements that institutionalized its hegemony (NATO and the US–Japan alliance) and continued to play a central role in politico-military developments (Bosnia, Serbia, Korea, Taiwan). In the Middle East, it strengthened its position both by imposing its military presence in the Gulf and by managing the drawn-out peace process between Israel and its Arab neighbours. If the political and security structure of the post-Cold War world was to be understood as unipolar, then the US's 'swing-power' position as the only state with a dominating role in many regions was a far weaker construction of it than anything envisaged by neorealist theory. It was not unipolarity in the sense of being the potential suzerain core of a world empire or federation. It was not even global hegemony in the sense of having its leadership universally acknowledged and accepted.

The case for multipolarity rested on two foundations: the end of bipolarity; and an understanding that US power had been in long-term relative decline, and that there were too many other significant powers about to justify a unipolar interpretation. The relative decline of the US was easily measured by the steady shrinkage of its share of the global GNP, from nearly 50 per cent in 1945, towards a more natural level of around 20 to 25 per cent. Before September 11, it could also be seen in the marked shrinkage of US willingness to take on overseas commitments or risk sustaining military casualties. In such an environment, there was more room for other powers to assert themselves, and by the end of the twentieth century there was a considerable list of states able and willing to do so, though mostly only within their own regions (e.g. Brazil, China, Egypt, India, Iran, Israel, Nigeria, Russia, South Africa, Turkey). One problem with the multipolar image was where and how to draw the line under what counted as a 'pole'. How did one deal with big but partial powers such as Russia, Japan and the EU? And after them, what? The list of potential candidates faded steadily from rising transregional powers (China, India) down to powers influential only in their region (Brazil, Nigeria, South Africa and suchlike). South Africa was a great power in a sense, and perhaps not all that different from Italy or the Ottoman empire in 1914. But including it would make the list absurdly long, suggesting not even multipolarity but a diffuse power structure.

In the event, as already noted, by the late 1990s unipolarity emerged as the dominant interpretation of the international power structure, albeit with some thinking of it as prospectively durable (Kapstein 1999) and others taking the more Waltzian line that a shift to multipolarity could not be long delayed (Kupchan 2002).

4.4 Conclusion

This chapter has summarized briefly how polarity has been interpreted for different periods. Since the idea itself was invented during the Cold War period its application to earlier times represents a retroactive assessment, although the diplomatic histories and records, with their focus on balance of power, suggest that a designation of 'multipolar' would not have inspired controversy had it been used during the pre-1945 period. During and since the Cold War polarity language represents both an analytical and a contemporary usage. With a few exceptions (Schweller 1993) one would probably not now find controversial a general statement along the lines that the pre-1945 international system was multipolar, the Cold War one bipolar, and the post-Cold War one (at least at the moment) unipolar. But this thinking rests on the understanding that 'great power' represents a single class of states distinct from all others. As already hinted, there are strong grounds for questioning this position.

5

Rethinking Definitions: Superpowers, Great Powers and Regional Powers

What is the thinking that lies behind the idea of great powers – or indeed hyperpowers, superpowers, middle powers, regional powers and all such classifications that designate a special status, capability and role in the international system? Given the tension between the need of polarity theory to count 'poles', and the very wide range of capabilities encompassed in the existing usage of 'great power', can this concept be tightened up? If it can, what are the consequences for thinking in terms of polarity in general and unipolarity in particular?

5.1   Classical definitions of *great power*

The term 'great power' has been common in diplomatic parlance since at least the mid-eighteenth century. Yet the term has not itself been all that stable. It nearly disappeared during the Cold War, being replaced by 'superpower' when the material capabilities of the US and the Soviet Union so greatly outpaced those of the next ranking great power(s) (initially Britain, later also Japan, Germany, France and China) as to require differentiation (Morgenthau 1978: 349). Neorealists have not much concerned themselves about this label change because it did not affect how the concept of polarity could be applied: bipolarity meant superpowers and multipolarity meant great powers.

Surprisingly, and with exceptions such as Schweller (1993), even among neorealists who stage themselves as devoted to the development of scientific rigour in IR there is a willingness to duck the task of defining great power. The most common dodge is the idea that, even though the power of states cannot be reliably measured, at any given time there is a practical consensus about who the great powers are. Waltz (1979: 131) says confidently: 'Any ranking at times involves difficulties of comparison and uncertainties about where to draw lines. Historically, despite the difficulties, one finds general agreement about who the great powers of a period are, with occasional doubt about marginal cases. . . . Counting the great powers of an era . . . [is an empirical question] and common sense can answer it.' Not surprisingly, those on the more historical side of IR agree. Wight (1979: 41) says, 'It is easier to answer it [the question 'what is a great power?'] historically, by enumerating the great powers at any date, than by giving a definition, for there is always broad agreement about the existing great powers.' But the game is given away by the fact that even Wight's own comments are inconsistent about which countries count as great powers (Wight 1979: 28, 41, 48, 54, 65) and a moment's reflection suggests that, if this assumption was ever true, it was not so during the 1990s, when there was no consensus other than on the US. As noted above, some thought the system durably unipolar, others that it was, or very soon would be, multipolar, and yet others that there were several types of power in play at the same time. Part of the problem is that the concept of polarity itself has disaggregated into different economic and military–political forms (Nye 1992; Buzan et al. 1993: 51–65), making it even more difficult than traditionally to compare like with like. How does one handle an economically weak but nuclear armed Russia in comparison with a rich but militarily feeble Japan?

Digging a little deeper into the 'classical' writings on great powers, one finds two clear threads in the attempts to formulate the criteria by which to distinguish great powers from other states in the system: material capabilities and social role. Kenneth Waltz's definition is perhaps the best representative of a hard realist tradition that is almost (but interestingly not quite) totally materialist in approach:

> In international politics, as in any self-help system, the units of greatest capability set the scene of action for others as well as themselves. (1979: 72–3)
> The economic, military, and other capabilities of nations cannot be sectored and separately weighed. States are not placed in the top rank because they excel in one way or another. Their rank depends on how they score on *all* of the following items: size of population and territory, resource endowment, economic capability, military strength, political stability and competence. . . . Ranking states, however, does not require predicting their success in war or in other endeavors. We need only rank them roughly by capability. (1979: 131)
> The greater the relative size of a unit the more it identifies its own interest with the interest of the system. (1979: 198)

Posen and Ross's (1996–7: 17) definition of great powers as 'powers that have substantial industrial and military potential' is a looser version of the same type of thinking. In this case 'potential' opens some scope for states such as China that are able to trade on capabilities they do not currently possess, but are thought likely to have in the not too distant future.

Waltz's definition emphasizes power as an all-round characteristic with multiple determinants. It offers no guidance as to how the different material elements are to be weighed against each other (the Japan–Russia problem), saying only that there must be some degree of balance across all of the elements. This definition is of course one that fits, and suits, the US perfectly. It also fits other all-rounders such as China and India, for whom the question is whether they have high enough levels of everything to make it into the top rank. It suited the Soviet Union for a time, but became problematic from the 1980s when the Soviet economy was conspicuously falling behind. It is problematic for all entities whose capabilities are 'great' but unbalanced: the EU because it lacks sufficient state-like qualities, Japan because it has only a powerful economy, and Russia because it has a weak economy. A curiosity in Waltz's definition is the criterion of 'political stability and competence'. Its importance is self-evident, but it represents a sharp departure from power conceived of in purely material terms. While political stability might be susceptible to a fairly detached analytical evaluation, political competence is almost certain to be highly contested. Think, for example, of the post-September 11 evaluations of the US's 'war on terrorism'. Some think this an exemplar of political competence in its measured, broad and firm response, while others judge it as short-sighted, hostage to special interests (the oil industry, Israel, the Bush family), and almost certain to fill the ranks of terrorist organizations with enthusiastic new recruits. A judgement about political competence is unavoidably itself a political act.

Hedley Bull's definition of great power has a materialist benchmark, but is much more concerned with socially constructed roles in the international system. It starts from the political issues that Waltz's definition tends to hide under the assumption that relative size is the key explanation for interest in and engagement with the management of the international system. Bull's definition comes out of the English school tradition, with its emphasis on international society, whereas Waltz comes from the positivist tradition in American IR, which starts from a more mechanical conception of international systems. Bull (1977: 200–2) stipulates that, in addition to being in the front rank of military capability (the key material condition), great powers must be:

> recognised by others to have, and conceived by their own leaders and peoples to have, certain special rights and duties. Great powers, for example,

assert the right, and are accorded the right, to play a part in determining issues that affect the peace and security of the international system as a whole. They accept the duty, and are thought by others to have the duty, of modifying their policies in the light of the managerial responsibilities they bear.

Note how this definition could exclude a state that had front-rank military capability but was not accorded recognition by others as a 'great responsible'. This contrasts with more material definitions that often accept victory in a great power war as conferring entry to the top rank of powers. There is ambiguity about the 'others' who confer recognition. Who are they? A self-constructed peer group of great powers? The society of states as a whole? Bull's social definition employs a recognition element that has to be accepted both by other members of international society and by the state concerned. This dual element means that great power identity (or indeed any international identity) is a reciprocal construction composed of the interplay between a state's view of itself and the view of it held by the other members of international society. Since each view affects the other, this social status is in a continuous state of flux (which does not preclude it from becoming sedimented and being quite stable for long periods). Bull's definition makes both self-conception and acceptance by others part of the criteria, but does not discuss whether one of these should be given more weight than the other.

India makes one particularly interesting case study for the interplay of self-conception and conception by others (Buzan 2002). It is easy to find voices among the leaders and people in India asserting Bull's 'right to play a part in determining issues that affect the peace and security of the international system as a whole', and even (the Gujral doctrine – Sen Gupta 1997) accepting 'the duty of modifying their policies in the light of the managerial responsibilities they bear'. But it is difficult to find many voices outside India that either accord it the status of great power or allow it to trade on its potential for development. At best one can find promises deferred into an open future, as in President Bush's (2002: 10) comment about 'India's potential to become one of the great democratic powers of the twenty-first century'. The US makes another interesting case, with present debates highlighting the possibilities for tension between material and social qualifications. One service of Bull's definition is that it draws attention to the importance of great power status to the identity and self-understanding of states.

It is worth noting that hegemonic stability theory (which is still strong in some parts of the policy community, however out of fashion it may be in academic circles) fits quite closely into Bull's way of thinking. Probably one would have to add first-rank economic capability to military capability as the material underpinning, but, from there on, the idea of HST is that one power both takes the lead in managing the international economic order (by providing collective goods and acting as lender of last resort) and is recognized by others as having special rights and duties in this regard.

Martin Wight (1979: 45–6), however, points out problems in formal recognition as a criterion for identifying great powers:

> it is only part of the truth to say that a great power is a power that is recognized as great by its contemporaries. Such recognition may contain an element of the wishful or the conventional, as when the Big Three coopted China and France at the end of the Second World War. . . . The existence of what is recognized determines the act of recognition, and not the other way round. . . . at any time there are likely to be some powers climbing into it and others declining from it, and in a time of revolutionary changes, formal recognition will lag behind the growth or decay of power.

Morgenthau (1978: 348–9) also comments on the problem of a disjuncture between material capability and diplomatic status, noting that in 1815 'the diplomatic rank of great power' was accorded to Portugal, Sweden and Spain 'only out of courtesy'. The move to permanent IGOs in the twentieth century has given legal standing to great power status (Wight 1979: 43), but this does not help much either. The US never joined the League of Nations, and several other substantial states were in and out of membership (Germany, Italy, Japan, the Soviet Union). Things were little better after the Second World War. Taiwan for long held China's Security Council seat, and Germany and Japan were excluded even after their economies had outstripped that of the Soviet Union/Russia. The position of Britain and France looked increasingly odd as time wore on, and the ending of the Cold War was not taken as an opportunity to remake the UN in line with the distribution of power in the 1990s. All of this suggests that there are 'real' great powers, defined by material capability, and 'virtual' great powers, that for particular reasons at particular times are allowed to punch diplomatically above their weight in the management of world politics.

These problems reflect a methodological divide within IR. Materialist approaches offer the theoretical possibility of formal, quantitative definition and analysis of great powers. This was attractive to the positivist wing of IR, but the attempt to measure power has so far been defeated by the multiplicity of components that comprise power in international politics. Some of these were difficult to measure even in themselves (the economic statistics of the Soviet Union and China; political stability and competence as noted above), and even those that could be measured in some more or less satisfactory way could not be weighed against each other. Could great wealth and technological skill compensate for not having nuclear weapons (Japan), or could large population and territory compensate for a backward economy (China, India)?

'Classic' definitions are useful in setting out a range of the factors needing to be taken into account, but they point in no very clear direction. By itself, the materialist definition is clearly unsustainable. It is impossible to define levels of relative power with anything like the precision and consistency necessary for positivist science. There must be a substantial material base if the term great power is to mean anything, but there must also be more than that. It has to matter whether or not a state possessing first-class capabilities chooses to take up the great power role or not. Think of Japan today, or the US in its pre-1914 isolationist phase. Materialists assume that behaviour will eventually be shaped by capabilities, but as the cases of Japan and the US show this can take decades or even centuries to happen. There is even room to think that 'civilian powers' might become a long-term feature (Maull 1990–1). What happens when, because of the spread of the democratic peace and/or the fear of weapons of mass destruction, the test of great power war is no longer available (or no longer used) as a means of exit from and entry to the rank of great power? It also has to matter whether a great power's claim is recognized by others or not. But the recognition approach is not workable by itself either, because there are too many situations when some great powers politically promote to formal great power status states lacking first-class capabilities. They do this to gain an ally, frustrate a rival or help the power in question manage a difficult transition downward or upward in status. Neither a purely materialist nor a formal recognition definition is convincing, and nor is an unclear combination of the two. Simple common sense might work at some times, but clearly does not at others, such as now. In the absence of any firm material or rhetorical criteria, some form of common sense may have to be the way forward, but it needs to be common sense guided by a firm framework of indicators.

5.2 Rethinking the definitions

The post-Cold War confusion about polarity is perhaps not as intractable as it first appears. The uni- and multipolarists are both still thinking largely in terms of great powers, and this concept has to remain the key to the matter. The most obvious (but not easy) solution lies down the path suggested in chapter 4: a differentiation between superpowers and regional great powers. The unipolarists are clearly thinking about superpower(s) as the key category. The multipolarists are less clear, but it can be argued that much of what they want to take into account is captured by the idea of regional great powers. It will immediately be objected that this 'solution' proliferates categories, ignores the rule that theories should be parsimonious, and poses serious problems for polarity theory. All of these points are true, yet the nettle has to be grasped. The point is (as shown in chapter 4) that an undifferentiated theory of polarity (i.e. one based on a single differentiation between great powers and other states – hereafter *simple polarity theory*) has *never* been sound. While an undifferentiated system of great powers is, in principle, possible, in practice reality over the last few centuries has deviated from that condition to such a degree that to use it as a theoretical assumption is more likely to confuse than to clarify.

A de facto differentiation between superpowers and regional great powers, whether recognized or not, has been the general rule ever since the European powers seriously began to make the world their stage. But the difference was hidden, first by the long conflation of European and world politics up to 1945, and then by the drama of bipolarity during the Cold War. One has to remember that a fully fledged global-scale international system is a relatively recent development, considerably less than two centuries old. It is therefore not surprising that we do not yet fully understand it, especially so given the distorting lens that Eurocentrism puts in front of our eyes. The fact of the matter is that a simple polarity theory will almost never work in any international system, and especially not in one as geographically large and diverse, and as politically fragmented, as the one we have inhabited for the last two centuries. It certainly does not work descriptively. Some might reply that theorists are less interested in description than in developing the sort of structural clarity from which deductions can be drawn. That is true, but the catch is that, if the price of structural clarity is a level of descriptive distortion so high as fundamentally to misrepresent what is being studied, then such clarity is counterproductive. Structural theory does not need or want thick description, but its simplifications cannot totally detach themselves from the nature of the reality on the ground. An excess of parsimony is as damaging to the pursuit of understanding as a shortage of it.

While simple polarity theory worked well enough most of the time in the relatively narrow focus of European international politics, it does not (except for some special cases discussed in part II) work when transferred to the wider global stage. The truth of this is obvious not only in the particular story of Europe, but also in contemporary regional security. Simple polarity theory generally works quite nicely in thinking about relatively compact geopolitical spaces, where states have few options for isolationist policies and regional powers and global ones are all crammed into the same small space. This is why simple polarity theories also play a significant role in regional security theory (Buzan et al. 1998: 9–19; Buzan and Wæver 2003). One can usefully see South Asia as bipolar, the Middle East and eighteenth-century Europe as multipolar, and southern Africa and North America as unipolar.

In the contemporary international system the great powers are widely spaced both geographically and in level of capability. There is only one superpower, and there are no other plausible candidates on the horizon for that status for at least a couple of decades. A world of several super-powers and no regional great powers is theoretically possible, but unlikely in the near or middle-term future. If it occurred, then simple polarity theory could be applied. If the US abandons its present role and status, then a world with no superpowers, only regional great powers, is also theoretically possible, and perhaps empirically a more plausible option within the forseeable future. Such a decentralized world would not fit well within any existing realist theory, and would require new thinking to conceptualize its character (see chapter 8).

Between these two extremes lies all of global-scale international history plus quite a large number of theoretical possibilities. It is perhaps difficult to imagine a contemporary international system with more than five or six superpowers, so that sets the limit on one side. Regional great powers might be somewhat more numerous. Recall that before the First World War the list of great powers stretched up to nine, and that was in a world in which most of Africa and large swathes of Asia were still colonized, and therefore not candidates. In the contemporary world, the question of where to draw the bottom line under the category of regional great power is quite challenging. The EU and Japan are problematic because of the lopsided quality of their capabilities, and one can still think of Britain, France and Germany as great powers in some senses. Countries such as China, India and Russia are almost certainly uncontroversial as candid-ates. As noted in chapter 4, substantial claims could also be advanced for a long list of countries which play a form of hegemonic role in their regions. From here on in, the question gets more difficult. The countries talked about as regional great powers all have either some claim to global importance (China, India, Britain, France, Germany, Japan) or a clearly dominant role within their regions (Brazil, South Africa, India, Indonesia, Nigeria), or both. But if we drop all the way into the regional level, how are we to label the states that define the polarity of their regions? Do Egypt, Israel, Turkey, Saudi Arabia, Iraq and Iran count as regional great powers? Do Pakistan, Argentina, Vietnam and South Korea? If they do, the list of such powers could stretch up to twenty. That would water down the category even more than the inclusion of the Ottoman empire and Italy in 1914, even allowing for the impact of the shift to a fully global-scale international system that took place with decolonization.

It is also necessary to think about what once could have been called 'the German question', and is probably now better called 'the China question': how to classify powers that fall between the regional great power and superpower stools? These are big powers in important regions that are potential candidates to make a bid for superpower status. The First and the Second World War can be read as bids by Germany, and then Germany and Japan, to raise themselves to superpower status by pursuing policies of imperial expansion. Both bids failed, but the German ones in particular came very close to success. Any system of classification throws up awkward borderline cases, but this particular problem is important enough to affect how one thinks about the whole exercise. Potential candidates for superpower status will register on systemic power politics in a quite different way from merely regional powers. That is why so much of twentieth-century international history centred on Germany and why China occupies such a special position in contemporary debates about world power.

The interplay between the historical record and the need to find categories that are coherent enough for theoretical application presses one to abandon the simple dual distinction between superpower and regional great powers used above, and to adopt a tripartite classification into *superpowers*, *great powers* and *regional powers*. It is inadequate to discuss, as Huntington (1999: 35–6) does, a tripartite distinction of this sort (in his case superpower, major powers, and second-level major regional powers) in common-sense terms without attempting to offer criteria for allocating actors to any given category. Among other things a distinction on these lines raises serious questions about the boundary between the system, or global, level and the regional one (Buzan and Wæver 2003: part I). Polarity theory is based on levels of analysis, and so requires that this boundary be clearly demarcated. If it is not, then neither the theory nor any variant of it can make coherent statements about structure, whether at the system level or the regional one. As the labels suggest, superpowers and great powers are global system-level phenomena, whereas regional powers are not. Consequently, the criteria by which these classifications are determined must reflect that difference in level.

Consider once again the discussion about definitions of great power in section 5.1. Taken individually, neither the material nor the constructivist approach worked all that well to pin down the essence of great power status. Materialist approaches faced a so far unsolved problem of measuring power, and did not easily offer satisfactory answers when power became disaggregated. Recognition approaches were distorted both by politically motivated 'courtesy' allocations of great power status and by self-claims of states to such status where the requisite capability was lacking. Simply adding the two together begged questions about what to do in cases where some criteria were met but not others. Contemporary Japan poses a classically difficult case. Before 1945 it was an undisputed great power. Since the 1970s it has had great economic capability which could easily be, but hasn't been, translated into military capability. Most of its people and leaders do not accept great power responsibilities, yet the country is widely looked upon, and expected to behave as, a great power by its peers, and has been talked of as a potential superpower. Whether or not it should count as a great power by these criteria is unclear.

On closer examination, the traditional debate on great power status embodies three criteria: the material one of relative capability and two more or less declaratory perceptual ones – self-declared status, and status as recognized by others, particularly the top-table peer group. But a brief reflection on Bull and Watson's (1984: 1) criteria for an international system – that a group of states 'form a system, in the sense that the behaviour of each is a necessary factor in the calculations of the others' – suggests that these three criteria are not sufficient. The idea that states calculate their behaviour in relation to the behaviour of others also needs to be taken into account in thinking about what distinguishes great powers (I am grateful to Ole Wæver for this idea). The key here is not just what states say about themselves and others, but how they behave in a wider sense, and how that behaviour is treated by others. A state may be formally accorded great power standing but not treated as a great power in the diplomatic and strategic calculations of others – a situation in which France and Britain and Russia increasingly find themselves. The declaratory criteria are obviously part of the behavioural one, but not all, or even most, of it. The behavioural criterion is about the full spectrum of foreign policy behaviour, about who to take seriously as de facto system-level powers. In this view, the main criterion for a state to be a system-level power is that it is treated as such by the other powers. Whether it acts on a global scale is less important: India and, sometimes, Sweden do, but are not treated as great powers by others; Japan mostly doesn't, and is. This rule also holds in declaratory mode: what others say about an actor is more important than what it says about itself. A system-level power acts on the assumption not only that its security depends on the global power structure but also that it is able to influence that structure. Others react to it as a potential hegemon and/or a crucial ally in relation to the global balance of power. This is in contrast to lesser powers which operate largely as 'takers' of such developments, and can only play regional level cards in establishing their status.

This behavioural element is of course influenced, often strongly, by the capability that states possess, the declaratory postures they take, and the formal status they are accorded by international society. But it is more than just the sum of these things. It is well understood, for example, that perceptions of capability are often out of line with reality (Segal 1999), but it is the perception that drives behaviour. Similarly, a façade of formal status may be kept in place, as it was for Russia during the later 1990s, while real behaviour proceeds according to a quite different calculation. Conversely, formal status may be denied notwithstanding capability and calculation of behaviour, as it was for the Soviet Union and Germany in 1919, and for Germany and Japan during the Cold War. Indeed, it might be argued that how states calculate their own and others' behaviour is the key to interpreting the other criteria, and thus to understanding how to rank powers. At the end of the day, it is not what states are, or what they say about themselves and others, that determines status, but how they calculate their own behaviour and, most importantly, how they respond to the behaviour of others.

If this argument is accepted, then two useful side effects result. One is to abolish the difficulty that neorealists have created for themselves by accepting Waltz's injunction that a great power, or a system-level 'pole', can only be a state. Waltz's argument was (rightly) directed against those who confused system polarity (the number of great powers in the system) with system polarization (the configuration of alliances in the system). However, the idea that a pole must be a state has run into endless difficulties in dealing with the EU, which becomes almost invisible through neorealist lenses despite its accumulation of actor quality. If one accepts the behavioural approach to determining status, this problem disappears. The EU can simply be judged by how others respond to it. If others treat it as a great power, then it qualifies as such regardless of its ambiguous, *sui generis*, political status. The English school always had a more sensible approach in their understanding that international systems were not necessarily comprised just by a group of states, but could in a more general sense be seen as 'a group of independent political communities' (Bull and Watson 1984: 1), a formulation that makes entities such as the EU easier to incorporate. The other problem that disappears is how to handle states with unbalanced capability profiles. Such states either will or will not be treated as great powers depending on how the actual and potential significance of their capabilities is calculated. Japan, for example, may not have nuclear weapons or long-range delivery systems, but everyone understands that on the basis of its civil nuclear power and space programmes it could very quickly develop them.

Taking both these definitional and historical criteria into consideration, I can now abandon the simple distinction between superpowers and regional great powers used above, and propose definitional criteria for a three-tiered scheme: *superpowers* and *great powers* at the system level, and *regional powers* at the regional level. The superpowers tier retains the meaning developed in the discussion above. The division between great powers and regional ones splits the category 'regional great powers' on the basis of those powers having primarily regional significance and those having substantial significance at both regional and global levels. Iran, South Africa and Brazil, for example, are clearly regional powers, whereas China, Japan and the EU have unquestioned weight both regionally and globally.

Superpowers

The criteria for superpower status are demanding in that they require broad-spectrum capabilities exercised across the whole of the international system. Superpowers must possess first-class military–political capabilities (as measured by the standards of the day) and the economies to support such capabilities. They must be capable of, and also exercise, global military and political reach. They need to see themselves, *and* be accepted by others in rhetoric and behaviour, as having this rank. Superpowers must be active players in processes of securitization and desecuritization in all, or nearly all, of the regions in the system, whether as threats, guarantors, allies or interveners. Except in extremely conflictual international systems, superpowers will also be fountainheads of 'universal' values of the type necessary to underpin international society. Their legitimacy as superpowers will depend substantially on their success in establishing the legitimacy of such values. Taking all of these factors into account, during the nineteenth century Britain, France and, more arguably, Russia had this rank. After the First World War, it was held by Britain, the US and the Soviet Union. After the Second World War it was held by the US and the Soviet Union. And after the Cold War it was held only by the US. Note that this definition leaves no room for a separate theoretical category of hyperpower. A hyperpower is simply a sole superpower viewed in critical perspective because of both its singularity and its particular character or behaviour.

Great powers

Achieving great power status is less demanding in terms of both capability and behaviour. Great powers need not necessarily have big capabilities in all sectors, and they need not be actively present in the securitization or economic processes of all areas of the international system. Great power status rests mainly on a single key: what distinguishes great powers from merely regional ones is that they are responded to by others on the basis of system-level calculations, as well as regional ones, about the present and near future distribution of power. Usually, this implies that a great power is treated in the calculations of other major powers as if it has the clear economic, military and political potential to bid for super-power status in the short or medium term. A state may be awarded great power status by successfully trading on its potential as well as its actual capability. This single key is observable in the foreign policy processes and discourses of other powers. It means that actual possession of mater-ial and legal attributes is less crucial for great powers than for super-powers. Great powers will usually have appropriate levels of capability, though China has demonstrated an impressive ability over nearly a cen-tury to trade on future capabilities that it has yet fully to deliver (Segal 1999). They will generally think of themselves as more than regional powers, and possibly as prospective superpowers, and they will usually be capable of operating in more than one region. But while great powers typically have these characteristics they are not strictly speaking neces-sary so long as other powers treat them as potential superpowers. Japan illustrates the case of a country thought of by others as a potential super-power (more during the late 1980s and early 1990s than now), but possessing unbalanced capabilities, and not clearly inclined to think of itself as a superpower candidate. Mostly, great powers will be rising in the hierarchy of international power, but a second route into the category is that of countries declining from acknowledged superpower status. Declining superpowers will normally have influence in more than one region and be capable of limited global military operation.

During the later nineteenth century, great power rank was possessed by Germany, the US and Japan (and Russia if not accepted as a super-power). After the First World War, it was still held by Germany and Japan, and France dropped into it as a declining superpower. During the Cold War it was retained by China, Germany and Japan, with Britain and France coming increasingly into doubt. Here there was the difficult question of how to treat the EU, which as time wore on acquired more and more actor quality in the international system, and was by the 1970s being treated as an emergent great power, albeit of an unusual kind, and with some serious limitations still in place. After the Cold War it was held by Britain/France/Germany–the EU, Japan, China and Russia. India was banging hard on the door, but had neither the capability, the formal recognition, nor the place in the calculations of others to qualify.

The justifications for designating these four as great powers in the post-Cold War international system are as follows. Russia qualifies by its recent exit from superpower status, and China, the EU and Japan all qualify on the basis of being regularly talked about and treated either as potential challengers to the US and/or as potential superpowers (Posen and Ross 1996–7: 17; Calleo 1999; Guttman 2001; Kupchan 1998, 2002; Mastanduno and Kapstein 1999; Wilkinson 1999; Waltz 2000). China is currently the most fashionable potential superpower (Roy 1994; Ross 1999: 83–4, 92–4, 97; Wilkinson 1999: 160–3) and the one whose degree of alienation from the dominant international society makes it the most obvious political challenger (Zhang 1998). But its challenge is constrained both by formidable internal problems of development and by the fact that a rise in its power could easily trigger a counter-coalition in Asia (Buzan 2004c). Assessment of the EU's status often hangs on its degree of stateness (Buchan 1993; Galtung 1973; Hodge 1998–9; Walton 1997; Waltz 1993a: 54; Waltz 2000: 30–2; Wilkinson 1999: 157–60; Walker 2000; Wohlforth 1999: 31) without it being clear how much state-like quality it has to achieve in order to count as a superpower. Kupchan (2002: 119–59) and Prestowitz (2003: 230–44) see it as potentially the leading challenger to the US as its integration processes continue to increase its actor quality. The EU clearly has the material capabilities, and could easily claim recognition. But given its political weakness and its erratic and difficult course of internal political development, particularly as regards a common foreign and defence policy, the EU seems likely to remain a potential superpower for some time. During the early and middle 1990s, there was a strong fashion, especially in the US, for seeing Japan as the likely challenger for superpower status (Huntington 1991: 8; Huntington 1993; Layne 1993: 42–3, 51; Waltz 1993a: 55–70; Spruyt 1998). With Japan's economic stagnation, this fashion has faded, but Japan could bounce back, and its standing as a great power looks firm. Like the EU, Japan is constrained mainly by its political inability to play a superpower role. India, despite its nuclear test, is not talked about or treated as a potential superpower, and so does not qualify.

Regional powers

Regional powers define the polarity of any given regional security complex (Walt 1987; Lake and Morgan 1997; Buzan and Wæver 2003): India and Pakistan in South Asia; South Africa in southern Africa; Iran, Iraq and Saudi Arabia in the Gulf; Egypt, Israel and Syria in the Levant; and so forth; and thus unipolar, as in southern Africa, bipolar as in South Asia, multipolar as in the Middle East, South America and Southeast Asia. The classification of *regional power* is much more important overall than traditional classifications such as *middle power*. Middle power is a rather specialized category, referring mostly to a handful of Western states such as Canada, Sweden and Australia that regularly play international roles well beyond their home regions. The capabilities of regional powers loom large in their regions, but do not register much in a broad spectrum way at the global level. Higher level powers respond to them as if their influence and capability were mainly relevant to the securitization processes of a particular region. They are thus excluded from the higher level calculations of system polarity whether or not they think of themselves as deserving a higher ranking (as India most obviously does). Regional powers may of course get caught up in global power rivalries, as happened during the Cold War to Vietnam, Egypt, Iraq and others. In that context, they may get treated as if they mattered to the global balance of power as, for example, during the Cold War when there were fears that escalations from Middle Eastern conflicts would trigger superpower confrontations. But the kind of attention received by an actor that is seen either as the spoils in a wider competition, or as a dangerous flashpoint with escalatory potential to the global level, is quite different from that received by an actor seen as a global-level power in its own right. Regional powers may not matter much at the global level, but within their regions they usually determine both the local patterns of security relations and the way in which those patterns interact with the global powers. Regional powers determine not only the polarity of their local security complex but also the way in which the dynamics of regional security interplay with the great power ones at the global level. In a surprising number of cases, regional polarity is the key to determining whether or not a state is able to reach great power status at the global level (Buzan and Wæver 2003). Parallel usages of polarity thinking can also be found in the literatures on regional integration, which often feature polarity as a key element in the analysis, for example in the unipolar/hegemonic structures in the southern cone of South America (with Brazil as the core of Mercosur), in Europe (with Germany as the core of the EU), and in southern Africa (with South Africa as the core of SADC).

*****

These definitions apply across the last few centuries, but they are also historically contingent. Before there was a global international system, there were no superpowers. During the last few centuries war was the primary determinant of entry into and exit from the ranks of global-level powers. But if, as many think, war is going to play less of a role at the system level from here on in, then other, more social, criteria will become important. Superpowers will still need first-rank military capability. But their standing will probably come to rest more on the capability to form and hold coalitions, to create and manage IGOs, or more deeply to create international societies (globally or regionally). In the absence of world wars, or the threat of them, recognition and acceptance by others of their leadership role in international society will become more central.

Also worth noting is a significant interplay between great power status and the place of the power concerned in its region (Buzan and Wæver 2003). This is especially true now that the distribution of power works on a global scale, with more chance that the major powers will be geographically separated from each other than was the case when nearly all of them were bundled into Europe. The easiest route to great (or super) power status is to be free of regional entanglement. The US, Britain and Japan have all had some success with this strategy. If geographical placement precludes that as an option, then the other route is via the achievement of regional hegemony. The US has no local challengers, and neither did the Soviet Union during its run as a superpower or China during its classical periods of imperial ascendancy in Asia. France and Germany both attempted it in Europe but succeeded only for a few years, as did Japan in East Asia. Modern India has so far failed to transcend its region, and this failure is one key to understanding why it is not treated as a great power. Russia's current desperation to control its region is because doing so is a necessary condition for hanging on to its great power status, which, as Freedman (1999: 34–8) points out, is now given, not taken. One of the critical points in the whole debate about China's future as a great, or even a super, power is whether it will be able to re-establish some form of hegemony over its region. Accomplishment of that would give it a platform for superpower status. Falling into balance of power relations with Japan, India and Southeast Asia would largely confine its sphere to Asia (Buzan 2004c). Hegemony within the region is not a guarantee of great power status. South Africa may dominate southern Africa and Nigeria west Africa, but this does not make them great powers (only regional powers in unipolar security complexes). And absence of hegemony does not preclude great power status (as demonstrated for most of modern European history). But seeing how a power is located within its region is often an important factor in its claim, or its potential to claim, global-level standing.

5.3 Consequences for polarity analysis: a new lens

On the basis of these definitions the global power structure over the last century can be summed up as follows.

- During the interwar period there was a 3 + 3 global power structure, with Britain, the US and the Soviet Union as superpowers, and Germany, Japan and France as great powers (for a different interpretation

along these lines, see Schweller 1993). Africa, the Middle East and most of Asia remained overlaid by the control of colonial powers.
- During the Cold War/decolonization period there was a 2 + 3 global power structure, with the US and the Soviet Union as superpowers, and China, Japan and the EU becoming great powers, albeit with the EU leaving room for questions about the standing of Britain, France and Germany as independent players, perhaps only of regional status when taken individually.
- During the first decade of the post-Cold War period the global power structure shifted to 1 + 4, with only the US remaining as a super-power, and China, the EU, Japan and Russia as great powers.

This scheme complicates polarity theory by putting two tiers at the system level, but clarifies it by providing a firm demarcation between global and regional powers. Regional powers can by definition be excluded from global-level structure. Their influence is largely within their region, and bears on the global level only when the interests of the global-level powers intersect within the region. With the regional level separated out, the contemporary international system polarity is exposed as one superpower plus four great powers. Such a system certainly cannot be adequately captured by simple designation as either unipolar or multipolar. Huntington's (1999: 35–6) idea of uni-multipolar goes in the right direc-tion, but fails to specify criteria for classification and locks itself into a single, static formulation. Interestingly, the general idea of a 1 + 4 world, differentiating the 'great power' category into two levels, was much more clearly articulated in US policy circles (Joffe 2001: 142–4) than it could be among neorealists still chained to Waltz's dictum of great powers as a single type.

If one follows the suggestion of differentiating the power classifications at the system level into superpowers and great powers, then there are four main consequences for polarity theory.

The first consequence is that there does not seem to be much theoret-ical mileage in hanging on to general hypotheses based on simple num-bers. The hypotheses from existing polarity theory would apply only to pure superpower systems (i.e. those composed of one or more super-powers and no great powers). Where both superpowers and great powers are in play (all of modern history so far) the possible combinations are too many to capture in simple number formulas. In addition, polarity theory depends on the assumption that all great powers operate over the whole international system. With the definition of great power given above, this assumption has to be abandoned as an out-of-date artefact of the origins of great power thinking in the smaller world of Europe. Given the size of the global system, mere great powers mostly do not operate globally, and only superpowers meet the requirements of simple polarity theory. One might easily imagine worlds with up to five or six superpowers, at least similar numbers of great powers, and potentially quite large numbers of regional powers. Even by confining regional powers to the regional level of analysis, the system level still contains a lot of possible combinations of superpowers and great powers: one superpower and anything between zero and ten great powers; two superpowers and anything between zero and ten great powers; and so on. In practice, the definitions used here mean that the number of superpowers and the number of great powers have a strong effect on each other. The more superpowers there are, the fewer great powers there are likely to be, and vice versa. Thus, a system of six superpowers and ten great powers is rather improbable, as is one with one superpower and no great powers (true unipolarity). In practice this interplay reduces the number of likely combinations, though still leaving it too large to base theory on a handful of categories as simple polarity theory has done. This sharp reduction in the ability to use simple number models of the international power structure points towards the use of scenarios, which is the approach taken in part II.

The second consequence, closely related to the use of scenarios, is the need to focus on the relationships between and among the two types of global-level power. The question is not just about how superpowers (or great powers) relate to others of the same type, but what kind of expectations one should have about how superpowers and great powers will relate to each other. The approach to this in part II will be to use a range of IR theories to derive expected rules of behaviour for both types of power, and then to see how these expectations line up with actual behaviour.

The third consequence is to open up the previously untheorized possibility of a world with no superpowers and several great powers. A steady decline in the number of superpowers has already been noted, with the next position on the spectrum being zero. This possibility poses interesting challenges to both realist and English school theory, which assume that great powers play over the whole system and consequently have system-wide interests in management. Mouritzen (1980, 1997, 1998) has pointed out how this assumption of universal operation is a curious and distorting feature of much IR theory. Because states are fixed rather than mobile, their interactions within the system will be affected by geography and distance. Only for superpowers does this localist bias largely disappear. Pure great power systems are thus unlikely to behave in the same way as pure superpower ones, because great powers are driven by less than global interests, and might interact with each other on a quite different logic from system-spanning superpowers. Friedberg (1993: 5) comes close to this idea with his scenario of great power regions and a world of 'regional subsystems in which clusters of contiguous states interact mainly with each other.' In the relatively short history of a fully global international system, no pure great power system has ever existed, and it is not surprising that such systems have not been the subject of theoretical attention. But a 0 superpower + x great power system is one of the main potentialities in the present 1 + 4 structure, and some theoretical attention to it is therefore a matter of urgency. More on this in chapter 8.

The fourth consequence stems from the importance given to regional powers as the third most important category of power. Traditional polarity theory is perfectly capable of looking at the relationship between the global power structure and the regional level (Hansen 2000; Walt 1987). But, by putting more emphasis on the regional level, this move forces the asking of specific questions about the relationship between regions and global-level powers. In a state-centric model of the international power structure, the next level down from the global one is the regional (Buzan and Wæver 2003). As already suggested, the status of great powers and superpowers is affected by their relationship with regions in a variety of ways. Great powers must operate in regions other than their own, and superpowers must operate in all regions. In some, perhaps most, cases, global-level status will hinge on the power concerned being able to dominate or detach from its local region. This issue will be a core theme in all of the chapters in part II. Before turning to the scenarios, however, it is necessary to add to the logic of polarity theory the whole element of identity and social structure.

Conclusions to Part I:
The Interplay of Polarity
and Identity in IR Theory

One of the attractions of simple polarity theory seen purely within the *Realists* neorealist frame is the sparseness of the motivational logic that then drives the system. Polarity theory ignores the element of identity or, put more accurately, reduces it to a fixed quality that is subservient to the distribution of material capabilities. In neorealist thinking, survival is the primary goal, and calculation of position is determined in material terms by relative capability (static comparison) and the pace, size and direction of relative gains (dynamics of change). This logic leads to straightforward rule-like expectations about balancing behaviour and could in principle be applied to complex polarities as well as to simple ones. Recall that, in Wendt's (1999) terms, neorealists assume that international systems *One + other Constructivist* are composed entirely of enemies and rivals. But Wendt's scheme offers three types of social relationship: enemy, rival and friend: 'The posture of enemies is one of threatening adversaries who observe no limits in their violence toward each other; that of rivals is one of competitors who will use violence to advance their interests but refrain from killing each other; and that of friends is one of allies who do not use violence to settle their disputes and work as a team against security threats' (Wendt 1999: 258). In a culture of enemies Self and Other are existential threats and easily fall into mutual securitizations based on fears of extermination (1999: 262–5). In a culture of rivals Self and Other recognize rights of coexist- *K. order* ence (1999: 279–80). In a full relationship of friends 'the cognitive bound- *B. Smith* aries of the Self are extended to include the Other' (1999: 305). One could *eftress* also understand this scheme of enemies, rivals and friends in terms of Wæver's theory of securitization (Wæver 1995; Buzan et al. 1998): enemies = mutual securitization unrestrained by recognitions of a right of (co)existence; rivals = mutual securitization restrained by recognition of rights of (co)existence; and friends = mutual desecuritization to a point of asecurity. While a system composed entirely of enemies, or even a mixture of enemies and rivals, might well conform to (neo)realist expectations about behaviour, ones composed mainly of rivals, or a mixture of rivals and friends, or purely of friends, will generate rather different expectations about how the powers will behave towards each other.

Thinking along these lines opens up the possibility that polarity is not a fixed determinant, as it is close to being within neorealism, but a factor whose impact plays through the social structure of the international system. In other words, to use Wendt's (1992) iconic formulation, if anarchy is what states make of it, so is polarity. This means that complex polarity theory takes on an interpretive element in which expectations about the behavioural impact of polarity vary according to the prevailing social structure. How the structural logic of polarity works in a system of enemies will be different from how it works in a system of rivals or one of friends. Among other things, opening up the possibilities in this way offers an easy resolution to the tension between neorealism and HST outlined in section 3.2 above. If the social structure is one of friends, or even of rivals, then the logic of hegemonic leadership makes sense in a way that it does not in a system of enemies. While not losing sight of the (neo)realist view, following Wendt's scheme opens the way to bring in both neoliberal and English school ideas about what to expect from different structures of polarity.

Neoliberals operate largely within the assumption that the prevailing international social structure is one of rivals. They start from the idea that international systems are composed of egoistic, self-interested, rational actors prepared to consider absolute as well as relative gains if conditions allow. Behaviour in this system is based largely on a logic of calculation about how best to pursue self-interest. Since this view depends on self-interest leading to cooperation, it does not assume any sense of international society as an independent variable. Its main focus is on the specific, designed institutions, such as regimes and intergovernmental organizations, that make such rational choice cooperation easier and more efficient and also allow states to deal collectively with problems (e.g. global warming, rules of trade) that they cannot handle individually. Interestingly, both ends of the neo–neo synthesis open the door to Wendt's ideas about social structure by accepting that the political climate of the international system matters. Waltz (1979: 126) argues that: 'In anarchy, security is the highest end. Only if survival is assured can states safely seek such other goals as tranquility, profit and power.' Keohane and Nye (1977: 27) argue that: 'Survival is the primary goal of all states, and in the worst situations, force is ultimately necessary to guarantee survival ... Yet particularly among industrialized, pluralist countries, the perceived margin of safety has widened: fears of attack in general have declined, and fears of attacks *by one another* are virtually nonexistent.' As Howes (2003: 683) observes, within the neo–neo debate there is a consensus that 'when states are reasonably satisfied with their ability to survive they are free to pursue absolute gains'. Howes goes on to argue (2003: 685–90), following Wendt (1999), that the key preferences defining national interest are the pursuit of economic well-being, physical survival and collective self-esteem.

English school thinkers and constructivists are not bound by the methodological strictures of rational choice. They assume that friendship is possible between and among states, and that international society is possible in a system of rivals and/or friends, and even, to a limited extent, in systems of enemies. In contrast to that of the neoliberals, English school thinking focuses on a deeper sense of institutions: not regimes and IGOs, but shared practices and values among states (e.g. sovereignty, diplomacy, international law) that evolve slowly over long timescales (Buzan 2004a: chaps 6, 8). The pluralist wing of the English school mostly hangs around an assumption of rivals, and therefore sees interstate society as built primarily around norms and institutions of coexistence (Bull 1977; Jackson 2000; Mayall 2000). In this view, the scope for international cooperation is limited to pursuit of a desired degree of international order. The core institutions typically comprise sovereignty, non-intervention, territoriality, diplomacy, international law, balance of power, great power management, war and perhaps nationalism. The solidarist wing of the English school looks to the possibility of rivals and friends, or even, in its more Kantian versions, of friends, in which states become more alike in their internal structures and values. Where powers have similar ideologies and similar structures of law, government and economy, scope opens up for the joint pursuit of shared values. What these values are depends on the type of states in play. Capitalist democracies might well pursue the joint development of a global market economy and liberal standards of human rights. Theocracies might pursue the spread of some shared universal religion. Communist states might pursue the spread of their ideology, the system of command economy, and one-party states. Allowing the idea of a social structure of friends means that the domestic character of the powers matters a great deal in determining how they relate to each other, and not just in whether they converge or not, but on what set of values they converge. A system of communist states would relate very differently to a system of liberal democratic ones, which is after all what the Cold War was about.

In thinking about the impact of polarity one therefore has to factor in some prior assumptions or observations about the social structure of the international system. In looking for guidelines about the expected behaviour of the powers, that is the approach I will take in part II. The three perspectives within which one can think about the impact of polarity on the behaviour of the powers can be summarized as follows.

- In a neorealist perspective, the assumption is of a social structure of enemies, or enemies and rivals, the principal motivations are survival and security, and, because military–political concerns are uppermost, the main concerns are with relative gains and balancing.
- In a neoliberal/pluralist perspective, the assumption is of a social structure mainly of rivals, the motivations are more mixed, with wealth and status issues gaining prominence to the extent that survival/ security problems move into the background. Concern with absolute gains gets more play, and concerns about balancing are reduced (not eliminated).
- In a solidarist perspective, the assumption is of a social structure of rivals and friends, or friends, the principal motivation is to advance joint projects within a framework of domestic convergence, and the main concerns are normative. Concern with balancing is low.

If this were a strictly theoretical work, I might proceed from here to deduce the expected behaviours of the powers from these three models in pure form. But my focus is on the contemporary international system, and specifically the relationships among the global-level powers within it, and these, of course, do not fall cleanly into any single model. Some relationships (those within the EU and, to a lesser extent, between the EU and the US) are broadly solidarist. Some (Russia and Japan in relation to the US, the EU and China) take the more neoliberal/pluralist form of rivals. There are no obvious pure enemy relations among the global powers (in the sense of high expectations of war), but those between the US and China show some clear neorealist elements. Beyond a focus on the global-level powers, the whole post-Cold War debate about 'two worlds' (Buzan 1991b: 432; Goldgeier and McFaul 1992: 467–91; Singer and Wildavsky 1993; and implicitly in earlier versions, Deutsch et al. 1957; Keohane and Nye 1977) suggests that no single model of the social structure can capture the contemporary international system. I am aiming neither at a hard application of theory nor at simple thick description, but at the space between them. My goal is a theoretically structured analysis of the contemporary international power structure and its likely evolution.

Taking all this into account, the task for part II is to think through the effects of the three most likely scenarios for complex polarity in the light of reasoned assumptions about the likely social structure of the system, given the set of global-level powers that will compose it.

PART II

Three Scenarios
for the Future

Introduction

The three chapters in part II focus on the interplay between the power structure of the contemporary international system in terms of polarity and the social structure of interstate society seen in terms of the identities and relationships of the major powers composing it. The aim is to identify the structural pressures on the behaviour of great powers and superpowers generated by this interplay. As argued in chapter 5, splitting the traditional great power category into two layers, great powers and superpowers, largely voids the simple polarity theory approach of counting the poles in any international system and deriving hypotheses from whether the system is unipolar, bipolar or multipolar. With two types of power in play at the system level, interest focuses not just on the numbers of major powers but also on how the different types of power relate both to each other and to regional powers. Here one needs to take into account not just the distribution of power, but also the type and distribution of identities of the major powers. The best method for exploring what I will call *complex polarity theory* is to formulate these relationships as scenarios, and to seek rules for the scenarios in those IR theories that are compatible with a polarity approach. This means taking a wider view of polarity than that found in neorealism, and bringing in the identity considerations developed in chapter 2 via neoliberalism and English school thinking. A scenarios approach is more complicated than simple polarity theory, but it does still narrow down the range of possibilities in a significant way.

I have argued that the interwar system was 3 + 3 (three superpowers and three great powers), the Cold War one 2 + 3, and the post-Cold War one 1 + 4. The next chapter will therefore start by looking at the 1 + 4 scenario, which is where we are now, and chapters 7 and 8 will look at the scenarios on either side of this, which are the most likely results of a structural change in global polarity. At the global level, changes in the number of superpowers are more important than changes in the number of great powers. A $1 + 3$ system may not be all that different from a $1 + 5$ one, but $2 + 3$ will be quite different from $1 + 4$. The key exception to this is when the number of superpowers falls to zero. In the next three chapters I will therefore focus mostly on the scenarios driven by changes in the number of superpowers. This argument does not surrender the position established in part I that it is necessary to distinguish between superpowers and great powers and thus sneak simple polarity theory in by the back door. While it is certainly the case that the number of superpowers is the most important variable in distinguishing one scenario from another, I hope to demonstrate in the next three chapters that it is the relationship between and among the superpowers and great powers that defines the operational character of the international power structure. The numbers of great powers and superpowers matter, but so to does their identity and how they relate. Imagine, for example, the difference between a $1 + 4$ polarity structure in which the one superpower is totalitarian and the four great powers are all democracies, and the same polarity structure in which all five are democracies. Or what if the fascist powers rather than the democracies and the Soviet Union had won the Second World War (Krasner 1995: 279)? Although I reject the extreme view of Haass (1999) that polarity only describes and does not explain, he is right that whether the major powers are friendly or hostile to one another makes a big difference to how polarity works. For each scenario, therefore, it is necessary to determine which states are most likely to occupy the main roles and what sort of identity each is most likely to carry. That determination is fairly easy for the scenario of where we are now, but has to be thought through quite carefully in scenarios that lie some way down the line.

If the present system is understood as one superpower plus four great powers, then its most probable futures in terms of polarity are:

- stay at $1 + x$, where $x = 3$, 4 or 5 (chapter 6)
- move to $2 + x$, where $x = 3$ or 4 (chapter 7)
- move to $0 + x$, where $x = 4$, 5 or 6 (chapter 8).

If the most likely development is continuity at $1 + x$, then the imperative is to understand how a $1 + x$ structure shapes the processes of international relations within it. This structure makes the US the single critical player, which in turn makes central the question of how the identity of the US interacts with that of the great powers. Whether the $1 + x$ structure is maintained or pushed towards change depends as much, or possibly more, on identity issues as it does on the distribution of material capabilities. The nature of US superpowerdom in a 1 + 4 structure and the strategy for maintaining it hinge crucially on how the US relates both to great powers and to regions. If there is a shift to 2 or possibly 3 + x, then we return to something similar in simple polarity terms to the international power structure of the Cold War, but probably not very similar in terms of its interplay of identities. If there is a shift to 0 + x, then we are in theoretical waters that have not been much charted in polarity terms but need to be anticipated. I argue that the US is central to all three scenarios, but it does not all lie in US hands. China is usually seen as the most likely to challenge US authority, having the will, and making good progress towards acquiring the means. The EU is another potential challenger, having the means, but not yet either the political will or the necessary degree of institutional cohesion. The decisions of both of these actors will have a major impact not only on which scenario wins out, but whether the operation of the international power structure will tend towards the benign or the malign. That, in turn, gives some key elements of choice to Japan, Russia and perhaps India. This may seem rather complicated compared with the parsimony of simple polarity theory, but it provides a lot more clarity than some of the despairing views from the globalist perspective in which the approach through polarity is either rejected or marginalized. As Cerny (2000: 642–6) sums it up, the globalist world is one of 'chronic but durable disorder, riddled with uncertainties' in which states of any sort play a decreasingly central role.

6

Where We Are Now:
One Superpower and
Several Great Powers

The present global power structure is a mixture of one superpower plus four great powers (China, the EU, Japan, Russia). Within this structure, the US remains the sole superpower, and the number of great powers either stays the same or rises or falls slightly (perhaps India makes it into the great power ranks, perhaps Russia drops out). A minor adjustment of the 'four' up or down by one will not significantly affect the way this structure operates and, Waltz's expectations notwithstanding, its social structure makes it potentially quite durable. What are the questions that theorists and policy-makers need to ask themselves about the operating characteristics of this 1 + 4 power structure, both in itself, and taking into consideration the particular set of states that occupy the one superpower and several great power positions? What expectations should one hold about the likely interplay between the US as the sole superpower and China, the EU, Japan and Russia as the four great powers? How do expectations derived from IR theories hold up against observed behaviour? Those who wish to maintain this structure need to think carefully about how it works. Those who want to change it need to be aware of the mechanisms for doing so and the consequences if successful. In the next section I justify the case for designating the polarity of the current international system as 1 + 4. Sections 2 and 3 explore the structural expectations about behaviour, first for the sole superpower, and then for the group of great powers. In each case, I start from the relatively simple assumptions of neorealism and derive expectations about behaviour from these assumptions, and see how those expectations stand up against the decade of operation since the end of the Cold War of the 1 + x system. Precisely because it is simple, neorealism is a convenient foil against which to start thinking about the effects of a 1 + x system, noting, as Hansen

(2000: 5) rightly points out, that one must distinguish between the turbulence of a structural change following the end of the Cold War and the emerging and ongoing effects of a settled structure. With an assessment in hand of how well or badly the actual behaviour of the powers fits with neorealist models, I then shift the assumptions away from enemies and rivals towards rivals and friends, bringing in insights from neoliberal, IPE, and English school thinking, and try to see whether they offer deeper insights into the practices of the contemporary 1 + 4 system. Section 4 examines the interplay between the 1 + 4 structure and regions.

6.1   Justifying a 1 + 4 designation of the post-Cold War power structure

Is it valid to talk about the post-Cold War polarity structure as '1 + 4'? Given the disparity of capability, role and status between the US as sole superpower and the group of great powers, the system clearly cannot be described as multipolar. Just as obviously, the US is nowhere near powerful enough to have eliminated the possibility of great power balancing, let alone being able to transform the international system from anarchy to hierarchy. If all the great powers aligned against it, that coalition would hugely outrank the US in all resources except immediately available high-tech military capability. If this is unipolarity, then it is a far weaker construction of it than anything envisaged by Waltz's theory. The US is neither a potential suzerain core of a world empire, nor is it about to construct a global federation. Indeed, the existence of a global polarity structure of 1 + 4, as opposed to true unipolarity of 1 + 0, should fit the behavioural expectations of Waltz's theory even better than 1 + 0. With several great powers in play the possibility of balancing against the superpower is much more real than in a system with one superpower and then only regional powers. A collection of regional powers is much less likely to be able to balance against a superpower than is a set of great powers. This makes the absence of serious balancing against the US since the end of the Cold War even more impressive, and suggests that powerful identity factors are in play which are not captured by the neorealist emphasis on balancing as the key response to a lopsided distribution of power.

The most obvious explanations for the absence of a counter-balancing coalition fearful of US power are found in the deeply institutionalized role of the US in so many parts of the system and its residual universalist ideological assets. Despite carrying a strong sense of its own exceptionalism, the US also believes itself to be the carrier of an inclusivist, universalist identity that, with the collapse of communism, is in a powerful position to dominate the future of humankind. This claim generates a powerful global resonance unmatched by anything that Russia, China or Japan have to offer. Only the EU could potentially compete with it, though it does not currently do so outside its own regional sphere. This rather Kantian explanation for the lack of balancing is the core of the 'democratic peace' position, and also plays to English school and HST ideas about shared values and solidarist international societies. It suggests that ideological convergence can reduce the impact of purely material considerations of power, and open up leadership possibilities that might not occur in a more ideologically divided system. Despite the worrying drift towards anti-internationalism in US policy, its two richest and most advanced potential rivals, the EU and Japan, remain firmly tied to it both in formal alliances and in an informal security community. Indeed, in the decade following the Cold War, inability to identify a credible global-level rival was something of a problem for foreign policy-making in the US. In the absence of an obvious enemy or crusade, it had to struggle against its own inward-looking tendencies, leading to recurrent rhetorical attempts to construct Japan (Campbell 1992: 223–40), China, 'rogue states', and fundamentalist Islam as a new global challenger. After September 11, the Bush administration successfully solved this problem, at least domestically, by promoting international terrorism as the mobilizing threat for US policy.

Despite the relative weakness of the US position by any serious standard of pure unipolarity, several attributes mark it out as a superpower, distinct from the ranks of great powers. These were discussed in chapter 4 (pp. 55–6) and included material capabilities, status as leader, and its strongly embedded position in four regions: Europe, East Asia, the Middle East and South America. The US has no similarly embedded position in Africa, South Asia or the CIS, though it is of course a strong outside player in all of them, and the first round of the 'war against terrorism' in Afghanistan pulled it strongly into Central and South Asia. On the basis of these considerations, depiction of the current system structure as either unipolar or multipolar risks serious misrepresentation, and 1 + 4 + regions seems both descriptively accurate and theoretically supportable.

6.2   Expectations for the superpower

In (neo)realist thinking states have no permanent friends, only permanent (national) interests centred around power and security. War is always a possibility, and the balance of power is the foundational guarantee of security. In pursuit of the balance, material capabilities are what matters, both one's own and those of others who might be enemies or serve as allies. Capabilities are relatively stable, and up to a point calculable, whereas intentions can change more rapidly. On this basis it is generally dangerous to lose relative power, and major powers of all kinds can be expected to try to maintain their position and status. There is assumed to be no international social structure distinct from the interests of the powers and able to provide a degree of order in its own right.

When applied to a polarity structure of 1 + x, these Hobbesian assumptions suggest three quite closely linked expectations about how the sole superpower will behave:

- that the superpower will try to prevent challenges to its status and will treat such challenges as a security issue (i.e. it will want to remain a superpower, and thus need to preserve the absolute and relative material capability necessary to retain that status);
- that it will want no superpower rivals and will thus act to delay or prevent the elevation of great powers (i.e. in addition to staying as a superpower it will also want to stay as the sole superpower); and
- that it will give priority to preventing the great powers from aligning against it (i.e. in addition to being the sole superpower, it will try to prevent the great powers from balancing against it, as Waltz's and Huntington's neorealist logics suggest strongly that they should).

In addition, Reisman (1999–2000: 62), following a fairly traditional realist line, argues that 'the larger the state and the greater its power, the more will bilateral diplomacy be preferred over multilateral, and the more measured will be the attitude towards multilateral institutions.' This logic can be applied to a variety of situations, such as the preference of India and China for bilateral diplomacy within their regions. Underlying it is the idea that powerful actors can wield their power more effectively in bilateral talks, and therefore have the most to lose by allowing themselves to be constrained by multilateral rules and procedures. In relation to a sole superpower, this reasoning suggests a fourth expectation:

- that the sole superpower will act unilaterally when it can, and will prefer bilateral diplomacy to multilateral.

How do these expectations stand up against US behaviour since the demise of bipolarity?

That the lone superpower will securitize challenges to its status

Interestingly, this expectation has been strongly questioned in the American debate about US grand strategy. Some writers, most notably

Wohlforth (1999), have been advocates of a unipolarist strategy for the US, but others, most notably Layne (1993, 1997) and Kupchan (1998, 2002), and also Waltz (1993a: 61, 75–6; 2000) and Huntington (1999: 37), either advocated, or saw as inevitable in the fairly near future, a multipolar world with the US as one pole. This academic debate about US policy suggests that lone superpowers (especially ones isolated by geography as the US is) are not compelled to securitize their status. If they try to maintain their status (as most of the participants in the debate believe the US is trying to do), then they generate the necessary securitization. As Kagan (2002) argues, the position of the US as the leading power is part of what attracts threats to it. If the US seeks to drop out, avoid the dangers of overstretch and free-riding (Carpenter 1991; Layne 1997: 96–112), and configure itself as one great power among several (as many of those just cited advocate), then more things open up for desecuritization. This interpretation could be either reinforced or countered by the US response to September 11: countered if the US stays on the offensive against international terrorism, and its people accept this; reinforced if the US decides to reduce threats to itself by disengaging from its more contentious overseas commitments.

In the event, however, this whole debate can perhaps best be put down to the effects of the transition period that Hansen (2000) warns about, when what prevails is the fact of structural change (end of bipolarity) rather than the logic of the emergent new polarity. By 2002, actual US policy, as reflected both in the maintenance of relatively high military expenditure and in the National Security Doctrine, was clearly committed to maintaining the country's superpower status. There was, indeed, increasing talk of a self-consciously imperial role for the US (Krauthammer 2001; Lipschutz 2002; Sick 2002), more in line with Waltz's original expectations of what unipolarity should look like. It must be noted, however, that the 1990s debate about US grand strategy was conducted without a clear distinction between superpowers and great powers. Consequently the effects of the US dropping out did not stand out as clearly as they needed to. As Waltz (1993a: 72) put it: 'the US will have to learn a role it has never played before: namely to coexist and interact with other great powers.' But the result of the US abandoning its superpower status would not have been a multipolar system structure as envisaged by his version of polarity theory. That would require three or more superpowers. It would have been a global system with no superpowers and several great powers (0 + x), an arrangment as suggested above that lies almost wholly outside the realm of existing theoretical speculation. Waltz (2000) still believes that no lone superpower can succeed for long in maintaining unipolarity because some combination of overstretch and counter-balancing will undermine it (a view also underpinning the work of Ikenberry, Prestowitz and Kupchan). Material factors may indeed shape the outcome in the long term. But, as I argue below, in the short term the key will be what kind of (de)securitization process dominates within the US. It is not unprecedented in US history for engagement with the balance of power itself to be securitized as the main threat to American values, rather than particular threats from outside powers (Schlesinger 2000: 18–25).

As judged by current US policy, this neorealist expectation about the behaviour of a sole superpower finds firm support.

That the lone superpower will want no superpower rivals and will thus act to delay or prevent the elevation of great powers, and that it will give priority to preventing the great powers from aligning against it

If the sole superpower decides to defend its status, then its strategies for dealing with these two expectations are broadly the same. For rising great powers, the superpower can oppose, suppress, coopt or encourage. Neorealist logic rules out encouragement because that would help create a superpower rival. In the case of a falling superpower rival, the superpower can try to support and bolster, or can encourage the fall. Neorealist logic more or less forbids that a superpower should try to prevent the demotion of its rival, but is open about whether it might try to sustain its ex-rival as a great power or allow it to free-fall to regional power level. US behaviour since 1989 tends to support these expectations. The US has not sought to restore Russia as a superpower, but has supported it as a great power conditional on reforms to make it more compatible with a liberal international economic order. By maintaining its alliances with Europe and Japan, the US has coopted the two wealthiest great powers whose identities are most closely aligned with its own, and thus both cemented an ideological consensus on the basic principles of the world economy and prevented any really serious great power coalition forming against it (Layne 1993: 5–7; Job 1999). It has sought to deal with a rising China by a combination of containment (a fairly traditional military–political response to a rising power) and ideological conversion to liberal principles, at least on economic practice (a longer-term attempt to reduce the identity gap between China and the West).

China and Russia are the two great powers with the biggest identity gap with the US. Like Japan their identities are towards the exclusive end of the spectrum, but unlike Japan they have not fully bought into the democratic capitalist model, and are therefore the two most likely great power opponents of the US. But they are also the poorest and most technologically backward of the great powers, and have a long history of antagonism against each other, both of which stand as obstacles to any serious anti-US alliance. If the 'war against terrorism' turns out to be a durable and dominating securitization, both are likely to be on the US side. As Layne (1997) and Kapstein (1999) argue, the US has it relatively easy here. The potential challengers are no match for it, and its geographical position is favoured: because the four great powers are all clustered in Eurasia, they are more impelled to balance against each other than to coalesce against the US. Layne's argument reintroduces geography into the equation, which neorealism tends to ignore. Layne promotes the extreme version of this argument which is that the US could safely abandon its great power alliances because balancing within Eurasia would automatically cancel out the rise of any superpower capable of threatening the US. This vision contrasts with those of Nye (1992) and Rosecrance (1992), who worry about the dangers of a return to balancing in the absence of US primacy and engagement. At least up until 2001, the US strategy of primacy (Mastanduno 1997) was based on a combination of coopting potential rivals and promoting 'universal' values congenial to itself (and many of its allies). This gave the US a strong role as balancer in Eurasia, and helped to suppress the development of balancing behaviour among the Eurasian great powers in relation to each other as well as to the US. Since September 11 a rather harder US policy has been emerging which cares less about maintaining alliances, and looks more to preserving and extending US military superiority.

The securitization perspective suggests interesting tensions within the US. Even before September 11 there was not much sign that the US was moving to Layne's position, which would require that it desecuritize the great powers. But in defending its status, the securitization processes within the US sometimes work at cross purposes. The securitization of China causes few contradictions. But the securitization of Japan during the late 1980s and early 1990s set against each other the need to respond to a potential superpower peer and the strategy of preventing a counterpole coalition by keeping the strongest great powers on side. Similar, but less acute, tensions could be seen between the US and the EU over the latter's attempts to create a European military force. Only if the 'war on terrorism' pushes the US towards extreme unilateralism does Layne's scenario of a hands-off policy by the US towards the great powers look likely. By 2002, the National Security Strategy of the Bush administration made it abundantly clear not only that the US was going to hang on to its superpower status, but also that it would oppose the rise of any others to superpower status:

It is time to reaffirm the essential role of American military strength. We must build and maintain our defenses *beyond challenge*. Our military's highest priority is to defend the United States. To do so effectively, our military must: assure our allies and friends; *dissuade future military competition*; deter threats against U.S. interests, allies and friends; and decisively defeat any adversary if deterrence fails. . . . The United States will require bases and stations within and beyond Western Europe and Northeast Asia, as well as temporary access arrangements for the long-distance deployment of U.S. forces. . . . *Our forces will be strong enough to dissuade potential adversaries from pursuing a military build-up in hopes of surpassing, or equaling, the power of the United States.* (Bush 2002: 29–30; emphasis added)

There is some room in these formulations for the interpretation that the US would allow an ally (the EU most obviously) to achieve superpower status on the grounds that it was not an adversary or military competitor. The 2002 National Security Strategy (Bush 2002: 26) even says: 'we welcome our European allies' efforts to forge a greater foreign policy and defense identity with the EU.' But since there is no immediate or even medium-term possibility of the EU bidding for superpower status, there is insufficient evidence to make a judgement on what the actual US reaction would be. During the tensions over the International Criminal Court, and more during the crisis preceding the invasion of Iraq, the US showed no hesitation about dividing Europe and disrupting its (already weak) attempts to build a common foreign and security policy.

On balance, like the first expectation, these two are also robustly supported by US policy since the demise of bipolarity.

That the sole superpower will act unilaterally when it can, and will prefer bilateral to multilateral diplomacy

It is surprisingly difficult to come to a clear judgement on this expectation. Surprising because, given the fact that there has been so much comment, both celebratory and critical, on increased US unilateralism and waning of support for multilateralism, it might look like an open and shut case. It is easy to compile a long list of instances over the past decade in which the US has downgraded, withdrawn from, refused to participate in, or opposed, multilateral projects (more on this in chapter 9). It has also upgraded bilateralism both in its dealings with the EU (Hoffmann 2003: 16) and in its approach to trade policy. The whole policy of 'coalitions of the willing' can be understood as preferring bilateralism to multilateral institutions such as NATO (Gnesotto 2003b: 33–7). This empirical evidence, has, however, to be set against both continued US support for many other aspects of multilateralism, including the IMF, the WTO, the G8 and APEC, and the general expansion of multilateralism over recent decades. Against an expanding background of multilateralism, various US opt-outs might reflect disagreements about particular issues rather than a general turn towards unilateralism. There is also the fact that US unilateralism stands out strongly, both because the US is the sole superpower and its defection carries a lot of weight, and because it has played a leading role over the last half-century in building up the practices and institutions of multilateralism as a central feature of international society. There can also be little doubt that the rhetoric and attitude of the Bush administration is much more openly sceptical about, even antagonistic towards, multilateralism as a general way of doing business than has been the norm in recent US administrations. The US National Security Strategy of 2002 says that: 'In exercising our leadership, we will respect the values, judgment, and interests of our friends and partners. Still, we will be prepared to act apart when our interests and unique responsibilities require' (Bush 2002: 231). Like US behaviour, this leans in both directions at once, suggesting that the US will pick and choose by issue, without adopting a principled preference either way. This represents an instrumental attitude towards multilateralism rather than a commitment to it as an institution of international society. On balance, the expectation of bilateralism is supported by the evidence from US behaviour, but not overwhelmingly. Ikenberry (2002a) identifies one constraining factor when he argues that multilateralism has been a significant part of US grand strategy, and is one of the key reasons enabling identity factors to weigh against expectations of behaviour defined in purely neorealist terms.

*****

Expectations about sole superpower behaviour derived from neorealism thus stand up rather well to the record of the past decade. The US does seem to be behaving as if it lived in a world composed mainly of (potential) enemies and rivals. It seeks to retain both its military dominance and its sole superpower status. While this conclusion will no doubt warm the hearts of (neo)realists, it still remains something of a puzzle. The behavioural logic of the (neo)realist position rests on an assumption that the system is composed of enemies and rivals, and that the relevant set of actors is *not* all of the states in the system, but the relatively small set of superpower(s) and great powers. While it was true during the Cold War that this group was defined primarily in terms of enemies and rivals, since

1989 that has no longer been the case. What has been remarkable about the post-Cold War world has been the extent to which the three main capitalist powers (the US, the EU, Japan) have stayed together in a security community that is hard to describe other than as Kantian, solidarist and based on the social relations of friendship. Since these three powers count for much more than half of the wealth and techno-logical prowess in the system, this is a hugely significant development. Russia has abandoned being an enemy of this group and, since it seems mainly to aspire to membership of it in some form, is not even much of a rival. China is the principal outsider. It is mainly a rival, and although it has some potential to become an enemy (especially over Taiwan) it also seeks, or has obtained, membership in some of the key Western clubs, most notably the WTO. The post-Cold War social structure among the global powers is one of rivals and friends, which suggests that neoliberalism/pluralism and even solidarism should have something to say about the expected behaviour of the powers.

The difficulty with investigating this point is that both neoliberal-ism and the English school are process-orientated theories more than structural ones. They have a more open view about what motivates states, and therefore do not generate a single rigid portrait of the international system in the way that (neo)realism does. This makes it more difficult to derive rule-like expectations from them. Nevertheless, the distinction between international social structures composed of enemies and rivals versus those composed of rivals and friends does give a starting point. Both neoliberalism and the English school expect to find cooperation among states, although within that expectation there is a lot of room for variation about how much cooperation and of what type. Both look for institutions as the manifestation of cooperation, but have different, though complementary, understandings of what 'institution' means. Neoliberals expect rational cooperation on the grounds of calcula-tions of self-interest, and look for what I call *secondary* institutions in the sense of specific, designed things such as international law, regimes, and IGOs (Buzan 2004a: chap. 6). English school thinkers expect to find a second-order type of society among states based on what I call *primary* institutions in the sense of organic, evolved sets of practices and principles that provide a framework of order in international relations, for example: sovereignty, balance of power, diplomacy, nationalism and suchlike. In this perspective, international law is itself a primary insti-tution whereas particular laws or groups of laws are secondary ones. Pluralists expect that primary institutions will be confined to those neces-sary to sustain an orderly coexistence among sovereign states. Solidarists look for a wider range extending into the pursuit of shared values/

beliefs (the market, human rights), and perhaps involving giving standing to non-state actors and individuals in the framework of international society.

On this basis, one needs to look to the institutional structure of the post-Cold War world. (Neo)realists see institutions only as an epiphenomenon of the distribution of power, whereas neoliberals and English school thinkers see them as having independent standing and effect in their own right. Both neoliberals and English school thinkers would expect institutions to become thicker and more significant as the social structure moved through rivals, towards and into friends. How do such expectations help one to understand the actual development of international relations since the end of the Cold War? One clear insight is that they explain the non-collapse of various Cold War institutions, most especially NATO and the EU, which in neorealist thinking (Mearsheimer 1990) should have disappeared along with the Soviet Union. The endurance and, in the case of the EU, strengthening of these institutions reflect the logic of a social structure of rivals and friends holding them in place after the logic of enemies that was part of their formation has disappeared. It also reflects a subsystemic logic: one would expect institutions to be best developed in those places where the international social structures are most strongly towards the 'friend' end of the spectrum, as they are within Europe. The case of the US–Japan alliance is less clear cut. It remains partly held in place by a (neo)realist logic because of the rival–enemy aspects of US and Japanese relations with China.

But the key question for this section is about the behaviour of the sole superpower. How should one expect this particular distribution of power to work in the rivals and friends half of the social spectrum? Hegemonic stability theory (HST) provides a useful pathway into this topic. In some respects, a $1 + x$ power structure is almost ideal for HST, bettered only by $1 + 0$. A sole superpower (so long as it is liberal in its economic and political domestic structure) is in a very strong position not only to provide the collective goods for the management of a liberal international economic order, but also to develop the institutions to support that order and to discipline others into accepting the rules of the game. One problem with HST is that hegemony can range from something unilateralist, coercive and quasi-imperial (and thus closer to the neorealist model) to something more multilateralist and consensual, involving leadership rather than command (and thus more in keeping with a rivals and friends social structure). By analogy, this way of thinking extends beyond the economic domain to shared value projects other than the market, such as human rights and environmental stewardship.

The empirical record on all this is distinctly mixed, and fails to fit clearly overall with any of the models, though each model can claim partial validation. I do not have the space here to unfold the huge amount of evidence that would be necessary to document the case in detail, but the general shape of it can perhaps be indicated by considering the contemporary debates about globalization and the role and place of the US in it. In one sense, globalization might be taken as a validation of the idea that international institutions, both primary and secondary, have become stronger and more widespread since the end of bipolarity. If the principal features of globalization are taken to be the spread of communication capacity and access to it, the increasing organization of production, trade and finance on a global scale, and the deterritorialization of many aspects of human activity and identity, then all of these depend on, and have been facilitated by, states and the international institutions created or encouraged by states. The very concept of globalization carries the idea that, since the end of bipolarity, the scale of these features has moved up from the West to encompass the former communist world and to consolidate the economic grip of the industrial powers on the states and societies of the periphery/third world. The existence of globalization, and the strength of the attitudes towards it, both positive and negative, support the idea that since the end of the Cold War not only has there been a shift from a social structure of enemies and rivals to one of rivals and friends, but that that shift has been accompanied by the widening and deepening of institutions that neoliberals and English school thinkers would expect.

Sole superpower status defines a distribution of capabilities that offers the superpower both the option to lead the development of international society (for example along the lines of HST) and the option to exit from it by using superior capability to pursue self-reliance and/or unilateralism. The US does not seem to have made up its mind to go clearly down one path or the other and appears to be torn on the whole question of institutions. Having played the leading role over the past half-century not only in creating a host of secondary institutions but also in elevating multilateralism to the status of a primary institution of international society, consequently marginalizing great power war and the balance of power as the key drivers of international politics, the US is now ambivalent. It still supports some multilateral institutions, but is hostile to others, and cannot be said to be playing a leading role in pushing the further thickening and extension of international society. In some ways it is on the defensive, seeking to preserve its autonomy by exempting itself from the rules that apply to others. Given this ambivalence it is ironic that some of the negative reaction to globalization sees it as an imposition of Americanization. This reaction would make sense in (neo)realist terms if it came from other states, but instead it comes mostly from non-state actors and movements.

On the one hand, much of the US-led liberal international economic order developed during the Cold War has stayed in place and has been extended to most of the former communist world. Under US leadership the trade regime has been strengthened by transforming the GATT into the WTO. Some of this, particularly in the third world, operates on a logic of coercion where reluctant states are bullied into line by threats of exclusion from trade, credit and key political forums. But the bulk of it clearly reflects either the rivals' logic of calculated self-interest (China, Russia) or the friends' logic of shared belief in the rightness of the market economy as a path to development and prosperity. On the other hand, US leadership is patchy, and in some noteworthy areas the US is not the leader, but the principal source of resistance to strengthening the institutions of international society (various arms control agreements such as that dealing with landmines, the BWC and the CWC; human rights agreements – the ICC, and those concerning the rights of women and children; environmental stewardship such as the Kyoto protocol). The US's commitment to the classically pluralist primary institution of sovereignty, at least for itself, remains in many areas overriding.

To sum up, (neo)realist expectations seem to provide a fairly good fit with the US behaviour of seeking to preserve its sole superpower status and prevent great power coalitions from forming against it. Yet (neo)realist assumptions are a poor fit with both the rivals/friends social structure of relations among the major powers over the past decade and the institutional structure that supports globalization. None of the theoretical approaches give clear expectations about how a sole superpower should behave in an institutionalized environment, leaving open the question of whether it uses its power advantage to take leadership of international society or to insulate itself from international society. In practice, the US has been doing both.

6.3   Expectations for the great powers

In a 1 + x system, (neo)realist assumptions about power suggest three expectations about the behaviour of the great powers:

- that their primary security and political concerns will be with the superpower;
- that the interdependence of security and politics among great powers will vary with distance; and
- that the great powers will collectively react against the unipole or, in Huntington's (1999: 44–6) words, that a counter-pole coalition is 'a natural phenomenon in a uni-multipolar world'.

That the primary concerns of great powers will be with the superpower, and that the interdependence of (de)securitization among great powers will vary with distance

The behaviour of the current four great powers and the leading aspirant (India) broadly confirms these two expectations, as does the behaviour of many regional powers from Israel and Turkey to Pakistan and the two Koreas. The EU is concerned primarily with the US, secondarily with Russia, much less with China and Japan, and hardly at all with India. Russia is concerned primarily with the US, secondarily with the EU and China, and rather less with Japan and India. China is concerned primarily with the US, secondarily with Russia, Japan and India, and rather less with the EU. Japan is concerned primarily with the US, secondarily with China and Russia, and rather less with the EU and India. India is concerned primarily with the US, secondarily with China, and, aside from the residuals of its Cold War relationship with the Soviet Union, not that much with the others. All of the great powers give the US first priority in their relations, and all prioritize their relations with the other great powers on the basis of distance.

That the great powers will collectively securitize the unipole

This expectation is in line with the (neo)realist logic which dictates that all will fear any power whose capability threatens to transcend the possibilities of balancing. The reasoning is nicely captured in Waltz's often-repeated refrain that 'Countries that wield overwhelming power will be tempted to misuse it. And even when their use of power is not an abuse, other states will see it as being so' (Waltz 1993b: 189; 2000: 13, 29). Huntington (1999: 44–6) also asserts that a counter-pole coalition is 'a natural phenomenon in a uni-multipolar world'. The logic that makes it 'natural' is the assumption that the social structure is one of enemies and rivals, though even this might be overridden if war, whether hot or cold, was itself securitized, in which case the incentives to pursue desecuritization in relations with other global powers would be strong. Huntington acknowledges that cultural barriers and the temptations to bandwagon with the US work against the formation of a counter-pole coalition, but in a social structure of rivals and friends it is not clear why such a coalition should occur at all. A counter-pole coalition would make sense if, and only if, *all* of the great powers felt that the superpower threatened their status and their independence. If the great powers were divided, then any counter-pole coalition would be weakened, non-participants would appear as free-riders, and the superpower would have options to make alliances. Given that most of the great powers share at least some 'universal' values with the US, that many of these values are liberal ones, and that the EU and Japan share quite a lot, the necessary sense of threat has not been generated. Even if one or two of the great powers did and do feel threatened by the superpower, the great powers may well be more concerned with securitizing neighbouring great powers than with challenging the distant superpower. Fear of such securitizing dynamics among themselves may even give some of the great powers incentives to prefer the existence of a relatively benign superpower capable of holding the ring among them. This logic is still visible even within so well-developed a security community as the EU, where 'keeping the US in' remains important to the management of the EU's internal politics.

If securitization is going to occur in a $1 + x$ power structure, the key question is whether the great powers will securitize each other or the superpower. This is a rather trickier question than is suggested by the crude assumptions about balancing in simple polarity theory. The fact that all of the great powers give priority to their relationship with the superpower skews the picture considerably, as does the well-developed institutional position of the US in Europe and East Asia. Another distorting variable is the relatively removed geographical circumstance of the current single superpower. The US has options to engage or withdraw (securitize, or not) that are not available to the Eurasian powers. In Eurasia, both propinquity and a shortage of shared values increase the incentives for the Eurasian great powers to securitize each other rather than the US. With the sole exception of a unity of all of them, the Eurasian great powers would find it difficult to form coalitions among themselves without triggering securitizations against each other. A serious Sino-Japanese alignment, for example, could easily trigger securitizing responses in Russia, and a serious Sino-Russian one would have the same effect on Japan. What this boils down to is an argument that counter-pole balancing is far from automatic or 'natural', but that the US could bring it about by working hard to undermine its own leadership assets and alienate the other powers. A good illustration of the requisite dynamics was provided by the dipomacy leading up to the US–British invasion of Iraq. Washington's open disdain for international legitimacy in general and the UN Security Council in particular, and its conspicuous determination to invade Iraq regardless of what others thought, not only split the EU wide open but for a time created a Franco-German-Russian axis. It alienated several European governments from their people, and heavily reinforced the growing impression that the US was shifting from a relatively consensual style of leadership to a more imperial one in which loyalty and obedience mattered more than legitimacy and friendship. The

Iraq invasion did not by itself shift the great powers into a counter-pole coalition, but it did show how US behaviour could work to encourage just such a shift.

Another way of questioning Huntington's hypothesis is to focus not on the imperative of balancing against the superpower, but on the aspirations of one or more great powers to rise to superpower status. Pursuit of such an aspiration is much more conditional on domestic developments (the ability to pursue internal balancing) than it is on forming coalitions against the existing superpower. In order to establish their credentials and status, aspirant superpowers are more likely to have to break any alliance they may have with the existing superpower than to form coalitions against it. Any moves towards coalition formation with other great powers would be likely to trigger anxieties among the remaining great powers, thus offering opportunities for the existing superpower to play balancer to its own advantage. And while some great powers may harbour aspirations to become superpowers, there is no reason to assume that this will be a universal trait that emerges in direct proportion to capability. As the case of Japan illustrates, identity also matters. Just as Japan has had for some decades the capability, but not the will, to play a 'normal' great power role, so it is possible for other great powers to construct their identity in ways that work against aspirations to be a superpower, even if the capability exists. Japan and, so far, the EU have historical disinclinations to take up that kind of political role. Some might fear the popular theories of overstretch and decline that are said to be the price of global leadership (Kennedy 1989). Some might want to avoid the pressures on their domestic politics created by global responsibilities and engagements, a sentiment that dominated US domestic politics right through the nineteenth century and up to the Second World War. Notwithstanding the assumptions of traditional *Machtpolitik*, it is far from clear that an aspiration to superpower status is a general feature of all great powers. It seems safe to assume that great powers will be concerned with maintaining status and avoiding demotion to regional power, but, in the twenty-first century, desire for superpower status may be exceptional rather than normal. The scenario for 'benign tripolarity', based on centred regions in North America, Europe and East Asia (Kupchan 1998; Gilpin 1987: 394–406), can be read as assuming that a system of great powers with no superpower(s) could be stable (see also Buzan 1991a: 174–81, 261–5, on 'mature anarchy'). Looking at the behaviour of the EU and Japan, and to a much lesser extent China, it is also possible to conclude that most, if not all, of the great powers that have risen up into that rank (rather than falling into it, like Russia) are happy to remain where they are and do not aspire either to superpower rank for themselves or to challenge the existing superpower. Calls for multipolarity by Russia, China and others (Ambrosio

2001) are not so much about making themselves into superpowers (a 2 or
3 + x system) as about wanting the US to give up its sole superpower
pretensions (0 + x).

Thus while the first two of the (neo)realist expectations are supported
by the practice of the great powers since 1991, the crucial third one is not.
The idea that the great powers should give first priority to their relationships with the superpower is not just compatible with (neo)realist
expectations, but also fits easily with neoliberal and English school ones.
The same can be said for the expectation about distance mediating the
priorities among the great powers. The (neo)realist expectation about
counter-pole coalitions only makes sense in a system of enemies and
rivals, and the observed absence of it supports the neoliberal and English
school expectation that institutions make a difference. Over the past half-
century the US has consistently, and with considerable success, promoted
both the primary institutions of multilateralism and the market and the
many secondary institutions necessary to implement them. This project
has been the main driving force behind the shift from a world of enemies
and rivals to one of rivals and friends. It certainly supports the claim
that, in terms of world history, the twentieth century was the American
century. Even during the Cold War the success of this project within the
Western camp meant that the more solidarist primary institutions represented by multilateralism and the market began to reduce the significance
of some of the classically pluralist institutions, particularly war and
the balance of power. The promotion of multilateralism and the market,
and the host of secondary institutions accompanying them, reduced the
attractiveness of war by setting in place a collective project of the pursuit
of joint economic gains that was incompatible with war. It reduced the
incentives to balance both by creating a joint interest, and by establishing
a framework of rules and institutions within which differences could be
negotiated and expectations of peaceful conflict resolution could be built
up. In addition, as Ikenberry (2002a, 2003) argues, it made US hegemony
acceptable and legitimate (see also Kapstein 1999; Joffe 2002). Since
the end of the Cold War multilateralism and the market have become
increasingly global in scale, and this social structure seems to provide a
much better explanation for the observed behaviour of the great powers
than the (neo)realist assumptions.

*****

Taking stock of this discussion of superpower and great power behaviour
in a 1 + x power structure, one can conclude that this structure might well
be stable for quite some time. The sole superpower wants to keep its
position, and most of the potential challengers do not want superpower

status for themselves. The material logic of neorealism suggests that, even if they did want to challenge for superpower status, the current great powers have a lot to do in order to get the necessary material and political requirements in place. This material logic gets tempered in two ways. First, by domestic considerations in some of the great powers which make them disinclined to bid for superpower status. Second, by globalist/ HST/institutionalism reasoning – or in the English school version by international society – in which the US-led international order carries considerable legitimacy and rests on shared values which are fully internalized by some, though are more the product of instrumental calculation or coercion in the case of others. These factors work powerfully to desecuritize relations between the sole superpower and the great powers. They suggest that continuation of a 1 + 4 system is a real possibility provided that the US does not itself work to bring it down. This conclusion might be thought vulnerable to the traditional realist worry that material factors are relatively stable, while intentions can change more rapidly. But from a neoliberal or English school perspective, in a social structure of rivals and friends, intentions can become sedimented in relatively stable and institutionalized relationships. Indeed, it is precisely the function of institutions, both primary and secondary, to stabilize expectations about behaviour in this way.

6.4 The significance of regions in a 1 + x power structure

It is beyond the scope of this book to look in detail at the regional level, a task already undertaken elsewhere (Buzan and Wæver 2003). But in one particular respect, the regional level is a crucial factor in sustaining the US position as the sole superpower. As noted previously, the US has adopted a *swing-power* strategy in which it positions itself as a member of three macro-regions (Asia-Pacific, North Atlantic, Western hemisphere) as a way of legitimizing its actual presence as an outside power in Europe, East Asia and Latin America. As much as, and perhaps even more than, its relative material strength, this unique political position defines US superpowerdom, and enables it either to play the other powers and regions off against each other or to coordinate them. In a similar vein, Ikenberry (2002b: 24) describes the US alliance system as 'the global spinal cord of unipolarity'. The basic pattern was put in place during the Cold War, and is likely to remain the dominant one so long as the US does not abandon, or lose, its superpower status. It depends not only on US power, but also on a specific, and so far durable, framework of institutionalization.

What is remarkable about the US position in Europe, East Asia and South America is the degree to which it has become institutionalized through the construction of super-regional projects: Atlanticism, Asia-Pacific (or Pacific-Rim) and Pan-Americanism (Buzan 1998). These super-regions are designed to prevent the consolidation of East Asian, European and South American regions that might either shut the US out or, in the East Asian and European cases, even develop as global power rivals to it. US support for the European integration project has for long been anomalous in this respect, and though understandable in the context of Cold War alliances looks more exposed in the absence of any threat from Russia. The Middle East was different because, although the US was consistently and heavily engaged there in defence of oil and Israel, it never constructed the overarching frameworks of shared identity that it created in the other three regions. Whether it will try to do so now that it has occupied Iraq, and may have entangled itself locally for the long haul, is an interesting question. These shared identity projects usually contain a strong mixture of super-regional economic integration (or aspirations thereto) and mutual defence and security arrangements, the particular mix varying according to the local circumstances and history. Their attendant labels and rhetorics enable the US to appear to be an actual member of these regions rather than an intervening outside power, and thus help to desecuritize its role. Interestingly, the US is not commonly thought of as a *member* of the Middle East, though the strong influence of religious lobbies in US politics does create the basis for an identity bond. But where super-regional projects exist, it is quite common for the US to be thought of, and perhaps to think of itself as, a member of those security regions. In this view, the US is part of the Americas, part of the Atlantic community, and an Asia-Pacific power. By seeming to put the US inside these regions, super-regional projects blur the crucial distinction between regional- and global-level security dynamics, and make them difficult to see from within the US. This blurring becomes an important tool for the management of the US's sole superpower position, not least in preventing the emergence of more independent regional integrations that might threaten its influence.

This is not to deny that these super-regional projects have substantial and sometimes positive political effects. But they can also hide the distinction between being a superpower and being a great or regional power. Buzan and Wæver (2003) argue that the US role in East Asia, South America and Europe is comparable to its role in the Middle East – an outside global power penetrating into the affairs of a region. The key point in support of that theory is that there can be, and are, debates about the US withdrawing, or being expelled, from the region concerned. Germany cannot withdraw from Europe, nor Japan from East Asia, nor

Brazil from South America. But the US can remove itself (or be removed from) Europe, East Asia and South America, and there are regular debates both in the US and in those regions about the desirability or not of such moves. US superpowerdom is expressed in its ability to act as a swing power, engaged in several regions but not permanently wedded to any of them, and in principle able to vary the degree and character of its engagement according to its own choice. A degree of shared identity with the US is the crucial ingredient in the construction of these super-regional projects and, like the US's relationship with the great powers, is therefore dependent on maintaining a specific social structure.

Because it has the option to delink from, or reduce the priority of its engagement in, any region, the US can use threats and inducements of increasing or decreasing its levels of engagement as a means of playing one region against another. This pattern of behaviour was visible during the Cold War, but constrained by the overriding need to hold together a common front against the Soviet Union. Now that there is no super-power rival, the US swing strategy is the dominant pattern. Since East Asia and Europe contain all four great powers, the swing option between them is the key to US post-Cold War strategy. As Wyatt-Walter (1995: 83–97) notes, this has been perhaps easiest to observe in the GATT/WTO negotiations, where the tactical quality of the shift by the US from globalism to regionalism was an attempt to gain more leverage over the EU and East Asia by playing them off against each other. The object of the swing strategy is not for the US to choose one of these regions over the others, but to use the possibility of such choice to maintain its leverage in all of them. Since each of these regions is dependent on the US in important ways, it is not impossible to imagine a kind of bidding war among Europe, Latin America and East Asia to engage US attention and commitment. Mahbubani's (1995) polemic in favour of a new and rising 'Pacific impulse', as against an old and declining Atlantic one, might be seen as an example of just this kind of wooing. Seen in this light, Simon's (1994: 1063) argument that the US is becoming a 'normal state' in the Asia-Pacific community, 'neither its hegemon nor its guarantor', is almost wholly wrong. While the US may be becoming more normal in playing traditional foreign policy games of balance, its overall position is highly exceptional. It is the key partner for many other states both economically and militarily–politically, and it is the only successful purveyor of 'universal' values.

US engagements in other regions do not have this core quality and reflect more instrumental concerns. Although the US is at the moment heavily engaged in the Middle East, that region is peripheral to the swing strategy. The American interest there hinges on its special relationship with Israel (Prestowitz 2003: 193–218) and its concerns about oil, and more recently terrorism, and is unlikely to outlast them should those ties weaken or concerns fade. The US has never been heavily engaged in South Asia, and were it not for the issues of nuclear proliferation and terrorism would have little interest there. That, however, could change should China come to be seen in the US as a global challenger. In that case the US might well look to India as a major ally and fellow democracy. Africa is almost out of this big picture, and likely to remain so, though even the marginal US engagement there has substantial impacts in the region.

6.5 Conclusions

Taking all this into account, a reasonable case can be made that the present sole superpower structure is potentially durable. (Neo)realist logic suggests that it should not be stable, and although expectations derived from it make a good fit with some behaviour, particularly of the US, the underlying assumption of a social structure of enemies and rivals does not fit well with the contemporary reality. That leaves space for neoliberal and English school thinking about institutions, which fit better with the social structure of rivals and friends, and which provide good explanations as to why the great powers have not, and perhaps will not, either form a counter-pole coalition or seek superpower status themselves.

Nevertheless, the tension between the rather good fit of (neo)realist expectations with US behaviour and their rather poor fit with great power behaviour is worrying. The argument that this polarity structure could be stable rests on the existence of liberal/pluralist and solidarist conditions of international society. It also requires that the US not act to undermine these. Since US behaviour fits best with (neo)realist expectations, this gives cause to think that the US itself could be the primary agent of change away from both the present polarity structure and the present social structure.

7

Options for the Future I: Two or Three Superpowers and a Few Great Powers

In order for the number of superpowers to increase from one, the sole superpower has either to allow, or even to encourage, the elevation of one or more of the great powers, or else be unable to prevent it. As argued in chapter 6, (neo)realist theory expects a sole superpower to try to retain its position, and there is nothing in either English school theory or neo-liberalism to counter this expectation. The conduct of the US over the past decade suggests that it is indeed behaving in this way. By itself, this expectation points towards tension, turbulence and even war as likely features of any transition from one superpower to more than one. Yet even if the process is highly likely to fall into the track of the sole superpower being unable to prevent (rather than welcoming) the rise of a peer or peers, history suggests that the sole superpower still has two options. On the one hand, it can acknowledge its inability to stop the rise of a rival (or at least to do so at an acceptable cost) and therefore take an adaptive view. Arguably this was how Britain treated the rise of the US. On the other hand, the sole superpower can try to resist and delay the rise and recognition of a rival power, a position perhaps exemplified by the US response to the Soviet Union during the first two decades of the Cold War.

At this point in the argument it becomes clear that, for this scenario, the interplay between the domestic identities of the leading powers, or in the case of unipolarity the domestic identity of the unipole, and the power structure of the international system as a whole becomes extremely important. During the Cold War, as noted above, bipolarity expressed not just the shape of the power structure, but also the fact that the political project of each was in zero-sum competition with the political project of the other. The opening question for this book is: what would bipolarity have looked like if the Soviet Union had also been a liberal democracy?

In neoliberal and English school terms, ideological closeness along liberal lines would mean that the two superpowers would share a wide range of values, and thus have incentives to cooperate in institutionalizing those values in international society.

Applying this line of thinking to the present situation throws up some interesting possibilities. I will focus on the two most likely scenarios: either that one great power gets elevated to superpower status (a 2 + x polarity) or that two do so (3 + x). The 2 + x scenario would return us to the familiar polarity structure of the Cold War. By the argument in part I, a 3 + x scenario would take us back to a polarity structure not seen since before the Second World War. There are four great powers at the moment, with two being liberal democracies (the EU and Japan); one being a communist state, albeit having adopted some aspects of market economy (China); and one (Russia) being a rather shaky democracy, and an even shakier market economy, with the possibility either to revert to authoritarian statism or continue down the long road towards some form of market democracy. In principle, therefore, combinations of two and three superpowers are available, some of which would contain ideological splits, and some a high degree of domestic similarity along broadly liberal lines. In a power structure with two superpowers the maximum harmony of identity would be the US and the EU, the maximum disharmony the US and China. In a three-superpower system it would make a difference whether there was relative ideological harmony (the US, the EU, Japan), a two-to-one split of some sort (the US, the EU, China), or a three-way split (not really available from the current position, but imaginable from the ideologically tripolar game before the Second World War, with democratic, communist and fascist powers manoeuvring in relation to each other).

Superpower status can be achieved either with the acquiescence of existing superpowers or against their will: the US eventually acknowledged the status of the Soviet Union on the basis of its military capability even though it remained adamantly hostile to its ideology. But the degree of ideological harmony or disharmony between existing and aspirant superpowers should make a considerable difference to whether the structural transition upwards from unipolarity is smooth or turbulent, especially given that the only options for harmony are liberal ones. Other things being equal, one would expect the transition to be rougher in proportion to the degree of ideological disharmony and/or illiberality, and vice versa. One would expect liberal democracies not to go to war with each other, but communist powers (on the model of Sino-Soviet relations during the 1960s and 1970s) might well fall into severe opposition despite their ideological 'harmony'. The nature of the transition from unipolarity up to bi- or tripolarity could be either turbulent or smooth.

The first task of this chapter is to think through how likely any increase in the number of superpowers is under current conditions, and who are the most likely candidates among the present four great powers. This will be done in the next section, which argues that there are no candidates for promotion in the short term, but that the EU and China are at the head of the queue in the medium and longer term. Section 2 explores the expectations for behaviour that might attend different combinations of superpowers, and section 3 looks briefly at the position of the remaining great powers.

7.1   Are there any candidates for elevation to superpower status?

On the face of it, the scenarios in this chapter are unlikely during the next couple of decades because none of the existing great powers is well positioned for early promotion (Kapstein 1999; Waltz 2000: 29–39; Hansen 2000: 79; Kupchan 2002: 4–5). Reflecting back on the three criteria for great power and superpower status set out in chapter 5, it is apparent that superpower status is rather demanding. Not only must a superpower have the capability to operate globally, and to do so in practice, but also it must see itself as having that status and be accepted by others (especially other superpowers) as doing so. By contrast, great power status rests on the fact that the state in question is responded to by others on the basis of system-level calculations, as well as regional ones, about the present and near future distribution of power. To make it into the superpower ranks today a great power clearly has to develop both the capability for, and the practice of, global operations militarily, politically and economically. It has also to acquire the perception of itself as a superpower and the acknowledgment of its peers. The third criterion, as argued by Buzan and Wæver (2003), is that any great power seeking superpower status will almost certainly either have to achieve some form of suzerainty over its own region, or else have a stable, settled and deeply desecuritized relationship with its neighbours. The US has long since achieved this in North America, and the Soviet Union unquestionably had it over its region during the Cold War. That Germany never achieved it except for very brief periods during the First and Second World Wars goes a long way to explaining its inability to win superpower status. This is the same logic that keeps India from rising up the ranks from regional power to great power. Only rarely can powers escape the link between their regional status and their global one. The US did not escape its region, but had an easy task because its neighbours were all much weaker than it. Britain, aided by its offshore geography and a strong navy, probably came closest to escaping its region during the peak of its imperial power in the later nineteenth century. But such opportunities are rare and, among the present great powers, only Japan is favoured by geography in the same way.

In the rest of this section I will examine each of the existing great powers in the light of these three criteria.

Russia

Russia is the least likely candidate for (re)promotion to superpower. Indeed, it remains a plausible candidate for further demotion into the ranks of big regional powers alongside India and Brazil. To achieve promotion back to superpower would require Russia to stage a miraculous, across-the-board recovery from the very severe economic, political and status shrinkage that followed from the implosion of the Soviet Union. As Freedman (1999) argues, Russia's problem is the huge disjuncture between its status needs and its economic and military weakness. Except for nuclear weapons, the massive military legacy from the Soviet Union has largely decayed. The Russian economy is routinely compared in size with that of the Netherlands, and in general health, prospects and stability Russia is identified with countries much lower down the ranks. Aside from its nuclear weapons, and its enormous political geography, Russia does not really have the material capability to sustain even its great power status, which is consequently more something given by its peers than taken by right. Russia's problems of redevelopment are deep and do not seem likely to be solved soon. The first problem blocking Russia's path is thus both lack of adequate capability to play a global role and lack of any prospect of being able to recover from that situation any time soon. Without adequate capability, Russia has no chance of achieving recognition by its peers, and thus faces a long disjuncture between its self-perception as a global power and the largely charitable basis on which it currently holds great power status.

The fragility of Russia's position is underlined by the uncertainties over its standing within its own region. In the post-Soviet space (CIS) Russia is acting as a traditional great power, seeking, not without some success, to reassert a degree of suzerainty over most of the former parts of the Soviet Union (Buzan and Wæver 2003: chap. 13). If it fails to create a centred regional security complex (RSC) it ends up with the same problem as India (having active rivals within the region), and risks sinking to regional power status. Russia has already 'lost' the three Baltic states, though since these are heading into the EU they are unlikely to be local challengers to Russia. It still faces internal problems of secessionism, most obviously in Chechnya. Belarus is Russia-leaning, even integrationist, but the torn and indecisive Ukraine has experimented with counter-balancing and may eventually try to follow the Baltics towards the West. The Caucasus and Central Asia are the most closely integrated into the CIS, especially in terms of military security, and begin to look firmly placed within the Russian sphere. The main overarching question in the post-Soviet region is whether a counter-coalition will form against Russia within the current regional boundaries, which looked possible for a time during the 1990s; whether countries will drift out of Russia's sphere; or whether Russia manages to reintegrate the region as a centred RSC. The outcome of this regional-level game will crucially influence not only the role Russia can play outside the region but also the international status it can claim. On all three grounds, therefore, and even though its position has improved a bit since the nadir of the 1990s, Russia is too weak to bid for superpower status during the foreseeable future.

Japan

The problem with thinking about Japan as a possible superpower is in distinguishing between the current gloom surrounding it because of its decade-long economic slump and its real capacity to meet the requirements for superpower status. Against the fashionable discounting of Japan one has to set both the serious and decade-long discussion of the 1980s and early 1990s about 'Japan as number one' and Japan's record in the past of making rapid and spectacular internal changes in response to serious outside pressures (mid-nineteenth century, post-1945). This latter talent makes it a more interesting and important variable among the four great powers than current discussion about its prospects might suggest.

In terms of capability, Japan's strong cards are its formidable indus-trial and technological capability and its wealth. By the standards of other superpowers, its territory is small, its population at the lower end of the scale (and shrinking), and its indigenous raw materials resources very thin. Japan could certainly generate a sophisticated arsenal of nuclear weapons and delivery systems quite quickly. It already has a 'recessed deterrent' in its space launcher programme and its large civil nuclear power industry. It could upgrade its existing self-defence forces into some-thing more substantial, but, given its ageing and dwindling population, it would be hard pressed to generate the kind of large-scale conventional armed forces that it possessed in the first half of the twentieth century.

If the picture on capabilities makes Japan look a bit marginal as a prospective superpower, the issue of status stands as a major roadblock. The most obvious problem is the unwillingness of a majority of Japanese to conceive of their country even as a normal great power, let alone a superpower. Public commitment to the pacifist article 9 of the constitution, and to a highly constrained role for the military, remains strong and there seems no reason to question Katzenstein and Okawara's (1993) and Berger's (1993) arguments that it is likely to remain so (Twomey 2000: 193–8). These domestic constraints are reinforced both by Japan's weak political institutions, which are ill-suited to the conduct of a robust foreign policy (van Wolferen 1989), and by its continued strong linkage to, and dependence on, the US in a lopsided alliance (Soeya 1998: 198–200; Van Ness 2002). They are also reinforced by Japan's unreconciled position in its region, where China, the two Koreas and, to a lesser extent, Taiwan and the ASEAN countries all cultivate negative memories of Japanese imperialism before 1945, and remain suspicious of any hint of revival of Japanese military power (Buzan 1988, 1996). As already observed in earlier discussion, there is less resistance in the rest of the world to thinking about Japan as a great power.

Japan's status problems in its region reinforce, and are compounded by, its inability either to dominate or to pacify East Asia. East Asia is an unusual region, both because it contains two great powers and several substantial regional powers, and because the impact of the US presence on the dynamics of the region's security relations is particularly strong and longstanding (Buzan and Wæver 2003: part 2). Most notably, the US plays a big role in relation to the two great powers in the region, balancing China, and keeping Japan so closely tied to itself that the latter does not really have to develop a security policy of its own. This US position means that it is very difficult to assess what Sino-Japanese relations would look like if the US was not involved in this way. It has been commonplace to argue that Japan does not feel much threat from China (Drifte 2000: 451–2; Twomey 2000: 169), but it is much less certain whether this would remain the case if the US ceased to play ringholder for the East Asian powers. Yahuda (2002) argues that attitudes towards China in Japan are in fact now deteriorating, and that the failure of both states to cultivate sensitivity towards the other's security concerns makes both them and the whole of Asia dependent on the US to hold the ring. Japan could certainly mount its own deterrent against China if need be (Twomey 2000: 185–93), but it is no longer capable of dominating East Asia by itself, and might be tempted to bandwagon with a rising Chinese power (Ross 1999: 115; Buzan 2004c). A Sino-Japanese condominium might be a possibility, but it would require very radical departures from existing arrangements. Some observers see potential for abrupt change in the differences between Japan and the US over policy goals in East Asia, particularly on China and Taiwan, but also on Korean reunification (Stokes 1996; Twomey 2000: 204–5; Drifte 2000), and speculate whether these will corrode the US–Japan alliance. The key point of vulnerability is a crisis over Taiwan, in which Japan might fail to back a robust US policy against China, so precipitating a breakdown in the alliance. Such events are within the realm of possibility but, if they were Japan's path into partnership with China, it is hard to see how Japan would avoid becoming the junior partner in any such arrangement, thereby reproducing its existing unbalanced partnership with the US. Given its economic ties to East Asia, Japan no longer really has the option of exploiting its offshore geography to play the old British game of pretending not to be a member of any region.

In sum, Japan seems a pretty unlikely candidate for promotion to superpower status anytime soon, or possibly ever. It is probably also true, in respect of both domestic attitudes and profile of capabilities, that a civilian power cannot be a superpower.

China

Since the economic downturn took the shine off Japan as a challenger, fashionable talk in Washington has focused on China as the leading candidate for 'peer competitor'. This fits into a more longstanding post-Cold War view that, if challenges to the US are to come, they will almost certainly come from Asia (Friedberg 1993). Although I share the widely held view that the emergence of a second superpower within the next two decades is unlikely, China certainly presents the most promising all-round profile as a potential challenger. In terms of capability it has a fast-growing and rapidly modernizing economy. Although still technologically and organizationally backward in many respects, China has been successful both in mastering the technology for nuclear weapons and manned space launchers and in presenting an image of itself as making sustained progress across the board in economic development. On the back of this expanding economy it maintains strong conventional forces and a modest nuclear deterrent. China has behaved sensibly in not allowing its military development to outpace and compromise its economic one. There is a price to be paid for this in a certain military technological backwardness, but the longer term prospects of this policy look formidable. Serious questions can nevertheless be raised about China's prospects for an inexorable rise to levels of capability sufficient to support a superpower bid. In part there is just the pattern of boom and bust that attends all forms of capitalist development. There is no reason to expect that China will escape from the pains of adjusting its culture, social practices and internal distribution of power to the demands of market-based development, and at a minimum one might therefore expect periods of setback and turbulence in its development. How China will be received externally depends heavily on how it evolves internally, and there are too many variables in play to allow any certainty of prediction. China could falter economically and politically, succumbing for a time to the many internal contradictions building up from its rapid development, and so fail to fulfil the material aspirations to power as quickly as some predict. Just as plausibly, it could continue to gather strength with relatively minor ups and downs in the process. In the latter case, it could become politically either more nationalistic, authoritarian and assertive, or more liberal, democratic and cooperative.

Unlike Japan, China certainly suffers few doubts about the legitimacy of its claim to be treated as a world-class power. Especially if the transition away from communism and towards the market is accompanied, as seems quite likely, by a nationalistic phase, China's domestic environment might well support assertions of superpower status. Unlike Russia, about which most anticipations are neutral or gloomy, China can and does successfully play on expectations about its future capability in order to enhance its status in the present. Unless the country suffers a major internal crisis, the tendency of the rest of the world to believe in the inexorability of China's rise to power will help it to bid for superpower status perhaps even before its material capability is fully up to scratch. This means that, as its capability rises, it should find a receptive environment internationally to its status claims, regardless of whether those claims are welcomed or feared.

The question of China's relationship with its region is both interesting in itself and crucial to its superpower potential. If China could position itself as the dominant power in East Asia, reasserting some form of effective suzerainty over its neighbours, then its claim for superpower status would be enormously strengthened. But if it gets bogged down in its region, as India has done, and as Russia fears doing, then it will have much greater difficulty in attaining the global reach and status necessary for superpower status. In Asia, the demise of the Soviet Union contributed strongly to the relative empowerment of China and its move towards the centre of the US debate about possible 'peer competitors'. The withdrawal of Soviet power from the region meant that both India and Vietnam lost their main external balancer against China, and that China became the central focus of East Asian (and up to a point South Asian) regional security dynamics (Buzan and Wæver 2003: part 2). But although its hand was strengthened in East Asia, China certainly does not dominate the region, and not only because the US remains heavily engaged there as an external balancer. In its position within the region there is some historical parallel with Japan in that China also inspires fear among its neighbours. But in the case of China, such fears reflect a much older and more longstanding experience of suzerainty which in some cases (Vietnam) go back more than a millennium. Neither country is therefore well placed to take up a consensual leadership role in East Asia, and both would risk triggering local balancing reactions if they tried to assert hegemony in a coercive way. China also has the additional complication of its unresolved dispute with Taiwan. China sees this as a domestic question, but much of the rest of the world, including the US, sees it additionally as an international one, and this contains much potential for poisoning China's relations both with its neighbours and with the US.

China's regional position bears some resemblance to that of Germany between 1870 and 1945. Although it is a big and relatively powerful state within its region, many of its neighbours are formidable powers in their own right. Some (Japan, South Korea, Taiwan) possess not just military capabilities more modern than China's but also very substantial financial and economic resources. Others (India, Vietnam) can put large conventional forces in the field. Several either have (North Korea, India) or could quite quickly acquire (Japan, South Korea, Taiwan) nuclear weapons capability. China is neither in the happy position of the US (having only weak powers as neighbours), nor in that of the EU (having legitimacy as a basis both for keeping its region peaceful and, up to a point, for integrating it as a single actor on the global scale).

Given China's lack of soft power resources among its neighbours (Van Ness 2002: 143), and the generally weak international society in East Asia, China faces the (neo)realist logic that its neighbours would balance against it if its material power began to look preponderant. Such balancing would mean that China faced serious obstacles within its region to any bid for superpower status. Given the historical fears it attracts, its lack of leadership legitimacy in the region, and the actual and potential military and economic strength of its neighbours, China might well expect to remain trapped within its region. At this point, however, a cultural interpretation specific to East Asia comes into play to question whether regional balancing should in fact be the expected response to increases in China's power. This interpretation rests on the possibility that the Asian international subsystem is dressed in Westphalian costume but will not perform according to a Westphalian script. It projects Asia's past into its future (Fairbank 1968; Huntington 1996: 229–38; Kang 2003) by assuming that what Fairbank labelled the 'Chinese World Order' – a Sinocentric and hierarchical form of international relations – has survived within the cultures of East Asia despite the superficial remaking of the Asian subsystem into a Western-style set of sovereign states. Its principal effect is to subvert the expectation of balancing as the normal response to threat and power imbalance in a Westphalian system, and to replace it with a propensity among the weaker powers to bandwagon. The idea is that hierarchical behaviour remains so deeply ingrained in Asian cultures that it makes their international relations not conform to the (neo)realist models of IR. If this is true, then China has much better prospects for gaining some form of suzerainty over East Asia as its power rises. China is therefore a quite plausible candidate for superpower status at some point in the not too distant future. Given all the conditions that still have to be met, however, its elevation is not inevitable and, if it does occur, is unlikely to happen for at least a couple of decades even if everything works smoothly towards that end.

The EU

The EU is the most novel of the contemporary great powers because it is not a state. For Waltzian neorealists this political fact alone would exclude it from being either a great power or a superpower. Although I argued above that the EU does meet the criteria for designation as a great power, its political limitations do lie at the centre of its potential to become a superpower. In terms of material capability, the EU is unquestionably the leading candidate for elevation to superpower status. It is not without significance that it contains four states that counted as great powers during the interwar years: Britain, France, Germany and Italy. Unlike Japan, the EU does possess the geographical size, population and raw material resources to be a superpower. Unlike China and Russia, and in parallel with the US and Japan, the EU has a stable, large, and highly developed advanced industrial economy. In principle the EU is capable of being a formidable military power, though the fragmented way in which it now spends its military budgets means that, apart from a few first-rate units and some nuclear weapons, its overall military capability is small compared with that of the US. The central issue, in some ways comparable to Japan, is about the political cohesion of the EU and its willingness to sustain a coherent and robust foreign and defence policy. Although cooperation on foreign, and up to a point defence, policy is well institutionalized, progress towards integrated policy has been slow and patchy. The EU as such is much more of a presence in the economic sector than in the politico-military one. The constituent states still retain a great deal of autonomy in matters of foreign policy and defence, and at the current rate of progress it will take many decades, if ever, before this balance shifts in favour of the EU as the main actor. Kupchan (2002: 119–59) and Prestowitz (2003: 230–44) are bullish about Europe's superpower prospects. But its politico-military weakness is a big missing element in the EU's capability profile, and one that will almost certainly take a long time to fix, if indeed it can ever be fixed. There is a real possibility that the EU will remain a loosely confederated postmodern entity (Cooper 1996) with the characteristics of a civilian power. There is often more outside demand that the EU should play a larger politico-military role than there is internal desire that it should become constituted in such a way as to make that possible.

This is a matter not just of capability, but also of status. As with Japan, domestically the EU has little will to seek superpower status, and would have to overcome a whole series of difficult issues in its own development before it could bid for that status. Not least because it is so closely aligned with, and institutionally tied to, the US, the EU tends not to feature much in US discussions of 'peer competitors', which have focused mainly on Asian candidates. US policy continues to reflect this attitude, despite the collapse of the Cold War rationale that justified US support for European integration as a way of strengthening forward defence against the Soviet Union. Recall the National Security Strategy quote from chapter 5 (Bush 2002: 26): 'we welcome our European allies' efforts to forge a greater foreign policy and defense identity with the EU.' Clearly the social and historical bonds that define 'the West' or 'the North Atlantic community' are still strong enough to keep the EU out of the 'peer competitor' spotlight that turned so ruthlessly on another close US ally, Japan, during the late 1980s and early 1990s. The role of shared identity in keeping the EU out of the US's threat perceptions is perhaps the same as that which makes the US not care about Israel's nuclear weapons while making Iraq's and Iran's nuclear weapon aspirations a justification for war. Or if shared identity is not the explanation, then the alternative is that, because most US policy-makers and foreign policy specialists discount the EU for not being a state, they miss its potential as a rival. That view comes clear in Kagan's (2002, 2003) much commented-upon work which builds around a contrast between a super-strong US and a relatively weak Europe, even though he is impressed by the postmodern political accomplishment that the EU represents. Kupchan (2002) is a rare case of someone putting the EU as the likely challenger to the US as its integration processes strengthen. Huntington (1999: 45) can also be read as leaning in this direction when he characterizes the ongoing integration of the EU, and especially its adoption of the Euro, as 'undoubtedly the single most important move toward an antihegemonic coalition'. This remark, however, reflects the self-imposed inability of most (neo)realists to see the EU clearly. Huntington views the EU itself as the coalition, and is not, in my terms, talking about an EU great power making anti-hegemonic alliances with other great powers.

It is perhaps at the regional level that the EU is most impressive, especially if one recalls the difficulty that disorderly and/or hostile regional security environments pose for Russia, China, Japan (and India). Wæver (1996a, 1996b, 1997, 1998, 2000; Buzan and Wæver 2003: part 5) has done more than anyone to develop the idea that what is most important about the EU is the way in which it pacifies and integrates its region. These effects have for decades had power well beyond the borders of its membership, though, given the recent and likely future expansions of membership, the EU itself will stretch all the way to, and in the Baltics beyond, the borders of the former Soviet Union. Nevertheless, its concentric circles of influence still reach strongly into the Balkans and Turkey, and across the Mediterranean to the Maghreb. In Europe, it is the power of the EU's integrating dynamics that is responsible for the emergence and reproduction (or not, if the integration process starts to unravel) of a great power. The EU-dominated part of Europe is a uniquely interesting contemporary instance of a strongly centred regional security complex being formed without a single dominating power at the centre (the only parallel being the way the US formed from the late eighteenth to the late nineteenth century: Deudney 1995). In Europe regional institutions have to work if the EU is to count as a great power. The formal construction of the EU is therefore a large part of the story; its ability to structure (dominate) the rest of the region (in a friendly way) as well as, to some extent, emerging as a global actor is another part.

Despite this remarkable accomplishment of pacifying and integrating its region, unmatched by any of the other three current great powers, though also achieved by the US, it is still tempting to come to a similar conclusion about the EU as I reached for Japan, namely that, while a civilian power can stand as a great power, it cannot become a superpower unless it abandons the civilian model. Although a few of its member states are military powers (Britain, France), the EU as a whole is still a civilian power. Other things being equal, and taking into account the deeply rooted internal difficulties facing serious EU integration on foreign and defence policy, one has to conclude that the chances of the EU becoming a superpower any time soon, or even ever, are small. The main probability is that, for many years and even decades, the EU will remain preoccupied with its internal development and expansion, not to mention the formidable problem of how to pacify and absorb the Balkans, and perhaps in the longer run even Turkey. An EU superpower is possible but, as Ole Wæver has usefully reminded me over the years, 'anything is possible, it only depends on how many other things have to change to make it so.'

I conclude from this survey that there are only two plausible candidates for elevation to superpower: China and the EU. China has further to go in material terms than the EU, but is probably more plausible on political grounds than the EU. Neither elevation is inevitable, and while

China's may be a case of 'when', the EU's is more one of 'if'. Even on the most favourable assumptions neither is likely to be ready to make a bid for two decades or more.

7.2 Expectations for the superpowers: three models

Notwithstanding the conclusion from the previous section that rival superpowers are unlikely to arise soon, it is still worth exploring the expectations that would result from the changes in polarity structure that would occur if either or both of China and the EU became superpowers. The first thing to note is whether and how the (neo)realist expectations for the sole superpower, given in chapter 6 for the present scenario, change in a system with two or three superpowers.

- The expectation that a superpower will try to prevent challenges to its status, and will treat such challenges as a security issue, seems likely to hold even when there are two or more superpowers. No superpower will want to be demoted.
- The expectation that the superpower will want to stay as the sole superpower becomes irrelevant, or rather becomes subsumed in a more general expectation that superpowers will not want to see their club expanded. Certainly the US and the Soviet Union behaved that way during the Cold War, and a corollary of this expectation is therefore that the rise of additional superpowers will tend to be a turbulent and tense process. Perhaps the most important exception to this rule is where a superpower in decline seeks to pass the torch to a rising power that shares its ideology. The exemplary case here is Britain and the US.
- The expectation that a superpower will give priority to preventing the great powers from aligning against it becomes irrelevant. The (neo)realist assumption is that, as during the Cold War, two super-powers would be opposed, and so concerned mainly with each other, and only with great powers as members of rival alliances. A three-superpower world is much harder to evaluate. Certainly the three superpowers should be concerned mainly with each other, and from that assumption it follows that each would be keen to prevent the other two aligning against it. Following the logic of the Cold War, it might also be expected that each would seek to construct and protect its own sphere of influence.
- The expectation that the sole superpower will act unilaterally when it can, and will prefer bilateral diplomacy to multilateral, becomes largely irrelevant. The superpowers will have to negotiate with each other over

some issues, but some of them may well be drawn to multilateralism, as the US was during the Cold War (Ikenberry 2002a, 2002b; Hendrickson 2002) as a strategy for constructing and maintaining a bloc.

Thus while some expectations remain the same or similar as the number of superpowers rises from one, some change substantially. As already noted, the obvious structural comparison of the two cases of two super-powers is with the Cold War. All three cases involve the US and one other superpower so, while the polarity structure and one of the super-powers remain constant, the question is: what difference does it make who the second superpower is? Posing the question in this way focuses the enquiry on to the interplay between the domestic character of the leading power(s) and the polarity structure of the international system as a whole. If one accepts the conclusion from the previous section that China and the EU are the only plausible candidates for elevation to superpower status in the foreseeable future, then there are three concrete scenarios involving a world with two or three superpowers: the US and the EU, the US and China, or the US, the EU and China. In terms of assumptions about the social structure of the system, bringing in the domestic character of the powers concerned reveals that even the two scenarios for two superpowers are quite different from the Cold War situation. During the Cold War, the two superpowers were at opposite ends of the ideological spectrum, and any gain by either was not just a question of relative material power, but also one about the force and legitimacy of their ideological claims to own the future. None of the scenarios on offer duplicates that particular social structure. A two-superpower system composed of the US and the EU would be marked by rather low levels of ideological difference and real possibilities for friendship. A two-superpower system composed of the US and China would certainly contain some significant ideological difference, but just as certainly nothing on the scale, or of the intensity, that marked the relationship between the US and the Soviet Union. China and the US could be enemies, but more likely they would be rivals. A US–EU–China system would contain two superpowers quite close in ideology and one with more difference: a social structure of rivals and friends. What expecta-tions might one have about superpower behaviour under these three sets of conditions?

Since the (neo)realist expectations received quite strong empirical support in relation at least to the sole superpower in the first scenario, I give them the benefit of the doubt here. On that basis the bottom-line expectations are that the superpowers will try to avoid demotion, will resist the rise of new entrants into their club, and will mostly be con-cerned about their relationships with each other.

Two liberal democratic superpowers: the US and the EU

(Neo)realist thinking suggests that the transition from one up to two superpowers should always be a fraught process, but if there is any set of conditions under which this expectation would *not* be met it is this one. The US and the EU have both intertwined identities and longstanding friendly relations which are deeply institutionalized. Although it is easy to imagine sharp differences between the US and the EU on issues ranging from the Middle East through the environment, to trade and human rights, it is extremely difficult to imagine them becoming enemies (Gompert 2003: 43). The US consistently supported the project of European integration during the Cold War, and at least until 2001 continued to do so. Although they do have a range of differences on a number of issues, some significant, they share a wide range of basic values rooted in liberal democracy and market economics. As Prestowitz (2003: 244) notes, the existing world order rests more on the good relations between the US and Europe than on any other relationship. If the second superpower was the EU, then the neorealist hypotheses would have a hard test. Would two closely interdependent democracies securitize each other, or would the outcome be something more Kantian (Wendt 1999; Cronin 1999), perhaps involving a condominium arrangement of some sort in which the two would try to co-manage international society. If the two superpowers were both liberal democracies, then their incentives to construct spheres of influence would be weakened by the desire to build and maintain a relatively open world economy. There might be spheres, but they would be much less mutually exclusive and zero-sum than those of the Cold War or the 1930s. If condominium was the outcome, then the remaining great powers would have even fewer possibilities to balance than they do under a single superpower. In this sense, the international politics of a condominium two-superpower system might look much like those with a single superpower.

Against this more liberal/solidarist interpretation stand the specific arguments of Kupchan (2002), Huntington (1999) and Kagan (2002, 2003) and the general ones of Waltz (1979), all pointing in the opposite direction towards the erosion of the North Atlantic community, and the growth of a perception in Europe and elsewhere that the US has become more of a unilateralist 'rogue colossus' with an uncongenial agenda (Kagan 2002: 26; Huntington 1999: 42; Prestowitz 2003) than a reliable ally with whom one shares a wide range of basic values. Indeed, a shift of perceptions along these lines might also be a necessary condition for stimulating the EU into abandoning its civilian power character and getting serious about constructing a robust common foreign and defence policy. Discussion of an Atlantic rift has to be taken seriously. The evidence pointing towards

it may mostly be in the form of warning shots aimed at influencing immediate policy, but it has deeper theoretical roots in neorealist expectations
about the behaviour of great powers, and is not an entirely implausible
outcome of differences over Middle Eastern, environmental and economic
policy pushed to extremes. If one follows this logic it leads to a scenario
in which two liberal democratic superpowers live in a (neo)realist social
structure of enemies and rivals. It is not impossible to find examples
of democracies treating each other as potential enemies (Anglo-French
naval rivalry and various Anglo-US tensions during the nineteenth
century), but these are pretty marginal in the historical record overall,
and much harder to imagine in the conditions of the twenty-first century.
There is a huge inertia of history, habits and institutions standing in the
way of the EU and the US falling into a relationship of enemies, or even
of rivals. To do so, they would have to disentangle their identities from
each other – not impossible, but not a task lightly done for either. Among
other things a development along these lines would require not only
sustained and radical changes in US and European behaviour and identity, but also the complete breakdown of democratic peace theory. Such a
development is possible, but an awful lot of things would have to change
to make it so.

Two superpowers, one liberal capitalist, one authoritarian capitalist: the US and China

A US–China scenario most obviously raises the prospect discussed in
section 2.2 about clashes between universalist/inclusive identities (the
US) and exclusive/particularist ones (China). Would a two-superpower
system composed of the US and China simply replay the Cold War, or
would it be something quite different? The answer(s) to this question
depend(s) on the degree of ideological difference and disharmony between
the US and China. On the assumption that the US retains its present
form of political economy, most of the possible variation in this equation
lies with China, whose possibilities for development seem much more
open than those of the US. Debates about China can be placed within a
matrix formed by two variables:

- does China get stronger (because its economic development continues
  successfully) or weaker (because its development runs into obstacles,
  or triggers socio-political instability)?
- does China become a malign, aggressive, threatening force in international society (because it becomes hypernationalist or fascist), or does it
  become more benign and cooperative (because economic development

brings internal democratization and liberalization and moderates its exclusivist identity)?

Obviously if China becomes weak, then it will not make superpower status, and whether it becomes malign or benign then becomes more a regional than a global concern. Because of its spillover consequences, a weak, disintegrating China would be as much of a nightmare for its neighbours as a strong and malign one. But if China becomes strong enough to attain superpower standing, then the malign or benign question matters a great deal both regionally and globally. Both options are possible, and the many variables in play make it impossible to predict which is most likely to occur. Indeed, both could happen, with a malign phase giving way to a benign one, as happened with Germany and Japan during the comparable phases of their industrialization.

A China much more powerful, but still in the ideologically Maoist mode of the 1960s and 1970s, might well trigger a replay of the bipolarization of the Cold War. Yet given the apparent contradiction between Maoism and efficient economic development, reversion to such a scenario looks all but impossible. Much less impossible would be a China that continued its current pace of development, but turned towards state capitalism and either or both of virulent nationalism and some form of fascism. Those wanting to take a malign view of China's future have plenty to draw on. There is the general idea that rising powers seek to assert their influence (Segal 1988; Shambaugh 1994). Attached to this are two ideas that seemed to amplify it. First is the idea that China is a revisionist power, not closely wedded to the existing international order, and with many territorial, cultural and status grievances. Second is the idea that China is a classic model of authoritarian modernization (Bracken 1994: 103–9), unrestrained by democracy and vulnerable to nationalism and militarism. Such views have been reinforced by China's lack of transparency, its willingness to resort to aggressive behaviour and threat or use of force against its neighbours (India, Vietnam, the Philippines, Taiwan), the continued cultivation of its historical hatred of Japan, and its robust opposition to US hegemony (To 1997: 252, 261; Soeya 1998: 204–6). If China became strong and threatening, then the (neo)realist idea that two superpowers *must* be enemies or rivals would probably be supported.

The more benign scenario depends on whether the process of development leads in time to a liberalization of China's society and politics, and therefore to a closing of the ideological gap between China on the one hand and the US, the EU and Japan on the other. This is the hope of those promoting economic engagement with China, and the implicit models are Japan, South Korea and Taiwan, all of which have developed through a period of authoritarian capitalism and into democracy, if not yet deep-rooted liberalism. Some argue that a benign scenario is supported by China's interest in development (Kang 1995: 12; Mahbubani 1995) and its adaptation to international society (Zhang 1998; Foot 2001). Some (Johnston 2003; Sutter 2002) argue that China cannot really be seen as revisionist, that in many ways it accepts substantial elements of the status quo both globally and regionally, and that it is already quite conscious of, and responsive to, the dangers of being seen as threatening by its neighbours, and indeed the US. China has already conceded much of the economic game to market capitalism, and, like Russia, it no longer offers an alternative universal model for the future. Recall that it was Gorbachev's moves towards economic reform that played a big role in winding down the Cold War (and the Soviet Union). Consequently, so long as China stays on its present course, and given that China is unlikely to reach for superpower status for a decade or two, it should be much easier (though not easy) for the US and China to coexist as rivals than it was for the US and the Soviet Union.

Because the malign and benign scenarios can be sequential as well as alternative paths, the timing of China's rise to superpowerdom – whether it took place during a malign or benign phase – could be very important both to the process of transition and to the subsequent relationship with the US. It seems unlikely under any circumstances that the rise of China to superpower status could be as potentially uncontested as the rise of the EU. The expectation is that the US would resist the loss of its sole superpower status, and the evidence to date is that the US would not take kindly to the rise of any Asian superpower. There is no reason to think that the concern that built up in the US during the late 1980s and early 1990s about the challenge from Japan, and that of the later 1990s and early twenty-first century about China as a peer competitor, would not be repeated if China began to meet the material, status and regional requirements for superpower status. Even on the most successful liberalization assumptions imaginable, China is not going to become like Europe in US eyes for many decades, if ever. An additional complication is Taiwan, which could become a spoiler in US–China relations even under relatively benign conditions of Chinese development.

Assume then that the US did not or could not stop China's rise, but was successful in tying it to a process of economic liberalization that would eventually have transforming social and political consequences. Assume also that China succeeds in becoming strong enough to reach superpower status, and that along the way it might or might not go through an awkward phase of extreme nationalism. Even for China to get to where South Korea and Taiwan are now in terms of domestic social and political liberalization would take a couple of generations. On that basis, a two-superpower world based on the US and China would not come close to having the potential for condominium inherent in the identity kinship of a US–EU two-superpower world. Almost certainly the transition from one to two superpowers would be a tense affair. Even on the most benign assumptions about China its exclusivist and economic nationalist instincts are likely to remain much stronger than Europe's. One could therefore expect less willingness on China's part to promote an open global economy. Indeed, given the dependence of China's superpower status on its being able to dominate or at least pacify the East Asian region, one might well expect spheres of influence to be an important feature of this two-superpower world. That would be even more the case if a Chinese superpower took the nationalist route. Yet even on this assumption the scope for China to try to mount the kind of challenge to the US that the Soviet Union attempted would remain small. In the face of a malign Chinese power, the US could expect most, or even all, of the great powers (Japan, Russia, the EU, possibly India) to swing to its side. China's lack of natural allies among the great powers, its assiduously maintained historical hostility towards Japan, and Russian and Indian fear of it, all combine to make an aggressive posture for China an expensive and dangerous policy. Like Germany within Europe, China has been dealt a particularly difficult geopolitical hand to play. Unless Russia somehow collapsed, leaving China with areas of weakness to its north and west, China is surrounded by strong powers. Soviet power after 1945 was hugely assisted by the fact that the country was surrounded by weakness: a collapsed postwar Europe; China in civil war; Japan destroyed and under occupation; and European empires unravelling in South Asia and the Middle East. China is almost certainly not going to enjoy a historical moment of that sort, and, if it does attain superpower status, its ability to sustain it will depend heavily on how successful or not it is at controlling its region without triggering balancing behaviour against itself.

Three superpowers, some ideological harmony, some disharmony: the US, the EU and China

Much of what has been said about the two scenarios with two superpowers can be applied to this scenario. This combination suggests strongly that one should expect an almost automatic alignment between the US and the EU. The addition of China would almost certainly reduce whatever chances there were that the US and the EU would fall into a relationship of enemies or rivals. For China, balancing against this alignment would be a futile and expensive option (at least until/unless China had become enormously stronger in material terms). Given that the ideological difference between China and the two Western superpowers would be nothing like as fundamental as that between the US and the Soviet Union, bandwagoning by China would be a viable option. For China, the basic logic would be nearly the same as in the scenario with just itself and the US, except that the incentives to be antagonistic would be even less and those for bandwagoning even more. It seems unlikely that the availability of China as a theoretical ally would cause either the US or the EU to worry much that the other might gang up with China against it in a general way. To the extent that China was malign, it would reinforce the natural tendency of the US and the EU to remain closely aligned. To the extent that China was benign, it would increase their incentives to draw it into a multilateral process of global management.

For this scenario, the sequence of who arrived at superpower status, and when, could have substantial implications for how the transition process unfolded. If the EU came into an established US–China system its elevation might well be welcomed by the US and resisted by China. If China came into an established US–EU system, both might resist its rise. If China and the EU came more or less simultaneously into a single-superpower system dominated by the US, then the US would be less able to resist a rise in the number of superpowers than it would be if facing only a single candidate.

Comparing this scenario with its only historical parallel, the interwar years, again suggests that identity matters hugely. During the interwar years the three superpowers split two to one ideologically (two democracies, the UK and the US, and one communist state, the Soviet Union) and faced two rising great powers (Japan and Germany), both fascist and seeking superpower status. A three-superpower system composed of the US, the EU and China would probably have a substantial degree of ideological harmony among the superpowers, and would face no ideologically hostile rising great powers. It would be a social structure of rivals and friends, not, like the interwar case, one of enemies.

7.3 Expectations for the great powers

As a rule, the more superpowers there are, the fewer great powers there will be. Nothing in the present line-up of powers suggests that this rule would not apply to the futures considered above. At the moment there is one superpower and four great powers. One of the great powers (Russia) could conceivably drop out of the class, and the largest of the regional powers (India) could conceivably make it into the great power ranks. With the rather remote possibility of Brazil, there are no other close contenders, so increasing the number of superpowers will almost certainly shrink the number of great powers. This close-to-zero-sum game means that the question of what to expect from the great powers in these scenarios becomes fairly residual. The more superpowers there are, not only the fewer the great powers, but also the less they count for. In (neo)realist thinking, a coalition of all the great powers becomes less likely than when they face a single superpower, and the great powers all together will weigh relatively less than the superpowers. In systems with more than one superpower, great powers at best become important because of their ability to affect the balance between or among the superpowers.

The pattern of events during the Cold War is an instructive place to start thinking. Given the extremely high ideological division between the US and the Soviet Union, and the many hangovers (occupations, enmities, alliances, military deployments, divided states) from the Second World War, the great powers faced great pressure to take sides, and all initially did so. The European powers and Japan built strong and durable ties to the US. China initially stood with the Soviet Union, but by 1960 had broken free, moving into a swing position as a balancer. China's actions during the Cold War were not based on capability. It was much the weakest of the three great powers, and in purely material terms put itself at great risk by, for a decade or so, making both superpowers its enemies. China's move was based on an internal ideological split within the communist camp. It was only the extremeness of Maoism that enabled China to escape from the pressures to align with one superpower or the other, and eventually to achieve some standing as a balancer between them. If nothing else, this episode demonstrates the importance of identity factors, and the existence or not of ideological differences, in determining how any particular structure of polarity operates in practice.

In all of the two- or three-superpower scenarios explored above, ideological differences are much smaller than during the Cold War, or for that matter the interwar years, and in some of them hardly an issue at all. There are still economic differences and policy disputes among the major powers, sometimes serious, but all are more or less firmly committed to market economies, meaning that there are no profound ideological differences and no zero-sum games about whose system will own the future. Barring unlikely political upheavals in the US, the EU and Japan, a majority of the major powers will retain this commitment. Should either Russia or China abandon it, they will also lose power in relation to those that don't. On this basis, any move to a system containing two or three superpowers is quite unlikely to generate the alignment pressures that marked the lot of the great powers during the Cold War. If a malign China became the second superpower, all of the others would probably lean towards the US. If it was the EU that became the second superpower, one might expect some rather mild counter-alignments like those between China and Russia against the US. But in a system without serious ideological divisions the great powers have the choice to stay unaligned at low cost, to take up varying degrees of association with either one or another superpower, or to become involved in a superpower condominium. In principle, this makes (neo)realist logic less compelling, and leaves more room for liberal and English school understandings of behaviour.

This argument rests on the understanding that (neo)realist thinking proceeds on a logic determined by relative power and a social structure of enemies and rivals, and that, other things being equal, the main response to preponderant power is to balance. The main counterpoint to this way of thinking has been that the identity and domestic character of the major powers make a difference to how they relate to each other, depending both on compatibility or not of ideology and on the particular character of the ideology or ideologies concerned. A third possibility, however, is sometimes labelled Confucian, in which preponderant power triggers bandwagoning rather than balancing behaviour. The main point of interest in this perspective is Japan, which does not really seem to have the option of becoming a superpower in its own right. Japan's Cold War and post-Cold War behaviour was understandable according to either (neo)realist or Confucian logic, and therefore gave no insight into which was operating. The test for Japan would come if China developed into a second or third superpower. If Japan operates according to Confucian logic, and not either (neo)realist or ideological, then when China's power became sufficient it could be expected to switch its alignment to China. In this sense, Japan is likely to be the only great power in a really pivotal position in the scenarios explored in this chapter. If it shifted alignment to China it would in one move both greatly weaken the position of the US and greatly strengthen China's position, not only in Asia but in the world. The deep entanglement of the US and Japanese economies works against this as an easy option, as does the carefully maintained (by China) historical antagonism between the two. But the US has already demonstrated an ability to treat Japan as a rival, and identity kinship between Japan and the US is not as strong as that between the US and Europe. In addition, being the front line in a tense relationship between the US and a rising China is not an attractive position for Japan. In thinking about how systems with two or three superpowers and the same number of great powers might work it would be imprudent to ignore this Confucian possibility.

7.4 Consequences for regions

How would regions be affected by increases in the number of superpowers? Picking up from the argument in the previous chapter, the main change would be a substantial weakening of the US's ability to play the swing-power role that is such a hallmark of its present sole superpower status. Since the most likely candidates for additional superpowers are in the two regions (Europe and East Asia) that are the lynchpins of the swing-power strategy, scenarios with two or three superpowers cannot but signal major changes in this pattern. In thinking about the impact of changes in polarity structure on regions it helps to distinguish between those regions which contain a great power (or powers) or a superpower, which I will call *home regions*, and those which contain only regional power, which I will call *other regions*. Since the regional level has been discussed extensively elsewhere (Buzan and Wæver 2003) I will not develop this aspect in any detail here.

Home regions

The rise of China and/or the EU to superpower status would have major consequences for their home regions. Compared to the present polarity structure, in each case, the local superpower would gain more influence within its home region, and the US would lose influence there. As argued above, the social structure in these scenarios is more likely to be rivals and friends rather than rivals and enemies, meaning that military strategic considerations are unlikely to be the main drivers of superpower relations. In addition, even in the three-superpower scenario, the US, China and the EU would all be geographically insulated from each other, which would tend to make military strategic considerations less prominent than they would be if superpowers (or their spheres) were directly adjacent. The US might still retain some options for leaning one way or the other diplomatically, but that policy would also be available to the other two. If the EU had become a superpower, it would have consolidated to the point where it no longer needed the US 'in' in order to help stabilize its internal politics. This development would pose Britain, which has traditionally played between the EU and the US, with a very difficult test of loyalties, even though relations between the US and the EU are likely to remain within the friends/rivals zone. In an Asia containing a Chinese superpower, Japan would face the toughest test: whether to go it alone, bandwagon with China, or try to stick with the US in some way as a more equal ally. This balance or bandwagon choice would face not just Japan, but also Russia and India, with relations among these three becoming a crucial variable. India might (or might not) attain great power status during the coming decades. As noted, controlling or pacifying its region is a key issue in China's ability to attain superpower standing. It could do so on the basis of huge material superiority, but that route is much harder than the more Confucian one in which it persuades its neighbours, particularly Japan, to bandwagon. The rise of China to superpower status might well draw South Asia more closely towards East Asia, most probably as part of a balancing coalition.

The rise of China would also pose serious questions for Russia. Assuming that Russia's material capability will continue to lag far behind both Europe's and East Asia's for a long time, the rise of these two will pose difficult questions for Moscow. In principle, its choices would be either to act as an independent insulator between the EU and China or to bandwagon with one or the other. Given the relative absence of disputes with the EU, and both historic Russian fears of Asia and the vulnerability of its positions in Siberia (very low population) and Central Asia (resentment against the former imperial power), the odds would have to favour a Russian drift towards closer relations with the EU. Russia might also seek alignment with Japan and India in an Asian balancing coalition against China, or with the US if it continued to play balancer against China.

Other regions

For regions not containing any great powers or superpowers, the rise of a two- or three-superpower system would also have implications different from those in a polarity structure of one superpower. Given that these scenarios are mostly towards the rivals and friends end of the social structure spectrum, the Cold War is not a good model for thinking about these implications. Perhaps the main general rule is that other regions adjacent to superpowers will tend to get drawn into orbit around their local superpower. (Neo)realist logic would suggest that other regions remote from superpowers would tend to experience competitive intervention, but this is not so straightforward in a social structure of rivals and friends. Whereas the US and the Soviet Union, as enemies, were forced to compete for influence globally, and thus staged competitive interventions in most remote regions, superpowers that are in the zone of friends/rivals have more choices. They might agree on spheres of influence, in which each acknowledges the primacy of the other(s) in their home areas. On that basis, the Western hemisphere would fall to the US, North Africa to the EU, and East and South Asia to China. Or they could agree to global-level rules which managed their competition worldwide. Africa is likely to be mainly of interest to the EU (adjacency, oil, colonial links), secondarily to the US (domestic ethnic links, oil), and probably not of much interest to China. Perhaps the most interesting 'other region' question under these scenarios is about the Middle East. In geographical terms, the Middle East is in the EU's back yard, but so long as the US remains a superpower it seems unlikely to let go either its interest in oil or its close ties to Israel. The occupation of Iraq in 2003 seemed to commit the US to a strong engagement in the Middle East for a long time. China's interest in Middle Eastern oil will grow as its economy expands, so it too is likely to become engaged there. Oil alone, as long as it lasts (or until some other energy technology replaces it), will ensure that the superpowers take a strong interest in the Middle East. Whether they manage their relations or compete is an open question, but either way the US would be unable to retain the near monopoly position as dominant external power that it developed during the 1990s. It seems also likely that 'clash of civilizations' issues will sustain superpower interests in the Middle East. So long as Islamic extremism rooted in the region is used to legitimize terrorist attacks against the global powers and their interests, engagement of some sort is almost guaranteed. Whether this engagement is primarily coercive, as it has increasingly become under US hegemony in the region, or takes more political, social and economic forms, is an open question.

Thus on this dimension, as in relations between the superpowers, the Cold War provides few lessons for systems with a similar structure of polarity but a different social structure.

7.5 Conclusions

Scenarios of two or three superpowers are unlikely in the near future because of the lack of great powers with the necessary foundations in terms of their combination of material capability, status and regional position. China and the EU become plausible candidates two or more decades down the line, but there is no inevitability about their achieving superpower standing. Assuming that either or both did achieve superpower status, a good case can be made that their domestic character would play a substantial role in shaping the relational dynamics between two or more superpowers. There would almost certainly be no replay of the Cold War, either in relations among the superpowers, or in their impact on regions. These scenarios suggest a weaker role for purely materialist (neo)realist logic and a stronger one for the social structural logic inherent in liberal and English school expectations.

8

Options for the Future II: No Superpowers and Several Great Powers

I have argued that the existing polarity structure of one superpower and several great powers is potentially quite stable, and that scenarios for an increase in the number of superpowers to two or three are probably not plausible before the 2020s. I have also observed as a historical fact that over the last century there has been a trend for the number of super-powers to shrink. Taken together, these points provide the basis for the scenario in this chapter, which rests on a further decline in the number of superpowers to zero, leaving a world with only great powers. What happens if the US either loses, or steps down from, its superpower status, leaving a polarity structure with only great powers and no superpowers? This scenario displays one of the main benefits of making the distinction between superpowers and great powers set up in chapters 4 and 5. It opens up the previously unexplored idea of an international system which has *no* truly global powers in it, but only a collection of great powers each influential mainly in its adjacent regions. Given the obstacles in the way of an increase in the number of superpowers, this possibility is arguably the main alternative to the present structure, yet it has been rendered largely invisible by the assumption of a single classification of 'great power' embedded in simple polarity theory. Some of the discussions of multipolar futures come close to this scenario (Kupchan 1998, 2002; Kegley and Raymond 1992, 1994), but by not asking whether the poles are great powers or superpowers they lose the ability to ask some important questions about how such a system might operate.

To say that a zero-superpower scenario is the most likely alternative to the present single-superpower polarity is not to say that it is therefore very likely. Indeed, given the intensity of the present fashion for 'unipolarity' interpretations of world politics, and the widespread acceptance that the dominant position of the US is unassailable, it might seem perverse even to suggest that the possibility of zero superpowers is worth considering. One has to recall, however, that fashion in this matter, as in others, can change with remarkable speed and on the basis of rather superficial evidence. Only a decade ago, the dominant fashion in relation to the US was declinism, and it is far from clear how or why the arguments underpinning that view have suddenly become irrelevant. Declinism was based on one empirical observation (that the US's share of global GDP was declining down to its 'natural' level from the artificial high just after the Second World War) and two general ideas:

1 that hegemonic powers carry leadership costs (especially military expenditure) that put them at a competitive disadvantage in relation to other powers, and that this disadvantage is exacerbated if the hegemon succumbs to the temptation to become overcommitted; and
2 that the steady spread of industrialization and modernization to more and more countries is diffusing the foundations of power ever more widely, with the consequence that it is increasingly difficult for any state to achieve the relative capability necessary for superpower status.

A corollary of this second idea is that it is not only relative capability that is affected by the spread of industrialization but also absolute capability. Absolute capability matters in how states relate to each other militarily. During the nineteenth century, the Western powers were able to dominate and colonize almost all other peoples on the basis of a vast disparity in military capability. By the second half of the twentieth century modern light weapons had become diffused very widely throughout the world, making it increasingly difficult for colonial powers to control their subject peoples by force. In effect, possession of modern light weapons enabled even weak powers to resist forceful occupation by strong ones in ways that they had not been able to do before. The present form of this lesson is the concern about the proliferation of weapons of mass destruction (WMD) and the capability to make them. The ability to manufacture crude WMD is a natural accompaniment of industrialization, and since many of the technologies have now been around for a long time, they are not that difficult to acquire. States that might otherwise be down in the ranks of regional powers (North Korea, Pakistan, Iran) can acquire WMD capabilities that give pause even to superpowers. So, of course, can non-state actors, including terrorists. This diffusion of absolute capabilities is distinct from, and in some ways as important as, changes in relative capability, not least in that it adds to the difficulties for any state trying to be a superpower.

None of these arguments has ceased to operate, and it is therefore a source of some puzzlement that relatively high US military expenditure (more than the next dozen countries combined) is now more cited as a measure of the country's impregnable sole superpower status than used as an indicator of overstretch and future decline. There are various reasons that might explain this perceptual turnaround. The threat of 'Japan as number one' has receded with the long stagnation of the Japanese economy. Russia has declined from superpower rival almost to regional power status. The US economy has recovered in some ways and has grown faster than that of the other advanced industrial countries. And the diffusion of industrialization has been slowed by the economic turbulence that started during the late 1990s. But these reasons are mostly quite superficial. If Japan has declined, China has continued to grow, and the EU to deepen and widen. If Russia has faded away as a rival and threat, terrorism and the spread of WMD have filled the gap. If the US economy has performed relatively well for a few years, it is nevertheless riddled with major problems of debt, unstable equity prices and corporate malfeasance that give no grounds for confidence about its future (Arrighi and Silver 2001). If the spread of industrialization has been slowed, that has also affected the US economy negatively and has not stopped the spread of WMD. There is no reason to doubt that the US is currently number one and has a long military lead over all of its possible rivals. But there are perfectly sound reasons for thinking that the US might not so much be passed by rival superpowers as itself slip back into the ranks of the great powers.

The scenario with zero superpowers is not implausible. It is worth investigating both as a real possibility for the next polarity structure of the international system whose consequences need to be understood, and because anticipation of those consequences could well be part of what keeps the present structure in place. As argued in the previous chapter, the consequences for the US of an increase in the number of superpowers were mostly fairly benign, or at least nothing like so malign as the bipolarity of the Cold War. The consequences of an all-great-power structure are rather more uncertain.

8.1   How might a zero superpower structure come about?

A polarity structure of one superpower and several great powers looks the most likely for the next few years, but it is not chiselled in stone. While it is hard to envisage the number of superpowers rising quickly, it is perhaps easier to imagine the number of superpowers dropping to zero.

There are two routes to this end, one material and one social. The material route is a simple extension of the declinist, imperial overstretch arguments from the early 1990s, and follows the model of Britain's relative decline as Germany, the US, France, Russia and Japan built up industrial economies. In this model, the US steadily loses relative economic, military and ideological power to the rest of the world, particularly Asia and Europe (Arrighi and Silver 2001), and to great powers (especially China) as well as lesser ones (the rising economies of South and Southeast Asia and of Central and Eastern Europe). At some point its share of the global GDP becomes too small to enable it to sustain its sole superpower roles.

The social route to the US losing its superpower status is about the loss of its ability to lead, and there are two obvious and potentially interlinked ways for this to happen. The first way is primarily internal: the US itself takes the initiative to abandon its leadership roles and alliance commitments, thus voluntarily laying down the mantle of superpowerdom. This could take place either as a conscious strategic decision – a political victory for those arguing that the US should pull out of Eurasia (Olsen 2002) – or as a result of neglect by US governments dominated by inward-looking agendas, the arrogance of power, and a loss of will to create and maintain the institutional machinery of international society. It is interesting to note how many commentators make the point that the US is more likely to be driven out of its superpower status by the unwillingness of its citizens to support the role than by the rise of any external challenger (Calleo 1999; Kapstein 1999: 468, 484; Lake 1999: 78; Mastanduno and Kapstein 1999: 14–20; Haass 1999; Spiro 2000; Kupchan 2002: 25–38).

The second way is primarily external: the US loses its followers because it ceases to represent the set of shared values that legitimated its leadership during the second half of the twentieth century. The importance of leadership legitimacy in underpinning the present US position is emphasized by Nau (2001: 585–6). He argues that the power of the US has not declined even though its relative material capability has, because the material weakening has been offset by the rise in the number of democracies sharing its values and identity: 'Communities of identity, or lack thereof, determine in large part how balances of power work', 'when national identities converge, as they have recently among the democratic great powers, they may temper and even eliminate the struggle for power.' To the extent that this is true, the superpower status of the US is substantially dependent on the legitimacy of its leadership. While it seems unlikely that the US, the EU and Japan will drift away from their strong commitment to democracy and market economies, it is more thinkable that they may fall out over issues ranging from the Middle East and world trade, to ballistic missile defence and environmental management. In this perspective, the argument hangs on the sustainability of the 'swing-power' role in defining the US's sole superpower status. The US is a superpower not just because of its material capability, but because of its institutionalized domination over the EU and Japan. If the US lost its institutional positions in Europe and East Asia, its material capability alone would not sustain its superpower status. It is easy to see how these two aspects of the social route could play into each other. Increasing US unilateralism driven by domestic imperatives corrodes the loyalty and trust of allies which in turn makes it more difficult for US governments to justify the expenditure of resources abroad.

Either or both of the material and social routes to the loss of US superpower status are possible, but the material path of decline would probably be quite long, whereas the social one could, in principle, be quite short. It is not difficult to spin a plausible scenario that would lead to this result by 2010. The main elements could include:

- increasing unwillingness among the US citizenry to pay the costs and take the risks of global engagement, especially if disillusionment with the effects of the 'war on terrorism' and/or the occupation of Iraq sets in;
- increasing difficulty in the US in maintaining a coherent foreign policy posture and a commitment to overseas responsibilities in the absence of any clear and overwhelming external threat to legitimize securitiza-tion, and the failure of the 'war against terrorism' to do this;
- a US shift to more unilateralist military postures, including some ver-sion of ballistic missile defence, and the cultivation of long-range strike capabilities to reduce dependence on overseas allies and bases;
- unilateral US pursuit of polices unpopular abroad such as those already in place regarding Cuba, Iran, Iraq, Libya and Israel, and possible extensions of the 'war against terrorism';
- exaggerated claims to sovereignty and special rights such as those already visible in relation to the International Criminal Court (ICC), the CTBT, various environmental agreements, and its use of contro-versial extraterritorial legislation. It is worth noting that Huntington (1999: 41) sees such a development as an expected feature of sole superpower status;
- withdrawal from existing international regimes and institutions and/ or refusal to adhere to new regimes widely supported in international society, as illustrated by US attitudes towards the landmine agreement, the ABM treaty and the ICC;
- a drift apart on key domestic values that underpin international society of the type already visible in relation to abortion, gun control, envir-onment, drugs and food;

*   increasing inability to agree on terms of trade, with a consequent erosion of the WTO and rising influence of regional economic arrangements.

China and Russia are already conspicuously uneasy about US leadership. Japan could easily become so if it feared that US policy was going to drag it into confrontation with China. Europe would be the most reluctant to let go of US leadership. But it might eventually come to that if the erosion of shared values exposed during the run-up to the invasion of Iraq became severe. Such erosion could occur if US unilateral policies towards international society generally and/or the Middle East in particular became seen as unacceptable or even threatening. It could also occur if the US played divide and rule among the members of the EU to such an extent that it came to be seen as a threat to the EU project itself. A model for a development along these lines is the resentment caused by heavy US diplomatic pressure on individual European countries during its 2002 campaign to wreck, or at least exempt its own citizens from, the ICC (Gnesotto 2003a; Brown 2002: 330, 337; Weller 2002). This social logic is not the same as arguing that simple rising power will cause these actors to have increasing differences with the US. It does not presuppose that these players increase in relative capability compared to the US, only that their willingness to accept US leadership declines. In the upper ranks of the regional powers India and Brazil also manifest conspicuous unease about a world in which the US has too much of a free hand to intervene in all parts of the world. As many authors observe (Huntington 1999: 42–3; Bobrow 2001: 6–8; Bacevich 2002: 88, 90; Prestowitz 2003), echoing Waltz's more general worry about reactions against excessive concentrations of power, there is already a disjuncture between a US self-perception of benign leadership and a widespread image of it elsewhere as a threat whose foreign policy, particularly on trade and the Middle East, is driven overwhelmingly by domestic politics. This could be moderated if the 'war against terrorism' comes to be seen as a general defence of civilization against extremists, but it could easily be exacerbated if that 'war' comes to be seen as an extension of either Israel's influence on US foreign policy or the influence of US corporate interests in backing whichever governments in the Middle East will be pliable on the question of the price and supply of oil, or both. Just as Japan's attachment to the US might be broken by a major US–China crisis over Taiwan, so European attachment to the US might be broken by the perception that US policy was fomenting a 'clash of civilizations' with the Islamic world on its doorstep. Geography matters here. Europe has to live next door to the Islamic world, and has historical and personal links with it that the US does not.

An interesting perspective on the external possibilities for the demotion of the US from superpower status can be found in thinking about possible developments in East Asia. The real key to US superpower status is that the next two biggest centres of capital and technology in the international system, Europe and Japan, accept its leadership and subordinate themselves to it by their membership in US-dominated alliances (Nye 2002). What Japan does is crucial both for the global status of the US and for the regional (and global) possibilities of China. Japan has four possibilities. It can continue remaining closely tied to the US. It can break that tie, and reinvent itself, as it has done in the past, as an independent 'normal' great power. It can combine these two by building a more equal alliance partnership with the US. Or it could bandwagon with China. Much favours a continuation of the tie to the US (Yahuda 2002). The US and Japanese economies are deeply entangled, and since the ending of the Cold War Japan began reforming its defence guidelines towards allowing a wider role for the JSDF and closer coordination with US forces in the region. Although there are some incremental signs of moves towards a more equal alliance, Japan's seeming unwillingness to take up a more robust military policy, or to challenge the US, or to develop a more independent foreign and military policy, suggests that this will be a long time in coming, if ever. If the existing lopsided US–Japan alliance remains robust, then a key prop of US global status is maintained. Either of Japan's other two options would pull away that prop and diminish significantly US claims to superpower status (even more so if they were matched by a similar breakdown of the Atlantic alliance).

The question then is what could cause such a breakdown? There are two possibilities. The first is the most discussed, and perhaps the most important. It is that Japan and the US will encounter policy differences so serious that their alliance will become unsustainable. Some observers see potential for such radical change in the differences between Japan and the US over policy goals in East Asia, particularly on China and Taiwan, but also on Korean reunification (Stokes 1996; Twomey 2000: 204–5; Drifte 2000), and speculate whether these will corrode the US–Japan alliance. The most widely mooted scenario that could quickly break the US–Japan alliance is a major military crisis over Taiwan in which Japan failed to support the US. Despite some formal revision of the US–Japan defence cooperation guidelines, doubts remained about whether, and to what extent, Japan would support the US in a crisis. China makes no secret of the fact that it is deeply opposed to this aspect of the US–Japan alliance, making the stakes for Japan very high no matter how it responded to a crisis over Taiwan (Johnston 2003: 43). The full and exact repercussions of such an event are hard to predict, and might include a general US disengagement from East Asia. The point is that it lies within China's power, and according to its rhetoric also within its will, to precipitate precisely such a crisis if it thinks that Taiwan is formally moving towards independence. There is still a constituency in the US for constructing China as the likely challenger to US hegemony, and these two things have a significant potential to play into each other. Hypothesizing a split between the US and Japan leaves open the question of whether Japan would then strike out as an independent great power, as it did after the First World War, or seek an accommodation with China. In chapter 7 I argued against the probability of Japan taking an independent line. Because the US plays such a big role in relation to the two Asian great powers – balancing China, and keeping Japan so closely tied to itself that the latter does not really have to develop a security policy of its own – it is very difficult to assess what Sino-Japanese relations would look like if the US ceased to play ringholder for the East Asian powers.

Whether or not a crisis over Taiwan or Korea could push Japan towards China is a question with too many variables to answer with any clarity: it might or might not. But the third possibility, as mooted in chapter 7, is that Japan might be tempted to bandwagon with a rising China simply on the basis of power considerations. Huntington (1996: 234–8) notes Japan's historic tendency to align with the dominant power in the system and, if such a tendency exists, it may well have been reinforced by Japan's dismal experience of going it alone during the 1930s and 1940s. The test for Japan would come if China's internal development produced rising relative power vis-à-vis the US. In this sense, Japan is uniquely in a pivotal position. If it took an independent great power line, it would both reduce the US position in Asia and the world and complicate China's prospects for hegemony in Asia. If it shifted alignment to China it would in one move both greatly weaken the global position of the US and greatly strengthen China's position not only in Asia, but in the world.

Superpower status in the twenty-first century hangs much more on the ability to create and sustain international societies (at which the US proved remarkably talented during the Cold War) than on warfighting ability (now relevant mostly at the margins, no longer in head-to-head world wars among the global powers). Consequently, the growth of US hostility to many of the IGOs and regimes that it led in creating suggests a distinct social drift away from leadership. This drift could prove central to determining whether the US sustains or abandons its sole superpower role. Kupchan (1998) notes that 'the U.S. lacks the societal commitment to self-binding present in Germany and Japan', but it isn't clear whether the explanation for this comes from system structure (i.e. its sole

superpower status) or from the unique and longstanding domestic character of American state and society (Bolton 2000: 51–5; Rabkin 2000:
111–19). Both explanations make sense, suggesting that the behaviour is
overdetermined. A system with no superpowers in the not too distant
future is thus not implausible, though neither is it a necessary or determined outcome. Its probability remains largely contingent on political
choices made in the US.

There is no doubt a lot of room for disagreement about both the
likelihood and the timing of the US either losing or laying down its
superpower mantle. But as with the scenarios for an increase in the number
of superpowers, it is nevertheless well worth looking at how a system
with no superpowers would operate if it did come about.

8.2   The dynamics of an all-great-power system

What would be the political and strategic character of a system composed only of great powers with no superpower(s)? As noted above, this
is largely uncharted theoretical territory. In a 0 + x system there would be
no truly global powers, only a series of great powers projecting their
influence into adjacent regions. A *Realpolitik* view would suggest that, in
an all-great-power system, one or more of the powers would bid for
superpower status. Any expectation of such an outcome would be a constraint on US options to abandon the sole superpower slot. While the US
might well feel comfortable in a system with no superpowers, it is much
less likely to feel comfortable in a system with one or more than one
superpower in which it is not one of those superpowers. But if all of the
great powers in an all-great-power system remained content with their
great power status (neither aspiring to superpowerdom, nor feeling obliged
to take on the role of providing international order at the global level),
then the result would most likely be a decentred system with which the
US could live. The relative geostrategic remove of the US from the other
main centres of power would, as in the past, make it easiest of all for the
US to find comfort in such a system. The arguments made in chapter 6
about the relative degree of contentment with their status of several of
the current great powers also suggest, in line with Nau's remark cited
above about how converging national identities will reduce the struggle
for power, that a stable great power system of rivals and friends might
well be possible. The benign version of an all-great-power system would
be something like that envisaged by Kupchan (1998), where one or more
great powers serve as the centre for macro-regional orders: the Americas,
some form of EU-centred greater Europe, and some sort of East Asian
system, perhaps based on a Sino-Japanese condominium.

In its most benign form such a system would have a relatively strong international society, with the different regions sharing some key values and maintaining an array of institutions to act at the global level. In this sense it might share some features with the three-superpower model discussed in chapter 7, where a lack of deep ideological differences underpinned a degree of cooperation and stability. Whether the US in great power, as opposed to superpower, mode would support such institutions or oppose them is an interesting question, particularly as regards the maintenance of the liberal international economic order. If the US's departure from the sole superpower role was accompanied by a wrecking of solidarist international institutions they could be difficult to replace. Keohane's (1984) work notwithstanding, it remains an unanswered question as to whether international society would be able to maintain solidarist institutions (such as those coordinating a market economy) without a hegemonic leader or leaders. How durable are solidarist institutions if they have no powerful champion? (Neo)realists would answer that, since institutions are a reflection of power, an all-great-power structure would be hard put to create or sustain them. Some English school thinkers and neoliberals would argue that ideology matters more, and that the existence of a substantial array of shared goals and/or values might well support solidarist institutions even where power was relatively diffuse. Others would lean towards the view that a world of great powers would most probably slip back to a more minimal, pluralist structure of international society, based mainly on classical institutions of coexistence. In other words, the sustainability, or not, of the international institutions of a relatively well-developed international society might well depend more on whether the great powers are rivals and friends or enemies and rivals than on the particular distribution of power.

A less benign version of the all-great-power world would have each macro-region going its own way, with fewer shared values and fewer global institutions, but no inclination towards conflict or intense rivalry either. This would be the benign mercantilist scenario from IPE, reflecting the inability to sustain an international economic order in the absence of a hegemonic leader. A moderately malign version of an all-great-power system would be where one or more macro-regions becomes the arena for rivalry among the local great powers. At present, the most likely candidate for that is Asia, where, in the absence of the US as the external superpower ringholder, a stark choice could emerge between accepting Chinese hegemony and organizing some form of counter-China coalition based around Japan, India and Russia. Exactly what sort of choices become the dominant ones depends not only on the relative power positions of China and its neighbours, but also on the character of China's internal political development: whether more liberal or more hypernationalist.

The most malign version of an all-great-power system would be where one or more of the great powers sought to assert itself as a superpower. Unless such a power was projecting widely acceptable values and was willing to clothe itself in binding multilateral institutions, the most likely outcome would be pre-emptive counter-pole securitizations, probably involving both competitive military build-ups and alliance formation. If this development was seen as likely, it might be the key consideration that prevented the US from abandoning the present arrangement with itself as the sole superpower. This logic is what places China in such a significant position. China is both the power most likely to be out of line with Western values, and the one least constrained in its domestic politics from seeking superpower status if its material capability was sufficient. So long as malign scenarios for China's internal development remain plausible, this version of an all-great-power system could be construed as threatening to the US and as a reason for not letting such a system structure develop. In other words, prudence would dictate that the US prefer to maintain the present polarity structure with itself as the sole superpower. Next best (in the sense of least risky) would be systems with two or three superpowers. Worst would be the zero-superpower scenario with a risk that China would bid for superpower status.

In the long run, the power structure at the global level rests on material capabilities, but the significance of different polarities will vary according to what kind of social structure (enemies, rivals, friends) prevails. Within any polarity structure there is thus quite a bit of scope for political choice about what does and does not get securitized and what roles are or are not sought. In the type of all-great-power system that could emerge from the present polarity structure, the key choices about social structure lie in the hands of the US and China. After the loss of the Soviet Union as a clear and easy focus for securitization, the US has real choices. It could decide to rest on its geostrategic advantages, desecuritize the global power structure, withdraw from its leadership responsibilities and forward deployments, leave the Eurasian powers to sort out their own relations, and step down from the role as the sole superpower. On the other hand, it could seek a new focus for securitization to support and legitimize its continued sole superpower role. This new focus would have to be some-thing more plausible than North Korea or Iran. Before September 11 there were two likely, and mutually reinforcing, candidates: China as an emergent 'peer competitor' and the potential instability of a $0 + x$ system. After September 11 the 'war against terrorism' became a third. This situation gives China some political choices as well. An abrasive and assertive Chinese stance towards its Asian neighbours and the US would ease the US path towards choosing securitization, while a milder and more conciliatory one would facilitate the desecuritization choice. But at the end of the day, China does not hold all the cards. If it chooses to play challenger to the US it probably could guarantee a US choice for securitization. But if it takes the more cautious route it by no means guarantees a US choice for desecuritization. US behaviour since the end of the Cold War suggests that it wants to find a focus for securitization. If that inclination is being internally driven, then there is probably not much that can be done by China, Russia, the EU or Japan to stop it. If it becomes driven by the 'war against terrorism', then a great deal will depend on the specific way in which that war plays out.

8.3   Consequences for regions

How would the impact of a zero-superpower world differ from the changes argued under an increase in the number of superpowers? Two general consequences would remain the same: the breakdown of the US's swing-power role as the key change from the sole-superpower scenario and the distinction between home regions and other regions. But since, unlike superpowers, great powers do not aspire to global roles, the particular dynamics of this structure would work differently from those in a system of multiple superpowers. The general expectation would be that each great power would have more influence in its home and adjacent regions, and that great powers would be unlikely to have much engagement in remote regions. In other words, a world of great powers would have a pronounced localist character.

Home regions

The removal of the US as the sole superpower would increase the influence of all the other great powers in their home regions. As in the multiple-superpower scenario the EU would have to learn to get along without having the US 'in', but in this scenario that might well not come about because the EU might already have been successful in its own widening and deepening project. In the all-great-powers scenario, the EU could be either weakened or strengthened by the removal, or sharp downgrading, of its links with the US, which would probably take the form of some winding down, Europeanization, or even dissolution of NATO. Whether the EU was strengthened or weakened by this development would depend on whether the European response was to deepen the EU institutions, or to increase tensions among the EU members by making the competition for influence among them more explicit. The crisis for Britain would be much sharper than under the multiple-superpower scenario because the

US would by definition have reduced its interest in strong overseas engagements and forward defence.

In Asia, the same phenomenon of US disengagement would mean that China and Japan would finally have to sort out their relationship without the US holding the ring between them. Japan would face the toughest test: whether to go it alone, bandwagon with China, or try to stick to the US in some way as a more equal ally (the unequal alliance with the US would no longer be an option). In other respects, this scenario would resemble that for a Chinese superpower, with the balance or bandwagon choice facing not just Japan, but also Russia and India, with relations among these three becoming a crucial variable. The outcome in Asia would depend more on the social structure than the polarity one, since this would be a multipolar subsystem. Russia's choices would be similar to those in the two- or three-superpower scenario (insulator between the EU and China or bandwagon with one or the other), but in this case the choice for insulator would be easier unless Russia still saw itself as becoming decisively weaker than China.

Other regions

In the other regions the key change would be the lessening or withdrawal of US interest and engagement and the probability that, other things being equal, geographical adjacency would become the key determinant of which great powers were influential in which regions. Under this logic, South America would be hard put to prevent an increase in US interest and influence in what would then be 'its' region. No other great power would be likely to challenge US primacy in the Western hemisphere. So unless Brazil could also make it to great power status, which seems unlikely for many decades, South America would probably be fated to fall under a new Monroe doctrine. The experience of Africa, and especially sub-Saharan Africa, might well be the exact opposite of South America's. Since there would be no adjacent great powers, the likely development would be a strengthening of the neglect already apparent since the ending of the Cold War. The exception to this would be North Africa, which would probably get drawn into the sphere of the EU, leaving the Sahara to act as an insulator.

As in the multiple-superpower scenario, the Middle East poses by far the most complicated and difficult questions, and for the same reasons: oil and 'clash of civilization' politics. I have argued elsewhere that the regional conflict dynamics within the Middle East are both strong and overdetermined (Buzan and Wæver 2003: chap. 7), and thus unlikely to be resolved in the near or even medium-term (several decades) future.

Since this region has experienced an exceptionally strong US presence both during and, even more, after the Cold War (Hansen 2000), the big question is what would happen if the US wholly or largely withdrew? The withdrawal of the Soviet Union from the Middle East allowed the US to intervene more deeply (the peace process, dual containment, the war on terrorism, the two wars in Iraq). A serious US step down to great power standing would mean a substantial reduction in its commmitment to the Middle East, or possibly disengagement from it. This could have huge consequences for the region by unleashing its indigenous conflict dynamics. On the assumption that oil remained of crucial interest to the industrial world, the EU, Russia, China and possibly India might take up greater roles or try to carve out spheres of influence. Here the open questions would be about whether the particular US commitments to Israel and to Gulf oil would survive its general retreat from great power roles, and that is difficult to predict. Even if they did survive, they would have to be exercised in much more complicated conditions, with several other great powers in play.

8.4 Conclusions

The zero-superpower scenario clearly shows the benefits of making a distinction between superpowers and great powers. In simple polarity theory, one is unable to differentiate between a system with several superpowers and one with several great powers. Yet, as I hope I have demonstrated in this chapter, there is a significant difference even if the assumptions about the prevailing social structure remain the same.

Among other things, this scenario reveals the potential instabilities that could result in an all-great-power system if one of the great powers goes for superpower status. This possibility provides one of the keys to maintaining the existing sole-superpower structure. Since the scenarios with more superpowers mostly look fairly benign, this one ends up being the most risky both for the US and for international society. Whether regions would be better off with more or less superpower intervention is an interesting and difficult question. It can hardly be argued that regions such as Africa, the Middle East and Southeast Asia benefited from the interplay of rival superpower interests during the Cold War. Post-Cold War, neither relative superpower neglect of Africa nor increased super-power engagement in the Middle East has been obviously beneficial, and it would be easy to argue that the negative effects have been many and strong. It remains an open question whether multiple superpower engagement under social structure conditions of friends and rivals would perform better than either the Cold War conditions of superpower enemies or the post-Cold War ones of a single superpower. Should the Middle East be left to fight its way to some local conclusion without outside involvement? Or would it be better with several great powers all intervening rather than one or two superpowers? Would Africa be better off if left to sort out its huge political and economic problems in its own way? These questions need to be thought about as part of any evaluation of alternative structures of polarity, and the way they are likely to impact on regions.

Conclusions to Part II:
The Interplay of Polarity and Identity in the Three Scenarios

The main conclusions from these three scenarios can be summed up as follows.

- It is unlikely during the next twenty or so years that the US will face other powers actively seeking to assert superpower status. The EU and China are the most plausible candidates, but both have much to do before they could qualify, and, especially in the case of the EU, it is far from clear that there is the desire to pursue that goal. If such a scenario did develop, the main probability would be for a relatively benign social structure with rather low levels of ideological disharmony, quite unlike that of the Cold War.
- It is by no means impossible that the US could step down from its superpower role, producing a world with no superpowers and a set of great powers. This is perhaps not likely any time soon unless the 'war on terrorism' produces such negative consequences as to precipitate a major rethink of American foreign policy along the lines of withdrawal from forward defence and global engagement. Should an all-great-power system emerge, its social structure could take any one of several forms, making this the most open and fluid of the three pathways.
- Most likely for the next decade or two is a continuation of the present polarity structure of one superpower and several great powers. The open question within this is about how the social structure will unfold.

The interesting question is how the three scenarios play into each other, with the prospect of either alternative being part of what sustains the present structure of polarity. The US seems clearly to have set itself against the emergence of any peer competitor, though whether this means any peer (even a friend) is less clear. But the possibility of that development is rather low anyway for quite some distance into the future, so the question is not so much about the US preventing the emergence of a world with two or more superpowers, but what impact its efforts to do so will have on the social structure of the sole-superpower scenario. There are also grounds for thinking that, despite the aggressive unilateral expansionism of the Bush administration post-September 11, it cannot be ruled out that the US itself will decide to give up the superpower role. Perhaps the main constraint against that is the fear in the all-great-power scenario that a new aspirant to sole-superpower status will emerge, making the US retreat into mere great powerdom untenable.

The interplay among the scenarios points to continuity of the existing one superpower and several great powers polarity structure, but with substantial question marks hanging over its social structure. Both in material and in social terms, the centrality of the US is inescapable. What stands out most strikingly is the increasing instability of the social structure inherited from the end of the Cold War, particularly the disjuncture between a US playing a game mostly of enemies and rivals and the other great powers playing one of rivals and friends. With the US now casting itself as the main enemy of the multilateral social structure that it did so much to put in place during the twentieth century, the disjuncture between the power structure and the social order is becoming rather stark. Most IR theory assumes that the greatest powers will be the ones with the most interest in world order, and that liberal democratic powers will be particularly inclined to take up hegemonic leadership roles built around markets and multilateralism. We are therefore not yet well equipped to deal with a situation in which the US seeks not to maintain and extend the institutions of interstate society that were previously central to its grand strategy, but to put itself above them, revert to aggressive bilateralism, and downgrade, or even cast aside, concerns about the legitimacy of its exercise of power. This imperial model is all too familiar from the long record of history, and it was precisely the contrast of the US to that model which gave its leadership such high levels of legitimacy during the twentieth century (Ikenberry 2001). The prospect of the US emerging as the principal threat to the stability of the existing polarity and social structures, and what, if anything, can be done about it, is the main focus of the last chapter. If the US seriously weakens or destroys the social structures that it inherited from the Cold War, it risks undermining one of the key foundations of its own status – its ability to embed itself in the regional structures of Europe and East Asia, and thereby to play the swing-power role that gives it a unique position of influence in world politics. US behaviour is crucial to the (in)stability of the existing structure. If it maintains or extends a social structure of friends and rivals, then its sole superpowerdom might last a long time. But if it forces the great powers into a game of enemies and rivals, then it both undermines the foundations of its own status and accelerates the possibilities of either a multiple-superpower world or a world with no superpowers. The behaviour of the great powers does have some scope for affecting which direction things go in, but the main decisions lie with the US.

PART III

US Foreign Policy and the Scope for Action

9

Understanding the Turn in
US Foreign Policy

As I have argued throughout this book, the focus on the US is justified
by its centrality not just to the present scenario of 1 + 4, but to whether
and how that scenario evolves into either of the other two. I have tried
to draw attention to the fact that the social elements in the position of
the US within contemporary international society matter as much as, or
possibly more than, the material ones. They matter not only because the
US claim to superpower status rests heavily on its social position, but
also because how the US plays its sole superpower role has enormous
implications for the stability and sustainability of the present international social structure. Particularly alarming is the apparent disjuncture between, on the one hand, a US policy which seems to be based on
neorealist assumptions about a world of enemies and rivals and, on the
other, the outlook of most of the great powers which is based more on
assumptions of rivals and friends. Since the position of the US is in
crucial ways dependent on this 'rivals and friends' assumption by Japan
and the EU, the disjuncture is potentially very threatening to the US
position, risking the creation of a highly counter-productive self-fulfilling
prophecy. The fact that this disjuncture is celebrated by some within the
US (Kagan 2002; Krauthammer 2001) as purely a function of disparities
in power is especially worrying because it closes the possibility of doing
anything about it other than changing the distribution of capabilities.
Other voices within the US policy debate (Ikenberry 2001, 2002a, 2002b,
2003; Nye 2002; Kupchan 2002; Prestowitz 2003) are perfectly aware that
the US has choices about how it plays its unipolar moment, but there is
nevertheless a danger that the distribution of power will itself become
seen as an immovable reason for the US staying with a unilateralist,
militarized relationship with the rest of the world.

The risk is that the US is moving sharply away from the practice of projecting its values by a logic of persuasion, and towards the coercive end of the spectrum. The US has been spectacularly successful over the last half-century not only in promoting the market, international law and multilateralism, but also in building a host of international regimes and intergovernmental organizations to reinforce the binding mechanisms of calculation and belief. In other words, the historic claim to fame of the US is that during the second half of the twentieth century it transformed the social structure of international society, building up multilateralism and a global market economy, and downgrading balance of power and great power war as the leading practices. Yet now the US vigorously attacks many of the institutions it was instrumental in creating; increasingly prefers unilateral over multilateral action; revels in the Manichean, 'with us or against us' rhetoric associated with the 'war on terrorism'; claims exceptional rights over international law; and asserts the right both to use force pre-emptively against targets of its own choosing and to change forcefully governments it doesn't like. In a nutshell, the question is whether or not the US is turning its back on the pursuit of a multi-lateralist liberal international order and restyling itself in more imperial mode. The empirical evidence for such a turn is mixed, and it is unclear whether present developments represent the peculiarities of the Bush administration (Daalder and Lindsay 2003) or some deeper shift in US politics. There are three prominent candidates for explaining this apparent turn: American exceptionalism, unipolarity and September 11. Conveniently, these three fall into a layered sequence. American exceptionalism has been around almost since the country's founding, unipolarity kicked in with the ending of the Cold War, and September 11 added its effects a decade later. To gain some insight into US behaviour, it is worth examining each separately, as well as the cumulative interaction among them. Because the potential consequences of this shift are so momentous, getting some sense of whether the change is temporary or durable is a matter of extreme importance.

9.1 American exceptionalism

There is a well-established tradition of thinking about US foreign policy in terms of American exceptionalism. Lepgold and McKeown (1995: 369), for example, argue that the exceptionalist view of American foreign policy 'holds that Americans deprecate power politics and old-fashioned diplomacy, mistrust powerful standing armies and entangling peacetime commitments, make moralistic judgments about other people's domestic systems, and believe that liberal values transfer readily to foreign affairs.'

Somewhat more harshly, Hassner (2002: 26–7) observes that 'Exception-alism carries with it a tendency to consider that the United States is empowered, because of the purity of its intentions and the excellence of its regime, to judge between good and evil, to award others good or bad points, to punish the wicked and troublemakers, not to recognize any superior legal authority above that which comes from the American people themselves, and to consider any external inclination to cast doubt on American intentions or to apply to it the criteria that it applies to others as an insult.' Anyone who finds that rendition suspect because coming from the pen of a Frenchman can easily find similarly expressed American views (Prestowitz 2003: 267–84; Bacevich 2002: 32–54, 116, 215; Kupchan 2002: 77–112). The idea that the US is special because its economic and political values are destined to shape the future of human-kind is the everyday stuff of American political rhetoric. Belief in the essential rightness of American values has been greatly reinforced by the fact that the US has been the winner in the three ideological world wars of the twentieth century.

Lipset (1996) argues that American exceptionalism explains a great deal about both what is good and useful and what is bad and problem-atic (for Americans and for others) about the behaviour of US state and society. Hoffmann's (1981: 10) argument that 'we have to start from a clear understanding of the aspirations, ambitions and problems of the local forces' represents a recurrent plea for the US to take more account in its foreign policy of the issues and dynamics that drive foreign societies and far-away conflicts, rather than filtering everything through its own domestic lens. By exceptionalism is meant the distinctive qualities that differentiate the US from other states. These range from its particular set of political and social values, through its unique historical trajectory, to the oddities of its constitutional structures and the way they affect its decision-making. That Americans claim exceptionality is not in itself exceptional. The same exercise could be done for Britain, Japan, Ger-many, China or many other countries. But because the US is the leading power in international society, the specific character and quality of its exceptionalism matter a lot. I do not have space here to do more than outline the key points that bear on how we are to understand and anti-cipate US behaviour. Four stand out: liberalism, moralism, isolationism/unilateralism and anti-statism.

Liberalism

The US is undoubtedly the most liberal of the Western states. Lipset (1996: esp. 31–9) notes the closeness of the American creed to the values of nineteenth-century liberalism (anti-state, laissez-faire, individualist) and the absence of conservatism in American politics – conservatism in the sense of *noblesse oblige* and the responsibility of the elites (or the state) to look after the masses. Yet in another sense, more closely linked to its economic liberalism, the US is the most conservative of the Western states. Moravscik (2002: 352–7) argues that the US lacks the left and centre political blocs that typify most other advanced industrial countries. The much mooted absence of socialism means that issues fall differently in American domestic politics than they do elsewhere. There is no general support for welfare rights or state intervention, and a general background of economic libertarianism and anti-statism. Human rights issues fall squarely into the ideological divide between Democrats and Republicans in ways untypical of other industrial countries. Lipset (1996) generally places the US at the extreme end of an individualism–collectivism spectrum, with Japan at the other end and the Europeans in the middle, and argues that individualism underpins many distinctive aspects of US society, from tolerance of high income differentials and thin welfare systems, through an emphasis on winning as opposed to how the game is played, to the relatively high participation in voluntary associations and the commitment to education and equality of opportunity that have been a distinctive feature of American life from its early days. Moravscik (2002: 354) stresses the degree of difference this makes between the US and other Western states, not just in its domestic arrangements, but in its attitude towards the establishment of universal rights by international society: 'Perhaps an even more striking divergence between the U.S. and other democratic governments lies in the status of socioeconomic rights. In comparative perspective, the United States has a relatively informal and underdeveloped (i.e., nonsolidaristic) conception of economic rights, particularly in the areas of labor and social welfare policy. . . . The tendency of the United States not to recognize socioeconomic rights finds few parallels in the former communist world, the developing world, or even among most other advanced industrial democracies.'

Yet while in some respects the US espouses a distinctive form of liberalism (more economic than social) that differentiates it from others and makes cooperation difficult, it is also in the grip of the belief that liberal values are universal, and that the intrinsic moral and practical superiority of liberal values gives them the right to claim the future of humankind. As Patrick (2002: 7) observes, 'the validity of the country's liberal principles derives from their presumed universality' and underpins a missionary element in US foreign policy. The force of this liberal universalist belief is visible throughout the Bush administration's National Security Strategy document of 2002:

we will extend the peace by encouraging free and open societies on every continent. . . . the United States must defend liberty and justice because these principles are right and true for all people everywhere. No nation owns these aspirations, and no nation is exempt from them. . . . America must stand firmly for the non-negotiable demands of human dignity: the rule of law; limits on the absolute power of the state; free speech; freedom of worship; equal justice; respect for women; religious and ethnic tolerance; and respect for private property. . . . Policies that further strengthen market incentives and market institutions are relevant for all economies – industrialized countries, emerging markets, and the developing world. . . . China is following an outdated path that, in the end, will hamper its own pursuit of national greatness. In time, China will find that social and political freedom is the only source of that greatness. (Bush 2002: 1, 3, 17, 27)

Liberalism has always been a prominent feature of US foreign policy, strongly linked to its leading role in creating the League of Nations and the United Nations, and, since the end of the Second World War, in its promotion of both a liberal international economic order and a political (not economic) version of human rights. But like all revolutionary states, the US has been torn between proselytizing to remake international society in its own image and preserving its own purity against foreign corruption.

Moralism

Moralism is also a much noted feature of US foreign policy, and according to Lipset the main explanation for this can be found in the distinctive religiosity that pervades American life. The US is the main, and strong, exception to the general rule that the advance of modernity erodes commitment to religion in society (Lipset 1996: esp. 61–2). 'The combination of capitalism and Protestant sectarian values, to be found dominant only in America, encourages conflict and moralism. . . . In America . . . Protestant sectarian moralism helps to produce adversarialness, since political and social controversies are more likely to be perceived as non-negotiable moral issues than as conflicts of material interest that can be compromised' (1996: 225–6). Many religion-driven controversies that preoccupy American political life, such as contraception, abortion and gay rights, are not central issues in other industrial countries (1996: 23–8). Lipset (1996: esp. 60–7) makes a big play about the fundamental impact of religion on the character of American political life, both for domestic and for foreign policy. He hangs a lot on the difference between dissenting Protestantism and established, or state, religions, seeing the former as underpinning American commitment to anti-statist views, including its low tax and low state provision of welfare, the importance of individual conscience, and moralistic views of political and social issues. State religions by contrast encourage obedience to the state. This aspect of American exceptionalism feeds strongly through into moralistic attitudes to war and foreign policy in the US, and the need to pose both support for and opposition to war in crusading and Manichean terms. The US needs to see its enemies as evil.

Again, this moralistic, Manichean tendency is clearly visible throughout the Bush administration's National Security Strategy document:

> For most of the twentieth century, the world was divided by a great struggle over ideas: destructive totalitarian visions versus freedom and equality. . . . Some worry that it is somehow undiplomatic or impolite to speak the language of right and wrong. I disagree. Different circumstances require different methods, but not different moralities. . . . our responsibility to history is already clear: to answer these attacks and rid the world of evil. . . . Freedom and fear are at war, and there will be no quick or easy end to this conflict. (Bush 2002: 1, 3, 5, 7)

This last point contrasts strikingly with Waltz's (1979: 112) argument that 'States, like people, are insecure in proportion to the extent of their freedom. If freedom is wanted, insecurity must be accepted.' The moralistic, Manichean tendency has long been apparent in the seeming need of the US to cast its foreign policy in terms of crusades, ranging from the extermination of fascism in the Second World War, through Reagan's rhetoric about the Soviet Union as an 'evil empire', to Bush's 'war on terrorism'.

Isolationism/unilateralism

The crusade aspect of US foreign policy links to its isolationist traditions, in which nothing short of a life-or-death issue can mobilize sustained support against the general indifference of the American polity towards overseas engagements. Isolationism and unilateralism are not the same, but they are linked. Isolationism is a long tradition in the US. It goes back both to the geostrategic position of the country, which until fifty years ago was substantially insulated from the other great powers by two oceans, and to the desire of its founding fathers that the American political experiment should not corrupt itself by engagement in the balance of power politics of Europe. It was strong enough after the First World War to pull the US out of the League of Nations of which its own president had been the principal architect. That said, the US has never been isolationist in the cultural and commercial spheres, though it has often sought to keep foreign policy commitments minimal (Bolton 2000: 60; Schlesinger 2000: 18). In this sense, isolationism is a type of unilateralism in that it involves a self-centred act of non-engagement. Schlesinger (2000: 18–25) argues that in this sense the US has been unilateralist for a long time, but that there has been a clear exception to its distaste for engaging in the balance of power, going back to Jefferson, which is when a concentration of power overseas becomes sufficient to threaten the liberty of the US. Traditionally, this fear was focused on Europe, which explains US engagements in the three world wars (First, Second and Cold) of the twentieth century. This argument can be extended to Asia, first as annexes to the Second World War (the threat from Japan as part of the fascist Axis) and the Cold War (China as part of the communist bloc), but from the 1980s in alternating concerns that Japan and/or China would dominate Asia and challenge the US for world leadership. So long as the other great powers played enemies and rivals with each other, geography kept the US safe and allowed it to be isolationist. But if one great power threatened to unite Europe (as Germany did twice during the twentieth century) or, even worse, Eurasia (as the Soviet Union did after 1945), then the US could no longer afford the luxury of isolationism.

The isolationist aspect of unilateralism has faded somewhat since the US became permanently engaged in great power politics at the beginning of the Cold War, though its residual potency is perhaps indicated by two ongoing features of US politics. First is the regular election of presidents who not only know and care little about the rest of the world and have to spend their first years learning from scratch (though one could easily find that in many countries), but more unusually are able to get elected, as Clinton initially did, on a promise *not* to be a foreign policy president. Second is the popularity of defence policies that, no matter how expensive and implausible, promise to insulate the US from attack (Lindley-French 2002: 45, 72). This idea of re-creating the barrier once provided free by the oceans has most obviously been manifest in the US since the 1980s, when Reagan's 'star wars' vision of national missile defence (NMD) began the ongoing expenditure of billions of dollars in pursuit of that dream (Bender 2003: 148).

The other side of unilateralism is the preference for acting alone rather than either coordinating action with others or binding oneself into multilateral agreements. Like the isolationist aspect, this type of unilateralism also relates to the tension noted above for all revolutionary states as to whether to remake international society in their own image or preserve their own purity against foreign corruption. Isolationism chooses preservation of purity against remaking international society (other than by the power of example). But unilateralism in the context of engagement can

go either way: imperial action to convert international society, or assertion of the right to be different and to take individual action against
threats on that basis (Schlesinger 2000: 27). The US has done both, but
the main concern about its current unilateralism is that it seems to be a
major turn away from the multilateralist strategy that the US pursued so
successfully during the second half of the twentieth century.

   This aspect of unilateralism is underpinned by a strong tradition of
'sovereigntism' in the US, by which is meant a disinclination to subordinate US law or politics to international institutions. Bolton (2000:
51) notes the contrast between the US and the EU member states at this
point in history regarding (un)willingness to bind itself to higher international laws and institutions: the US 'emphatically rejects the loss of
national autonomy.' Similar points are made by Legro (2000: 260), who
focuses on the longstanding desire of the US to preserve its ability to
'decide its own course in each instance'; by Posen and Ross (1996–7: 46),
who argue that the US public 'is against giving up much US autonomy'
to intergovernmental organizations; and by Brown (2002: 333), who argues
that the US has 'a long tradition of reflexive opposition to international
jurisdiction over U.S. interests'. The 'new sovereigntists' (Spiro 2000;
Krauthammer 2001) and the neoconservatives (Daalder and Lindsay 2003:
1–16) in the US take a particularly strong line. They believe that the US
should not be constrained by international society, in part because it is
powerful enough both to go it alone and maybe get others to follow after
when it does; in part because international society is weak and vague;
and in part because multilateralism threatens the autonomy of the US
constitution and domestic law. Rabkin (2000) explains this unilateralism
using a strict positive view of international law by the US, with a strong
emphasis on sovereignty and reciprocity as the keys to acceptability. Thus
GATT and the Geneva Conventions on war are OK, but many multilateral agreements on human rights and environmental standards are not
acceptable, and the ICC especially not (Rabkin 2000: 113–19). He argues
that the essential requirements for the US are that international law must
be explicitly consented to by the US government for each commitment,
that no commitments under international law must displace the authority
of the constitutional organs of the US, and that international law must
not impinge on how the US treats US citizens within the US (Rabkin
2000: 111). Unilateralism of this type has a variety of motives. In part it
is about sovereignty and law and the unwillingness of the US (in contrast
to the members of the EU) to subordinate its domestic practices to multilateral arrangements that sit above US law. In part it is about democracy
and the argument that, since multilateral arrangements and institutions
are not subject to the control of US citizens, there is no legitimacy in
giving them power over US citizens (Ralph 2002: 16). And in part it is

about instrumental calculations of national advantage or national security, as when the US unilaterally withdrew from the ABM treaty (in order to exploit a supposed technological lead in missile defence), or when it unilaterally denied the legal rights of so-called enemy combatants by interning them at the Guantanamo military base. Ruggie (2003) nicely styles this aspect of US behaviour 'American exemptionalism'.

In considering this aspect of unilateralism it is important not to lose sight of the fact that unilateralism is not in itself bad, nor multilateralism in itself good (Elliott and Hufbauer 2002: 408). A preference for unilateralism and opposition to multilateralism is sometimes perfectly rational. The EU's principle of subsidiarity reflects this, and a good case can be made that in military operations multilateralism easily leads to operational inefficiency whatever its political merits might be (Wedgwood 2002). There is also a difficult grey zone between unilateralism and leadership. More consensual forms of leadership work by persuasion in advance of action, taking on an explicitly multilateral form. Leading from the front might initially look a lot like unilateralism, and only become legitimate in retrospect if others have followed. Elliott and Hufbauer (2002: 397), for example, note that a round of 'aggressive unilateralism' by the US during the 1980s on trade policy had the effect of pushing others into transforming the GATT into the stronger multilateral institution of the WTO. These two styles of leadership are illustrated respectively by the first and second US-led wars against Iraq. Unilateralism or multilateralism is mainly a choice about form rather than substance. Multilateralism could be used for illiberal ends (e.g. to enforce apartheid or communist rule). But that said, multilateralism does have some element of good in its own right as an institution of international society – as a general expectation about how problems are solved, and order maintained, by international society.

Anti-statism and separation of powers

The fourth theme of American exceptionalism is the unusual anti-statism that is mainly reflected in the rather extreme separation of powers designed into the US constitution, and was already visible in the discussion of liberal, individualist and religious themes above. In much of continental Europe, and especially so in France and the Scandinavian countries, the state is closely intertwined with society and generally seen as being a crucial instrument for the realization of society's goals. This view is much less common in the US, where the state is more often regarded as a threat to society, and something to be kept to a minimum lest it obstruct society's pursuit of its goals. Lipset (1996: 20) notes that a distinctive American history created a state without a feudal past, defined by ideology rather than common history, and with a strong and deep influence of non-established Protestant religion: 'America began and continues as the most anti-statist, legalist and rights-oriented nation.' Lipset (1996: 44) sees this anti-statism as reflected in the constitutional division of powers and the high proportion of elected offices. This division opens space for 'numerous and powerful special interests and lobbying organizations', and the influence of these is enhanced by weak party structures and a political style that is 'more materialistic, more oriented toward special interests, and more personal, than elsewhere'. Along similar lines, Bolton (2000: 51, 80–1) argues that American exceptionalism is rooted in a strong commitment to liberty, which itself is rooted in two things: the individualist tradition of Protestantism and what he calls 'American constitutionalism'. This latter reflects not only a strong sense of sovereignty in relation to the outside world, but also a deep commitment to the division of powers, seen as essential safeguards against governmental control and domination over the lives of citizens.

In relation to foreign policy, the main practical consequence often hinges on the necessity for a two-thirds majority in the Senate as a major obstacle to US ratification of international agreements. No party of the president has ever commanded a two-thirds majority in the Senate, so all ratifications have to be bipartisan (which is easier during times of external threat, such as the Cold War, harder when external pressures do not work to produce a domestic consensus) (Patrick 2002: 8–9, 21; Lyman 2002; Moravscik 2002: 358–9; Jacobson 2002: 428). In itself this separation of powers poses a severe technical barrier to US participation in multilateralism. But it also allows the more general anti-statist and economic liberal sentiments room to play and creates opportunities for the many strong lobbying groups that operate so effectively within the constitutional separation of powers (Reisman 1999–2000: 76). Some (Ikenberry 2003: 10) celebrate the 'voice opportunities' that this system creates for outsiders seeking to influence the policy of the hegemon. Others (Prestowitz 2003: 225–6), reflecting on the huge success of the Jewish and Taiwanese lobbies, note the downside: 'Our system of government, with its separation of powers, facilitates capture of key positions by dedicated minorities that are sometimes heavily influenced by foreign elements whose interests are directly at odds with those of the United States.' The long career of Jesse Helms as influential chairman of the Senate Committee on Foreign Relations is an exemplar of how strongly opinioned individuals occupying key positions in the American political process can have a huge influence on what foreign policy does and does not get made.

Distrust of the UN in the US is linked to general dislike of government and to strong desire to retain democratic control. International agreements designed to encourage state-led and/or state-empowering policies, such as

environmental policies based on pollution quotas and human rights policies based on welfare provision, fall foul of liberal and anti-state sentiments, making ratification problematic. The US tends to prefer non-state
actor/market-based policies, and anything which looks like empowering
the state will fall into the centre of the political divisions within the US
between Republicans and Democrats. Dislike of statist solutions easily
leads within the US to charges that international measures are socialist,
or aiming at world government, and are against the rights of individuals,
the family, etc. Thus the US is inherently more resistant to agreements
that strengthen the state against civil society, because that issue is a central divide in US domestic politics in a way that it generally isn't, or not
to the same degree, in other advanced industrial countries (Moravscik
2002). A good example of this is the US opposition to the Kyoto protocol on the grounds that environmental controls would lead towards a
state-regulated economy (Jacobson 2002: 425–6). Even where national
majorities pretty clearly exist in favour, as for the Convention on the
Elimination of All Forms of Discrimination Against Women, the Senate
can block them (Moravscik 2002: 358–9), and this means that what might
appear as a difference of values between US and European societies
in fact reflects a difference of political procedure. Opinion polls suggest
that the US public is neither hostile to multilateralism nor in favour
of unilateralism. Its main discomfort is with over-engagement and US
domineering. But US political elites are less favourable to multilateralism
because it threatens their power (Kull 2002). The impact of constitutional
structure on US foreign policy also works the other way around, as
on the issue of extraterritorial sanctions, with Congress being the main
generator of these, often against the wishes of the executive (Mastanduno
2002: 299, 313). The strongly held domestic views on issues such as abortion, which as noted above resonate much more in the US because
of religion than they do in Europe, also generate tensions between US
domestic values and its participation in various multilateral regimes
(Reisman 1999–2000).

*****

These four themes of American exceptionalism point towards what in
a European perspective is the peculiar combination of a large, powerful
and hugely influential state and society that are in many ways extraordinarily inward looking and self-referential. The charge of being inward
looking and self-referential could be laid against most states and societies, but Europeans at least have historically conditioned expectations
that great power brings with it a more outward-orientated perspective.
In this respect, the tempting comparison is with classical China's view of

itself as 'the middle kingdom' (Kang 2000: 28; Lipschutz 2002: 7–8). What might be called 'middle kingdom syndrome' is about seeing oneself as the centre of the universe, being the exclusive holder of the only civilized values and standards that matter, and having nothing to learn from the rest of the world. While this is perhaps too strong a formulation to give an accurate portrait of the US, American exceptionalism, especially when combined with the dominance of domestic politics in the making of US foreign policy, does lean towards middle kingdom syndrome. As noted above (p. 137), many have commented on the substantial disjuncture between how Americans see their own foreign policy (as benign and well intentioned) and how others see it (often as threatening and as dominated by domestic interests). Bacevich (2002: 90) observes that 'American statecraft is not, in the first instance, about "them"; it is about "us"', and goes on to give a detailed, almost Leninist, portrait of how the needs of the US political economy to maintain its own prosperity drive its foreign policy with little heed for the consequences. In similar vein, Lindley-French (2002: 80) notes that 'The power of the United States externally is such that it tends to export domestic policy rather than construct classical foreign policy.' This combination of a benign self-image as the carrier of universal values and a domestically driven foreign policy insulates the US from the idea that peoples abroad oppose it, or even hate it, because of its foreign policies rather than because they oppose or hate its values. This deaf spot is all too apparent in the Bush administration's characterizations cited above of terrorism being about opposition to American values. Prestowitz (2003: 1–17) urges the necessity for Americans to see themselves as others do, saying, 'it is usually we who are the odd man out. As a nation we are an outlier'. . . . 'our sense of mission and self-righteousness makes it hard for us to hear' (2003: 14).

Reducing this to the parochial concerns of the IR community, Steve Smith (2002: 84–5; see also Hendrickson 2002: 4) worries that, because of its strong positivist, rationalist way of constructing 'knowledge', 'the discipline of international relations as currently practiced in the United States does not assist civil society in comprehending the complexities, and the many forms of life, of contemporary world politics.' This contributes to the failure of the US to understand why it is hated in so many places, and why the September 11 attacks attracted the degree of support, or at least understanding, that they did: 'A dominant version of U.S. patriotism has silenced many U.S. critics' [of the war on terrorism]. Smith sees the rational choice approach as fixing assumptions about identity and interest in ways that make it difficult if not impossible to understand the motivations of international terrorists, and therefore make it difficult if not impossible to devise appropriate policies, and likely that policies resulting will simply reproduce the problem by inspiring new generations

of terrorists. 'The hegemonic discourse of U.S. IR . . . omits by definition much of world politics, and competing notions of rationality, and
any other regimes of truth, and thus runs the risk of constituting the
common sense of tomorrow's U.S. civil society in a specific, and decidedly
political, way, all under the guise of being legitimate, neutral, value-free
social science.' This view chimes with Lipset's (1996: 19, 31) argument
that the ideology of Americanism, with its creed of liberty, egalitarian-
ism, individualism, populism and laissez-faire, means that 'those who
reject American values are un-American.' The ideological basis of American nationalism contrasts with the more exclusive historical, organic
conceptions of nation elsewhere, and opens up possibilities for a more
generalized tension between inclusive, universalist US self-conceptions
and other cultures. Because the US presents itself as a set of values rather
than as an organic, ethnic people, it is easier to question its legitimacy
and to take positions against it.

But while looking through the lens of American exceptionalism provides some useful insights, it cannot by itself tell us much about the
present problem of understanding US behaviour. Although these points
do reveal important things about the internal generation of policy within
the US, all of them have been in operation for much of its history. The
factors of exceptionalism can suggest various dispositions and problems,
but since they have been there for decades or even centuries they cannot
explain what to many seems a dramatic and disturbing shift in US policy.
For example, Kupchan (1998: 66) notes that 'the U.S. lacks the societal
commitment to self-binding present in Germany and Japan', but isn't
clear whether the explanation for this comes from the unique domestic
character of American state and society or from the position of the US
within the international system structure (its sole superpower status).
Both explanations make sense, suggesting that, if one wants to understand current US behaviour, more than American exceptionalism has to
be taken into account.

9.2 Unipolarity

American exceptionalism invites one to look inside the US to see how
its domestic character and processes affect its external behaviour.
Polarity, in this case unipolarity, invites one to look outside-in, to see
how the international position of the US affects its external behaviour.
The interesting thing is to see how these outside-in arguments play into
the standing themes from American exceptionalism. Does unipolarity
reinforce tendencies already there, or does it pull against domestic-driven
imperatives? Like bipolarity, unipolarity carries both a material and an

ideological meaning. Materially it means that the US has a massive, and for the time being quite easily sustained, politico-military superiority, and is effectively unbalanced in a politico-military sense by the other great powers. Ideologically, it means that the US leads a camp of Western states whose governing formula of capitalist democracy has no rivals in its claim to represent the future of (post)industrial society. To say that it has no rivals is not to say that it is unchallenged. There is opposition to it in much of the Islamic world, in the more authoritarian parts of Africa and Asia, and within the political left generally. But the Islamic world has been unable so far to develop its own form of modern political economy that is efficient, sustainable and attractive enough to offer an alternative model, and is therefore not an ideological rival in the same sense as the Soviet Union was. China's market communism is distinctive, but does not look sustainable, and is not offered as challenger for the future of (post)industrial society. The left does not now really have a plausible alternative outside the liberal frame. Ideologically, therefore, the world is unipolar, with the US in the lead position.

Two sets of arguments about US behaviour flow from unipolarity, one about unilateralism, the other about securitization.

Unilateralism

The general line of argument linking unipolarity and unilateralism is that the former should predispose towards the latter. In the case of the US, this means that its position as the sole superpower should reinforce the inclination towards unilateralism already present in American exceptionalism. Unipolarity can be seen as an extreme case of the general proposition that great powers are less disposed to multilateralism than weaker states because they have more to lose (by having their freedom of action constrained, and by having to support free-riders) and less to gain (because they can often get their way anyway) (Patrick 2002: 9–10; for a contrary view see Moravscik 2002: 348–50). In relation to the US specifically, Reisman (1999–2000) notes the tension between its responsibilities as 'custodian' for international society (which means that it is often pushed to exempt itself from the rules in the name of necessary action) and its role as the main promoter of international institutions (which pushes it towards rule-bound behaviour). The idea that unipolarity is itself a form of exceptionalism for the unipole is carried forward by Huntington, who argues that the sole superpower will make exaggerated claims to sovereignty and demand special rights on the basis of its unique position and role (Huntington 1999: 41). Arguments of precisely that sort appeared in the US campaign against the International Criminal Court

(ICC), that because the US has exceptional responsibilities, especially military ones, it could not risk putting its military personnel under legal threat (Brown 2002: 329–33) and could reasonably claim a unique '*lex USA*' legal regime for itself (Weller 2002: 712). There is much in this reasoning to suggest that, as with great- or superpower status, the idea of being a unipole can quite quickly become embedded in the identity of the state concerned, and therefore itself become securitized as part of what needs to be defended and preserved.

If these arguments are correct, one should have expected the onset of unipolarity to trigger increased unilateralism by the US. A move of that sort is widely held to be associated with the arrival of the Bush administration in 2001, which was not just publicly unenthusiastic about the UN in particular and multilateralism in general, but, cheered on by the neo-conservatives (Krauthammer 2001; Daalder and Lindsay 2003: 62–77), seemed to embark on a specific campaign to undo large parts of the multilateral order that the US had put into place since 1945. If this seems to be a delayed response, one has to remember that unipolarity did not kick in as the accepted social fact shaping US behaviour until quite late in the 1990s. During that decade, the power structure of the international system was an open question, and perceptions of the US were still affected by the hangover of the declinist debate. But by the late 1990s, the sustained slump in Japan, the Asian economic crisis, slow progress in consolidating the EU's CFSP, the relatively good performance of the US economy, and the longish time horizon before China could challenge the US as a global power, all supported the idea that the unipolar moment might in fact turn out to be a durable era. The Bush administration's assertion of a much more unilateralist position for the US, as well as the declining zeal for multilateralism during the Clinton administrations (Crossette 2002: 56–8), thus seem quite well timed. In effect, the Bush administration set about reversing the move initiated by Roosevelt towards the end of the Second World War that shifted the US from its longstanding tradition of unilateral isolationism to the engaged multilateralism that characterized its behaviour throughout the Cold War (Legro 2000: 260–2; Chace 2003: 1).

The catalogue of recent US unilateralism is quite impressive.

1980s and 1990s

- From the Reagan administration onwards, the US withheld its dues to the UN and other agencies with the declared aims of both creating pressure for reform and reducing its own share of the UN's costs. Its arrears mounted to around $1.5 billion, with a partial settlement achieved in 2001. Forman (2002: 447–8) notes that, during the 1990s, the US was in arrears 'to virtually every multilateral organization to which it belongs'. For contrasting views see also Gerson (2000) and Karns and Mingst (2002).

- In 1984 the US withdrew from UNESCO on grounds of corrupt management and anti-Western (and anti-Israel) attitudes.
- In 1984 the US Senate refused to ratify the Law of the Sea Treaty.
- The US refused to ratify (having signed) the 1989 UN Convention on the Rights of the Child, in part because twenty-three of its states allow the death penalty for those under eighteen, and also because the US allows recruitment into its armed forces at age seventeen. It has nevertheless ratified two additional protocols to this convention.
- The US made many reservations to its 1992 ratification of the International Covenant on Civil and Political Rights based on concerns about its sovereignty and the effect of the covenant on the balance between state and federal government.
- The US was the only industrialized nation not to ratify the 1979 Convention on the Elimination of All Forms of Discrimination Against Women, with opponents mobilizing around concerns about US sovereignty and implications for abortion rights.
- The US withdrew its acceptance of the ICJ's jurisdiction in 1995 after a ruling on US policy in Nicaragua.
- The 1996 Helms–Burton Act on Cuba (concerning ownership of former US property in Cuba) and the Iran–Libya Sanctions Act (concerning oil investments and trade) extended extraterritorial sanctions to those who violate aspects of US sanctions against those countries.

1997
- Despite intense pressure from Europe, Canada and many NGOs, the US refused to adhere to the landmine agreement because of its army's concerns about the effects of a ban on the safety of American soldiers.
- The US's implementing legislation for the Chemical Weapons Convention of 1997 seriously weakened the inspection provisions and seemed to 'allow the United States to create for itself a separate and less rigorous verification regime' (Smithson 2002: 258).

1999
- The US Senate rejected the 1996 Comprehensive Test Ban Treaty (CTBT), mostly on grounds of acrimonious party political issues.

2001
- The US refused to adhere to the Kyoto protocol on environmental emissions.
- The US alone rejected a verification protocol to the Biological and Toxin Weapons Convention.
- The US blocked agreement on a Small Arms Treaty by refusing to regulate civilian ownership of military weapons and to restrict arms supply to rebel movements.

- The US gave notice of withdrawal from the Anti-Ballistic Missile (ABM) Treaty and pursuit of its own national missile defence program.

2002
- The US refused to adhere to the International Criminal Court, and subsequently campaigned forcefully in Europe and elsewhere (Weller 2002: 697, 705–12; Hendrickson 202: 5–6; *The Economist*, 22 November 2003: 29) to get bilateral exemptions for all US soldiers, diplomats and citizens.
- The US announced refusal to abide by the 1949 Geneva Conventions on the treatment of prisoners of war in the case of its prison at Guantanamo Bay.
- The US vigorously opposed the Draft Optional Protocol to the Convention Against Torture which would have allowed international inspection of US prisons (including the one at Guantanamo Bay).
- The US announced major tariffs on steel and a $190 billion subsidy for agriculture.

2003
- The US went to war against Iraq without a new UNSC resolution specifically authorizing such action.

One cannot attribute causality to unipolarity in triggering the Bush round of unilateralism, particularly not with the shadow over the 2000 election and the clear possibility that a more multilateral Gore administration might well have been the winner. Ikenberry (2003: 18–20) also notes that there are significant countervailing pressures working against any automatic linkage between unipolarity and US unilateralism. But the coincidence of the timing with the consolidation of the unipolar understanding of world politics is suggestive, as is the fit with the predictions of neorealist theorists. The Bush administration's unilateralism on environmental and arms control agreements certainly played a role in the ejection of the US from the UN Human Rights Commission and from the International Narcotics Control Board in 2001. Yet despite this long list, one cannot conclude that the US has abandoned multilateralism completely. It remains engaged in the main economic institutions (IMF, World Bank, WTO), supported NATO expansion, and remains active in various regional arrangements such as NAFTA and APEC (Patrick 2002: 10–20). Jacobson (2002: 416, 430) also notes the swift US ratification of the UN Framework Convention on Climate Change in 1997. Neither is it clear whether the present surge of unilateralism represents a narrow agenda supported mainly by hard-line conservatives, both 'neo' and traditional, or whether it represents a deeper sentiment within the US body politic. Certainly there is evidence that substantial parts of US public opinion continue to support a multilateral posture (Leffler 2003: 1062–3). There are also spectacular individual moves by US citizens, such as Ted Turner donating 1 billion dollars to the UN as a reaction against US government funding cuts to that organization and many of its agencies. Bill Gates's well-funded 'foreign policy' on AIDS might be seen in a similar light, as can more grassroots campaigns such as '34 million friends' run by the US Committee for the UN Family Planning Association, designed to compensate for Bush's axing of $34 million from the UN Population Fund (*Guardian Weekly*, 168: 3, 2003: 29).

It is also important to register that US unilateralism, in line with the discussion on American exceptionalism, is not new. Such actions have been a feature of US foreign policy in the past, most notoriously in Congress's rejection of President Wilson's League of Nations after the First World War, and Nixon's exit from the IMF's regime of fixed exchange rates in 1971. In substantive terms, the present bout of US unilateralism has nothing on US behaviour during the 1920s and 1930s. What makes this round important is the degree of contrast it creates with the broadly pro-multilateralist stance of the US initiated by Roosevelt during the Second World War and dominant during the following half-century. The Bush administration is explicitly hostile to much multilateralism, and US rhetoric about 'coalitions of the willing' that featured in the campaign against Iraq reveals a much more conditional, instrumental and ad hoc attitude even where it does favour, or need, the support of other states.

Taking all this into consideration, it seems safe to say that unipolarity complements the factors in American exceptionalism that predispose towards unilateralism. Even the combination does not make unilateral behaviour a certainty, but the two forces working together do make it more likely, and certainly provided useful resources for an administration that was anyway committed to such policies for ideological reasons.

Securitization

The second set of arguments to flow out of unipolarity concerns the impact of that structure on the security perceptions of the unipole. The main proposition is that the sole superpower should feel an elevated sense of threat and should conduct its policy on that basis. Grounds for this view are easy to find in neorealism's commitment to balance of power logic as the fundamental consequence of anarchic structure. As argued above, Waltz's theory is firmly committed to the view that a sole superpower will inevitably appear threatening to all the other powers, who will balance against it on that basis. The sole superpower should therefore expect to have its status severely challenged. Huntington (1999: 44–6) supports this with his argument that a counter-pole coalition is 'a natural phenomenon in a uni-multipolar world'. Certainly the most influential recent statements of this position come from Robert Kagan (2002, 2003), a prominent neoconservative who, like the neorealists, bases his argument on the material distribution of power. Simply put, Kagan's (2002: 2–4) argument is that the good/evil, friends/enemies extremism of US foreign policy results from its position in the distribution of power, and is a function of being the leading power. In contrasting the political styles of the EU and the US, he says that the 'differences in strategic culture do not spring naturally from the national characters of Americans and Europeans' but reflect the fact that the US is now powerful and Europe weak. When the power positions were opposite, in earlier times, so were the strategic cultures, with the US being less militaristic and more inclined towards commerce and law and public opinion in its foreign policy. In short, according to Kagan, the US lives in a Hobbesian world in which its power attracts threats, and in which it acts because it can, whereas the EU attracts few threats because it is weak and pursues multilateral diplomacy because it has not the means to do otherwise. A similar position is taken by Graham and La Vera (2002: 226–7) and Lindley-French (2002), who argue that there is an interplay between securitization and unipolarity inasmuch as the US attracts threats because of its status and its policies and engagements. This creates a closed circle of power, threat and securitization. These arguments all reflect the material aspect of unipolarity, and they have been the dominant linkage of unipolarity to securitization.

Those who dispute this interpretation do so not by contesting the basics of the argument, but by adding the countervailing factor of a relatively benign 'rivals and friends' international society in which US predominance is not seen as threatening by others because they share a set of liberal values which makes its leadership acceptable. The key position here is the quite widespread observation that post-Cold War most of the great powers are members of a security community, and that this represents a unique development, largely removing great power war as a danger. Kapstein (1999) gives this a specific twist to argue that the effectiveness of multilateral institutions alongside US material power both explains the absence of balancing against the unipole and allows for the possibility that unipolarity might be stable. The salient point is not so much who is right or wrong in these arguments, but which interpretation of unipolarity gets accepted within the US – and indeed the other great powers – as the prevailing social fact. It is the accepted social fact that shapes securitization. There are two factors in play that could corrode the legitimacy of US leadership. One is the possibility that the more extreme practices of liberalism facilitated by a capitalism that is ideologically unbalanced (in both senses) will generate sufficient inequality to undermine the ideological basis of US hegemony (Kapstein 1999: 485). A measure of this can perhaps be found in the strength of the anti-globalization movement. The other, ironically, is that US behaviour, and particularly the US playing a game of enemies and rivals within an international society of rivals and friends, will trigger balancing reactions. From this latter perspective, the most worrying development is precisely that the Kagan interpretation of unipolarity will come to dominate perceptions of the US, both inside it and among the other powers. It is already strongly placed within the Bush administration's understanding of unipolarity, where it provides a handy justification for aggressive unilateralism. These two strands come together in Calleo's (1996: 63–4) argument that the removal of the Soviet Union takes away the threat that forced the capitalist powers to mute the competition among them that is a natural feature of their economic system. The Cold War was an interregnum in this competition, and, with its end, normal history resumes and 'the Marxist clock' starts ticking again.

To the extent that unipolarity generates structural pressures on the US to heighten its sense of insecurity, those pressures can find fertile ground in the predispositions set by American exceptionalism. The most obvious fit is with isolationism and the way in which the existence of two oceans and a set of militarily weak neighbours has conditioned the US to expect a level of national security that appears high to outsiders. Kagan (2002: 10; see also Lindley-French 2002: 45, 72; Hendrickson 2002) notes the widespread perception in both Europe and the US 'that Americans have an unreasonable demand for "perfect" security, the product of living for centuries shielded behind two oceans.' If unipolarity raises perceptions of threat in the US, then this easily plays against high expectations of security to generate what might be called *hypersecuritization*: a tendency both to exaggerate threats and to resort to excessive countermeasures. Another way of thinking about hypersecuritization is in Hendrickson's (2002: 9) terms, borrowed from Kissinger, of an 'inability to be reassured'. Adding to this is the interplay between unipolarity and the universalist aspect of American exceptionalism, which sees the US as the political embodiment of the future of all of humankind. This universalist element means that the US can justify the pursuit of its own national security not just on the basis of preserving a distinctive nation (already a very strong rationale for any country) but also on the basis of protecting the future well-being and rights of all of humankind. This additional element makes it easier both to claim special rights in pursuit of US national security and to discount the standard arguments that excessive pursuit of national security tends to be self-defeating because it threatens others, and so triggers security dilemma responses that raise the level of threat to be faced.

Two pieces of evidence suggest that hypersecuritization has indeed become a feature of US behaviour. The first is the widely observed militarization of US foreign policy (Bacevich 2002: 141–2; Lindley-French 2002: 33, 43), with the military increasingly being the preferred instrument despite America's abundance of soft power. Prestowitz (2003: 161, 144) observes how this militarization is enabled by the separation of powers within the US political system, and how this armed face is one of the causes of the growing disaffection with the US abroad. Bacevich (2002: 122–7) argues that the military has become a central element in American identity, and that during the 1990s the idea of maintaining military supremacy became a consensus position in American politics. The second piece of evidence, reflecting the first, is to be found in the very high levels of relative military expenditure and the concern, clearly set out in the National Security Strategy (Bush 2002: 29–30), that US forces: 'will be strong enough to dissuade potential adversaries from pursuing a military build-up in hopes of surpassing, or equaling, the power of the United States.' To that end, the US has maintained an unprecedentedly high level of military expenditure relative to the other major military powers. According to the data of the International Institute for Strategic Studies (IISS 2002), even in 2001, before September 11, the US was, at nearly 330 billion dollars, spending as much as the next eleven big military spenders combined, three times as much as China and Russia combined, and not quite twice as much as all of its major European allies and Japan combined. Despite a level of military superiority probably not exceeded since the height of the Roman empire (Bender 2003), and the palpable lack of military threat to the US from any other great power, the neoconservative Project for the New American Century still worries about 'the decline in the strength of America's defenses' and the need to extend its presently advantageous position 'as far into the future as possible' by increasing US military expenditure even further (Kagan et al. 2000: i–v).

9.3   September 11

The third layer in the sequence of factors that might explain the apparent turn in US foreign policy is the terrorist attacks of September 11, 2001, and all of the reactions that flowed from those events. There has been a huge amount of commentary on this, and by now there is probably a consensus around the idea that the US suffered a major collective trauma that radically affected its security policy (Hassner 2002: 8–9; Leffler 2003: 1049). More controversial is the extent to which this trauma has been manipulated, maintained and extended by the Bush administration because of the way in which a hypersecuritized political environment could help it achieve the radical political goals which it brought with it to office. The attacks on September 11 offered the Bush administration not only a huge opportunity to pursue their domestic agenda within the US, but also, as they thought, an opportunity to remake the world (Daalder and Lindsay 2003: 78–97). It is not my purpose here to try to resolve these questions. My aim is to track the impact of September 11 on US security policy and to relate that impact to the analysis already done above on American exceptionalism and unipolarity. The argument is that unipolarity and September 11 have acted as successive lenses in a two-stage process of selecting and intensifying particular aspects of American exceptionalism. Unipolarity selected and intensified predispositions towards unilateralism and hypersecuritization. September 11 amplified these two even further (Hendrickson 2002: 1) and added to them a highly charged rendition of the moralistic/Manichean interpretation of the world. But September 11 also threw up a potential contradiction with American exceptionalism in the form of the challenge posed to individual rights by the 'war on terrorism'.

The September 11 attacks represented an unprecedented violation of the American homeland. Their effect was amplified not only by the peculiarly horrific and cold-blooded nature of the attacks, and their symbolic brilliance, but also by the relatively high sense of insulation from the horrors of the world that were part of the American tradition. There was an overwhelming sense of sanctuary not only breached, but breached in a way that could be endlessly repeated because it exploited the very openness so fundamental to the American way of life. The response of the Bush administration was to intensify the hypersecuritization and unilateralism already under way as a result of unipolarity. Bush declared a war rather than a police action, and by doing so created a domestic environment in which security requirements trumped liberty and human rights, and an international one in which the priority of pursuing terrorists justified US claims for a wide right of unilateral and pre-emptive action against or within other states, and for establishing a US military presence much more widely than before. Reinforcing the reasoning behind NMD, deterrence was no longer seen as an adequate response to the threat of WMD, and pre-emption was to take its place (O'Hanlon et al. 2002: 4). September 11 reinforced the neoconservative project to keep the US as number one, increased its military expenditure still further, and even managed to support the NMD project despite its seeming irrelevance to the new threat exposed by the use of civilian airliners as missiles.

The new hypersecuritization focused around the combination of fanatical and nihilistic terrorists and WMD, with so-called rogue states as the supposed link between the two. It brought out strongly the moralistic and Manichean tendency in US foreign policy, with a universalizing rhetoric of civilization versus barbarians (Salter 2002: 163–7). 'The gravest danger to freedom lies at the crossroads of radicalism and technology. When the spread of chemical and biological weapons, along with ballistic missile technology – when that occurs, even weak states and small groups could attain a catastrophic power to strike great nations' (Bush 2002: 13); 'Like Saddam Hussein, some of today's tyrants are gripped by an implacable hatred of the United States of America. They hate our friends, they hate our values, they hate democracy and freedom and individual liberty. Many care little for the lives of their own people. In such a world, Cold War deterrence is no longer enough' (2001: 2); 'today's most urgent threats stem . . . from a small number of missiles in the hands of these states, states for whom terror and blackmail are a way of life' (2001: 2); 'We are menaced less by fleets and armies than by catastrophic technologies in the hands of the embittered few' (2002: 1). Characterizing the war in such essentialist terms of good versus evil conveniently pushed to the margins perfectly reasonable arguments that much of the problem lay in reactions against US policies, not against the US itself.

While there was widespread international support for the concern about the linkage between terrorism and WMD, there was much less support for the Bush administration's more self-interested attempt to locate selected 'rogue states' as the key nexus connecting the two. Bush's 'Axis of evil' speech was received badly, not only because it created the implausible spectacle of the sole superpower staging three minor powers (Iran, Iraq and North Korea) as its main security concern, but also because it excluded the whole problem of the US position in the Middle East, and particularly its strong support for both Israel and a variety of corrupt and authoritarian Arab regimes, as a main cause of the problem represented by al-Qaeda. The contrast with the Cold War was very striking. Then, the designated opponent and object of securitization was a power that represented what seemed a plausible political alternative: one could easily imagine a communist world. The post-September 11 securitization focused on neither an alternative superpower nor an alternative ideology, but on the chaos power of embittered and alienated minorities, along with a handful of pariah governments, and their ability to exploit the openness, the technology, and in some places the inequality, unfairness and failed states generated by the Western system of political economy.

The nature of the September 11 events meant that the reinforcement of unilateralism occurred largely within the sphere of military security and was closely entangled with hypersecuritization. And the response was by no means totally unilateralist. Initially, there was a huge outpouring of genuine sympathy for the US and a willingness to cooperate in combating terrorism. The invasion of Afghanistan as the first response was widely seen as legitimate and attracted a lot of support. The very nature of the 'war on terrorism' necessitated widespread cooperation on a range of issues, from police and intelligence coordination to the regulation of immigration, freight and banking. The three most conspicuous examples of unilateralism contingent on September 11 were the claiming of a right of preventive attack, the denial of rights to prisoners of war discussed above, and the invasion of Iraq.

The right of preventive attack was chillingly set out in the National Security Strategy statement of 2002, which made clear a commitment to:

> defending the United States, the American people, and our interests at home and abroad by identifying and destroying the threat before it reaches our borders. . . . We recognize that our best defense is a good offense. . . . We must be prepared to stop rogue states and their terrorist clients before they are able to threaten or use weapons of mass destruction against the United States and our allies and friends. . . . We will . . . when necessary, interdict enabling technologies and materials [for WMD]. . . . Given the goals of rogue states and terrorists, the United States can no longer solely rely on a reactive posture as we have in the past. The inability to deter a potential attacker, the immediacy of today's threats, and the magnitude of potential harm that could be caused by our adversaries' choice of weapons, do not permit that option. We cannot let our enemies strike first. . . . The United States has long maintained the option of preemptive actions to counter a sufficient threat to our national security. The greater the threat, the greater is the risk of inaction – and the more compelling the case for taking anticipatory action to defend ourselves, even if uncertainty remains as to the time and place of the enemy's attack. To forestall or prevent such hostile acts by our adversaries, the United States will, if necessary, act preemptively. (Bush 2002: 6, 14, 15)

As widely noted (O'Hanlon et al. 2002; Hendrickson 2002: 7), this claim extended the traditional right of pre-emption in the face of imminent attack to something closer to a right of preventive war and regime change. This was done with little regard either for the threatening image of the US it created abroad or for the consequences of the leading power changing the norms of international society in such a way as to enable other governments to claim similar rights and reasons to use force.

The consequences of this in action became apparent in the confrontation with Iraq, which reached its peak in 2002–3. What might have been a multilateral approach, in which the US and Britain provided the military pressure to back up UN weapons inspectors, quickly became a unilateral game in which it became clear that the US was going to invade Iraq on its own timetable and for its own reasons, regardless of the views of other powers. This move resulted in huge damage both to relations between Europe and the US, and to the EU, which split badly (Gompert 2003:

43–9). The subsequent furore over the inflated claims made by the US and British governments to justify the war demonstrated the dangers of unilateralism. Iraq itself clearly posed no threat of WMD attacks on the West, and neither was any convincing connection made between Saddam's regime and al-Qaeda type terrorists. That connection, indeed, seems to have been created by the war and the subsequent occupation, which gave supporters of Saddam and supporters of Osama bin Laden both reason and opportunity to join causes in attacking the occupation regime. The shortcomings of the intelligence information used to justify the attack raised huge question marks over the whole strategy of pre-emption, amplifying fears of a rogue superpower using inadequate or wrong information to lash out militarily against anyone it didn't like (Daalder and Lindsay 2003: 167). The shift to justifying the war on the grounds of removing a brutal, aggressive and tyrannical regime just made things worse. Although hardly anyone disputed this characterization of the Iraqi dictatorship, the idea that the US claimed a generalized right to replace any nasty regime not to its liking pointed towards the wholesale abandonment of the post-colonial settlement on institutions of sovereign equality and non-intervention, and their replacement by an explicitly imperial regime of inequality and an imposed 'standard of civilization'.

9.4 Conclusions

What one can see from this account is the way in which some of the predispositions embedded in American exceptionalism, particularly those towards unilateralism, hypersecuritization and Manichean world-views, have been selected and amplified by the arrival first of the structural pressures of unipolarity, and then by the trauma of September 11. As a result of this conjuncture, these behaviours are effectively overdetermined and therefore potentially durable.

I say *potentially* durable because in politics nothing is fixed. The consequences of policies, especially excessive costs and unexpected negative results, can generate change even when the momentum behind a policy is strong. Wars, which seem a likely accompaniment to a more imperial US, are notorious for having unanticipated side effects that vastly outweigh the initial purposes for which actors entered into them, as was the case with the Vietnam War, and as may well turn out to be the case with Iraq. Already there are concerns within the US about the rising costs of unilateralism, both financial and political. The risk of overstretch in combining rising military expenditures with massive tax cuts in the context of a large current account deficit could generate major financial instabilities (Chace 2003: 3–4). In addition, and in sharp contrast to the first US war against

Iraq, Washington's unilateralism means that few other states are willing to help the US with the huge financial costs either of the war in Iraq or of the subsequent occupation. It is unclear for how long the American electorate will remain tolerant of high military expenditures on such wars and occupations, especially if the associated policies fail to deliver either a diminution of terrorism and American casualties or an onset of mild-mannered democracy in the Middle East and Southwest Asia. Also to be considered are the political costs, in which US politicians and public have to deal with being more disliked and more isolated than at any other point in the country's history. This negative feedback from friends and allies challenges, and may make more difficult to sustain, the country's virtuous image of itself and its claim to be the vanguard for the future of humankind.

Neither is it clear how quickly the present US policy could be undermined by sustained failure. The defeat of the Taleban in Afghanistan has not generated a democracy in that country and, as the local warlords and drug barons reassert their power, seems unlikely to do so. The outcome in Iraq remains to be seen, but at the time of writing (December 2003) the prospects do not look promising. The offensive liberalism of the Bush administration (Leffler 2003: 1047, 1055) – the idea that if the US installs democracy in currently authoritarian countries this will generate 'democratic peace' in the regions – seems deeply flawed. Never mind the huge difficulties of installing democracy from the outside and the false analogies with the democratization of Germany and Japan after 1945 (where total defeat was inflicted on the whole nation, not just on the government, and where society contained substantial traditions supportive of democracy). If, against the odds, the occupation regime succeeds in putting a genuine democracy in place in Iraq, it is likely either to break up the country or to produce a government that is just as hostile to Israel as Saddam was. Democracy (the practice of installing and removing governments by elections based on a wide franchise) is not the same as liberalism (the constitutional embedding and protection of individual rights against the state). Electoral practices are much easier to install than liberal ones, and it is liberalism that is the key to ideas about democratic peace. Democracy in illiberal societies can easily produce extremism. If the occupation does not succeed in installing a democracy, or finds that democracy simply produces another government it doesn't like, the US has either to leave behind another dictatorship or else to try to prolong itself in openly imperial fashion against increasing local resistance. As Gary Sick (2002: 6) rightly observes (and to its credit), the US is 'not going to be very good as an imperial power' among other things because it fails to see how insufferable others find its 'combination of might and righteousness'.

In addition to the (mis)fortunes of war, new, perhaps unrelated, and often unanticipated events can have powerful impacts either for or against the status quo, just as September 11 did. Economic downturns or political scandals could undermine the authority of the Bush administration. A new terrorist outrage could either reinforce existing policy or bring it into question.

In the Middle East, the neoconservative project to make the region safe for Israel and oil companies seems highly unlikely to succeed. Even using quite positive assumptions about the US occupation of Iraq, it cannot have a good outcome for the region in the absence of a reasonably just settlement between Israel and the Palestinians. The US's more or less unconditional support for Israel regardless of its policies makes the probability of such an outcome remote. As Prestowitz (2003: 194, 211–12) notes, 'Israel is something like a fifty-first state.' The well-placed influence of Jewish and Christian lobbies, which play powerfully into the separated powers structure of American politics, both prevents the US from putting much pressure on Israel and means that 'the space for debate on Israel is less in the United States than in Israel.' Given the deeply entrenched hostilities in the region, and the overdetermination of its many conflicts, it is perhaps unlikely that any US policy could bring peace and democracy there within the foreseeable future even if the US was not constrained in these ways (Buzan and Wæver 2003: part 3). In addition, the enhanced US military presence in the region destabilizes many states and fuels the fires of Islamic extremism. Together these impacts feed the dynamics of terrorism and reduce the chances of a successful outcome to the 'war on terrorism'.

Failure for the imperial turn in US foreign policy could occur not just in the Middle East but on the wider scale of the West. As argued at length in the preceding chapters, a US policy based on assumptions of a social structure of enemies and rivals risks becoming a self-fulfilling prophecy. The splits over the UN and Iraq have already done grave damage to the EU and Atlantic relations. Does the US want to stall and reverse the consolidation of the EU, particularly its ability to conduct a common foreign and security policy? Although few Europeans like to think about it, the US does have the capability to wreck the EU project, either through unintentional damage such as that caused by its campaign against the ICC, or through purposeful wrecking designed to prevent the rise of a peer competitor, or even a peer companion. Hoffmann (2003: 16–19) observes the rise of precisely such an intentional wrecking in the talk in Washington of 'disaggregating' the EU and the much more circumspect attitude since the invasion of Iraq in the Bush administration towards supporting European integration. The internal stability of the EU still rests significantly on 'keeping the US in', and if Washington

forced European countries to choose between it and the EU several countries, and the EU itself, would face a major political crisis. All of this was
demonstrated very clearly by the crisis over Iraq, which displayed the
ease with which the US could split Europe, and the inability of the EU to
make foreign policy (other than on trade issues) against the US (Gnesotto
2003b). There is a view that US–Europe tensions are a kind of game, like
the interminable crises of NATO during the Cold War, and therefore not
fundamentally serious. Nau (2002: 18), for example, argues that: 'America
is not ready for greater European influence. And so its rhetoric urging
Europe to spend more on defence is just as suspect as Europe's com-
plaints about American unilateralism. Neither ally really wants the consequence of what it is asking for. America doesn't want greater European
influence, and Europe doesn't want America not to lead – because then
it would have to lead on its own. The unilateral/multilateral debate is
convenient for both, and thus never goes away.' Yet as Cox (2003) points
out, and as is inherent in Kagan's (2002, 2003) thesis, the challenge from
a neo-imperial US is sufficiently fundamental to bring this complacency
into question. If militant unilateralism in Washington is sustained, rather
than just the passing aberration of a particular administration, the EU
could well face an existential challenge unprecedented in its history.

An imperial Washington that targets China as a potential threat to its
hegemony could pose similarly profound questions to Japan. Though the
signs so far are that Japan prefers to bandwagon with the sole superpower, strong and sustained Sino-US antagonism would put Japan in an
extremely uncomfortable front-line position. If Europe and Japan begin
to fear or oppose the US, some extremely hard choices would follow.
Should they begin to distance themselves from the US, rethinking their
bandwagoning posture and weakening the West as a coherent core? Or
should they accept a more naked, more military, and less consensual
form of hegemony, with implications of suzerainty in the requirement to
acknowledge that American power legitimates the US standing outside
and above the institutions that form the framework of multilateralism for
the rest of interstate society? If Japan and Europe start to break away
from their longstanding allegiance to Washington, the question for the
US is whether that would be seen as a catastrophic foreign policy failure
or as an acceptable price for freeing the US to use its power to impose its
vision of the good life on the rest of humankind.

While failure, or the prospect of it, might (or might not) turn US
policy, so also could those other strands of American exceptionalism that
are negatively affected by current US policy. The most obvious of these
is the powerful commitment to individual rights, the rule of law, and the
separation of powers which lie at the heart of the US constitution.
Hypersecuritization by definition empowers the state against civil society

and enables legal and civil rights to be overridden. In the past, American society has shown considerable tolerance for allowing national security claims to trump civil liberties. That was the case with the internment of American-Japanese during the Second World War, and with McCarthyism and the witch-hunts against alleged communists during the early years of the Cold War. But in the long run the claim for security cannot be sustained without destroying the core values it is supposed to protect. Here the question will be for how long, and in what ways, the 'war on terrorism' will serve US governments as a legitimate reason for restricting civil liberties. While one might expect that the demand for civil liberties will eventually become a countervailing pressure against hypersecuritization, the specifics of that development will be hostage to how that 'war' unfolds.

In a still useful summary of the US debate about grand strategy, Posen and Ross (1996–7) identified four general positions:

neo-isolationism: in which geography protects the US, and the four great powers are caught up by geography in a relatively self-contained Eurasian game of balance of power (assumption of rivals and potential enemies);
selective engagement: in which the US has actively to preserve the political division of Eurasia in order to avoid being dragged into great power wars, as in 1917, 1941 and 1947 (mainly an assumption of rivals);
cooperative security: in which the US plays a leadership role in pursuit of a liberal order (mainly an assumption of rivals and friends); and
primacy: in which the US gives priority to preserving its sole-superpower status, prevents the emergence of rivals, and seeks to embed the legitimacy and the force of its leadership at all levels (mainly an assumption of enemies and rivals).

Even with the addition of the 'war on terrorism' these positions define fairly durable policy options for the US, and as such all of them remain potentially in play. But the main choice over the previous decade has been between the last two. With the Bush administration, depending on one's point of view, there has either been a sharp turn away from the foreign policy drift theories of the 1990s (Kupchan 2002: 3–35) towards the primacy option (the 'Bush revolution in foreign policy'; Daalder and Lindsay 2003) or a making obvious of the existence of an 'American empire' that has been in the making for many decades (Bacevich 2002; Prestowitz 2003: 19–49). The extreme worry here is the danger of the Bush administration extending to global scale the style of interventionist military imperialism that it has practised in Central America and the Caribbean for more than a century (Bacevich 2002: 69–71). The idea that an American empire has been around for some time is a counterpoint to the more benign views of liberals such as Ikenberry (2001: 210–73; 2003) of the US as a liberal hegemon leading a broadly consensual international order. Either way, the concern is that the drift towards unilateralism, Manicheanism and hypersecuritization, accelerated under the Bush administration and its response to September 11, will perhaps quite quickly result in weakening the global position of the US by one or more of:

• pushing the US into imperial overstretch;
• exposing the reality of its imperial position and triggering balancing;
• undermining the consensual multilateralism on which the stability of its liberal hegemony depends.

As very many of the writers cited above have already pointed out, a neo-imperial US policy is likely to generate increasing resistance and rising costs. It is also likely to damage the alliances and institutions that the US will need if it is to realize many of its policy objectives, ranging from the 'war on terrorism', through the pursuit of a more peaceful Middle East, to the maintenance of an open world economy. The US may be number one, and it may be capable of defeating any and all comers militarily. It may also still have the most soft power resources (Nye 2002–3). But it is nowhere near powerful enough to impose its will on the world against resistance. As the history of the Soviet Union demonstrated with great clarity, military power can defeat, but it cannot be used to manage political, economic and social relations in the long run. Soft power by definition requires the promotion and maintenance of shared values, and disappears when values cease to be shared. Outside of the more extreme conservative circles there is a widespread view that the US will eventually have to rediscover multilateralism if it is to sustain its position and achieve its goals (Ikenberry 2001, 2003; Leffler 2003: 1062–3; Prestowitz 2003: 267–84; Joffe 2002: 178–80), or even (Kupchan 2002: 292–301) to achieve an orderly transition to a multipolar world.

10

Conclusions:
Where To From Here?

10.1 Summary

In the preceding chapters I have set out a structural approach to understanding and anticipating world politics. I have combined a radical revision of neorealist polarity theory with an interpretation of international social structure inspired by the English school and Wendt. I have argued that, while polarity and social structure can and do interact in powerful ways, they are essentially independent variables. The apparent determination of social structure by polarity in neorealist theory results from the fact that neorealist theory has built into it an assumption that the social structure is one of enemies and rivals. Using this framework, I have argued that the present power structure of one superpower and several great powers is the most likely to prevail during the next decade or two. An increase in the number of superpowers is difficult to imagine for at least a couple of decades. A decrease to zero superpowers could happen quite quickly if the US chose it, and although such a choice is imaginable it does not at present look like the most likely outcome. The all-great-power scenario contains a number of risks, some quite serious, and fear of these helps to sustain the present single-superpower structure.

The seeming durability of the polarity analysis drew attention to the social structure of the 1 + x system. Here the key insight was a disjuncture between the behaviour of the US, which was playing a game of enemies and rivals, and that of the other great powers, most of which appeared to be playing a game of rivals and friends. In the case of the EU and Japan, their internal commitment against playing a Westphalian game of power politics looked very deep, and this in itself was a major stabilizing element in the 1 + x structure. Because of their internal commitment, it would take a lot to turn them against the US, but such turnings were not unimaginable in the face of sustained unilateralism, Manicheanism and hypersecuritization by the US. Russia was too weak to matter much in this equation, and anyway seemed to have committed itself to association with the Western security community. China was a bigger question in the social equation. A case could be (and was) made that China was simply biding its time and keeping a low political profile while increasing its strength before launching itself as a rival superpower to the US. In this view, while its day-to-day behaviour was consonant with a game of rivals, its real underlying objective remained one of enemies. To hold to that case, however, required discounting or abandoning both a weight of present evidence and the expectation that engaging China with the market would in due course liberalize its internal society and politics. There is much immediate evidence that China is in many ways committing itself to participate in international society, both in East Asia (e.g. ARF and ASEAN + 3) and globally (e.g. WTO, NPT). It is also clear that generational change in China's political, economic and intellectual elites makes a difference. The cases of Japan, Taiwan and South Korea provide powerful support for the idea that engagement with the market does restructure society and politics, though it takes two or three generations to work its effects. Since China's continued rise to power depends on sustaining its engagement with international society, there is a strong contradiction between US expectations that a powerful China must be an enemy and the whole thrust of US policy towards China, which is to transform it through sustained liberal engagement while containing it during the transition period. On balance, even China does not make convincing supporting evidence for the US game of enemies and rivals against the great powers.

The big question highlighted by the combined polarity and social analysis was therefore about the danger that the disjuncture between the 'games' of the US and the great powers would not only undermine the benign elements in the present social structure but also accelerate change in the power structure. Most of the determining factors in this equation rested in the hands of the US. I painted a portrait of the present situation, suggesting that the turn in US foreign policy that started during the 1990s, and intensified with the Bush administration and its reactions to September 11, was nothing less than an assault on the international social structure built up mainly by the US over the previous half-century, and therefore a seismic shift in US grand strategy. The significance of this turn hangs on whether the changes in US foreign policy are superficial and transitory manifestations of a particularly radical and hard-line administration, or whether they represent a deeper upwelling in the American body politic that is likely to be enduring.

To address this question, I added on to the structural analysis of the international system a social structural analysis of US foreign policy, looking at the cumulative effect of American exceptionalism, unipolarity and September 11. I argued that these three factors generated a powerful momentum behind unilateralism, Manicheanism and hypersecuritization. The growth of US hostility to many of the IGOs and regimes that it led in creating predates the Bush administration and suggests a deeper drift away from Washington's former style of leadership (Crossette 2002). While the Bush administration was not responsible for these effects, it welcomed them and sought to exploit them to the maximum for its own ends. There was therefore a real risk that the turn in US foreign policy would be durable, making frighteningly plausible the scenario of the rogue superpower pulling down the very international society that it had laboured long to build up. If it succeeded in such wrecking, it would not only undo a quite unprecedented international social structure in which the risk of great powers playing classical games of balance and war with each other had fallen close to zero, but also jeopardize the social foundations of its own superpower status in the acceptance of its leadership by the EU and Japan. As Guzzini (2002: 296) rightly argues, 'US primacy that is not embedded in a legitimate world order undermines US security.' The stakes, therefore, are very high. In terms of immediate practical politics, the danger lies either in a second-term Bush administration that carries on along the same lines as the first or in a change of government, but where the incoming administration is sufficiently influenced by the same combination of American exceptionalism, unipolarity and September 11 that its foreign policy would be substantially indistinguishable from that of its predecessor. Both of these alternatives would suggest a durable shift in the centre of gravity of US domestic politics: the first because the Bush administration would be re-elected on its record; the second, even more convincingly, because the new consensus would be cross-party.

There remains, however, some room for manoeuvre. Although structural analyses often suggest a certain inevitability about events, it is clear that the domestic game within the US remains open. As Waltz observes, structures shove and shape, but they do not determine. The momentum behind US unilateralism, Manicheanism and hypersecuritization is indeed strong. But American exceptionalism contains other strands which pull against this turn, some of which (most obviously civil liberties) are very negatively affected by it. There is also the question of the contradiction between sustained unilateralism and the powerful American economic interest in maintaining an open global economy. Multilateralism and the running of global liberal trading and financial regimes are so closely connected that it is hard to imagine the latter being possible without the former, and it is far from clear that 'multilateralism a la carte' (Gerson 2000) will be a sustainable solution to this tension. A third possibility in the realm of immediate practical politics is therefore that a new American government with a better sense of the importance of multilateralism will take the reins in Washington. A congenital structuralist like myself takes the view that the costs of present US policy will be so great that Washington will sooner or later rediscover the wisdom and necessity of multilateralism. What the structuralist cannot say (viz. Waltz's problem about when balancing will return) is how long this will take to happen. Immediate choices are often buffeted by a host of random and/or local events that can push policy in one direction or another. Change could happen in 2004 as a result of the deeply misconceived occupation of Iraq turning into a disaster not only in itself, but also because, as seems likely, it inflames the problem of terrorism rather than helping to control and contain it. In such a case, the damage done to the EU and the West as a whole should be quickly recoverable. But if it takes two or three administrations for the (re)turn to happen, then the damage inflicted on international society might be so great as to take a generation to recover. On top of this, it is far from clear whether sustained terrorist attacks will reinforce or undermine American commitment to the current strategies of the 'war on terrorism'.

One useful way to think about the consequences of the US's imperial turn is in terms of its effects on the primary institutions of international society. By primary institutions I mean the deep, organically evolved, organizing principles and practices that constitute both states and international society (e.g. sovereignty, non-intervention, diplomacy, balance of power, international law, nationalism, equality of peoples) (Buzan 2004a: chaps 6, 8). Primary institutions lie beneath the instrumental, designed IGOs and regimes (secondary institutions) that states create to manage their relations. The key to this argument is the closely linked rise of multilateralism and the market as primary institutions of international society (OECD 1998: 80–1). These primary institutions, and their associated network of secondary institutions, have been a critical factor in the downgrading of the role of balance of power, alliances, anti-hegemonism and to a lesser extent war. If multilateralism is itself downgraded by sustained US attacks on it, then a resurgence of these older institutions is a likely result. It could reverse the decay of war as an institution, and halt or reverse the rise of multilateralism and international law. In extremis, it could put a huge strain on sovereignty and non-intervention by asserting a right to change regimes on grounds either of support for terrorism or of attempting to acquire weapons of mass destruction that might be used against the US. It could revive anti-hegemonic balance of power logic by casting the US more in the role of a threat than as a carrier of acceptable shared values. In this sense the accumulation of empirical evidence by neoliberal institutionalists that secondary institutions do facilitate co-operation under anarchy is highly relevant. It is not clear that the Bush administration recognizes this fact, and therefore understands the probable cumulative consequences of its actions. Nor is it clear how far the US can go in downgrading multilateralism without beginning to jeopardize the market, and whether powerful US corporate interests in sustaining the market therefore act as a brake on its unilateralism. One of the remarkable features of US leadership over the past half-century was its ability to build a consensual international order that was increasingly held together by calculation and belief rather than coercion, and which operated multilaterally through a host of mediating secondary institutions. Empires do not work that way. Coercion is their first tool and loyalty their first demand. If the US turns strongly and durably in this direction, then the consequences for the underlying fabric of international society will be negative, large and long-lasting.

10.2 Options

What, if anything, can the great powers do to save the US from itself before it wrecks the much valued institutional structures and deep friendships that are not just its major historical legacy of the last half-century but also the vindication of that part of American exceptionalism which sees the US as unique among great powers, and as having something special and important to contribute to human history? How should they respond to the US's drift towards 'offensive liberalism' and its seeming commitment, for reasons far more internal than external, to playing a game of enemies and rivals? Given the depth with which unipolarity and September 11 have embedded unilateralism, Manicheanism and hypersecuritization into US behaviour, is there anything they can do?

They certainly have the incentive to try. For one thing, the odds are strong that they are stuck with the 1 + 4 structure for quite some time to come, and therefore need to make the best of it. For another, as Ikenberry (2003: 7–12) has pointed out, there are many reasons for the great powers to prefer US leadership to any of the likely alternatives. Even discounting some of Ikenberry's rosier views about the consistency of US foreign policy, and the benefits of its 'voice opportunities', a lot remains. With all of its faults (including the disposition not to see that there are any faults), the US remains by far the most acceptable and benign candidate for leading power. Its historical, geographical, social and political assets make it both a valuable carrier of shared values and, by historical standards, relatively unthreatening to the other powers. It has a large accumulation

of historical goodwill which is closely tied both to the security and economic services it has supplied to Europe and Asia and to the institutional
way of conducting international relations that it has embedded within
international society during the twentieth century. Even China, despite
its repeated calls for a more multipolar world, benefits from US leadership, both in not having to settle its historical account with Japan and in
prospering on the basis of the US being willing to accept a huge and
unbalanced volume of its exports. There are, of course, many things to
complain about, from the stupidity of the Vietnam War and the 'war on
drugs', through the inconsistency of policy on nuclear proliferation and
environmental controls, to the appalling consequences of US support
for a variety of dictators in Latin America, the Middle East and Asia.
But on balance, unless one is wholly opposed to capitalism, there can be
no question that the US has been an astoundingly successful and con-
structive international leader over the last half-century and that there are
no candidates around that look capable of doing the job equally well or
better. Having no power do the job looks risky for the reasons argued in
chapter 8.

The great powers have two types of leverage that are unique to them:
they can try to change the polarity structure and they can change the
social structure. These are not mutually exclusive, and they can be played
either to pressure US behaviour from outside or to unseat the US as
leader. The great powers can also, as other states, try to change the
domestic debate with the US by using the 'voice opportunities' provided
by the separation of powers in the American political process.

In a strict neorealist and Kaganite view the only option for the great
powers is to change the distribution of power, either by bidding for
superpower status themselves (chapter 7) or by doing what they can
to push the US down from sole superpower to being one of the great
powers (chapter 8). As I have shown in these chapters, changing polarity
is fraught with dangers. Although a world with two or more superpowers
might actually be quite benign, it is a long way off. In addition, there is
a risk that a material challenge of this sort would trigger yet more
hypersecuritization as the US sought to preserve its sole superpower
status. This would be more the case if China was the challenger than the
EU, but even the EU scenario contains significant uncertainties about
how the US would respond. As noted, the US has the political option to
disrupt EU integration, and post Iraq may well be more minded to do so.
It also has the economic leverage to make a lot of trouble for the rise
of China (by closing its markets to Chinese exports). In the other direction, the great powers cannot do all that much to bring about a world
of only great powers. For that to happen, the US would have to give up
its superpower status, and, as shown, the dynamics of that are largely

internal. This scenario contains considerable dangers, and to make it stable would require that all of the great powers visibly and credibly renounce any aspiration to replace the US as the sole superpower. It would also require the development of ways of managing global problems within a political framework that would be dominated by regional spheres of influence.

Changing the social structure offers the great powers a wider range of options, adding choices about whether international society with a 1 + 4 polarity is constructed on the basis of being enemies, rivals or friends with the superpower. In principle, Europe and Japan have the option to withdraw friendship from the US. China could choose to play a harder game of rivals or even enemies, though its present inclination is to avoid as much as possible the risks of having the US focus on it as a challenger. The great powers could pay more attention to coordinating their policies so as to restrain or isolate the extremes of US unilateralism. Yet given the entanglements of military, economic, political, environmental and social interests between the great powers and the US, it is a moot point whether it would be any easier or faster to change the social structure in this drastic way than to change the material one. The particular US practices of the 'war on terrorism', for example, may foment much dissension, but the fact remains that the combination of nihilistic terrorism and WMD poses a serious threat to all of the powers. As has already been shown, many of the key variables are more in the control of the US than of the great powers, and in reality the role of the great powers may lie more in how they react to what the US does than in any plan designed and driven by one or more of them. It is the US that is changing course, and by doing so challenges the others about what sort of international society they will or will not tolerate. The main options for the great powers are already clear from the crisis over Iraq: to resist US unilateralism by denying it political and material support (as France, Germany and Russia initially did); to go along with the US in the hope of keeping multilateralism alive and of moderating its policy (most obviously the policy of Tony Blair, and more quietly of Japan); or to keep quiet and neither support nor oppose (often the position of China). The Bush administration has complicated the choices of the great powers with its extraordinarily extreme formulation that everyone who is not with the US is against it. That posture expresses an imperial demand for loyalty. It excludes the crucial democratic roles of loyal opposition and friendly critic, and it should be a first priority of the great powers to restore those roles. Blair was quite right that close friends of the US have special responsibilities in these difficult times, but quite wrong that the only function of friends is to go along with US policies in the hope of gaining some influence from within.

The key to how the scenarios unfold will be how the reactions of the great powers affect both US policy and the social structure of the single-superpower world. If the US continues down the path of unilateralism, Manicheanism and hypersecuritization, will the other powers eventually acquiesce, thus fulfilling the predictions of those in the US who justify unilateralism as leading international society from the front? Or will they eventually defect, start to see the US as more threatening than benign, and move towards positions of detachment or even opposition? It is not possible to predict when, or even if, such a turning point will occur. What can be said is that the question becomes more relevant the longer the US's offensive liberalism turn continues, and the more extreme its unilateralism, Manicheanism and hypersecuritization become. As Guzzini (2002: 291–4) notes, unilateralism amounts to an abandonment of diplomacy, and that abandonment is closely linked to the much commented upon militarization of US foreign policy discussed above. Dunne (2003) is even more alarmed, seeing US unilateralism as a fundamental rejection of international society and a move towards a hierarchical international system. Given the degree of institutional entanglement and shared interest between the US and the other great powers, not to mention the internal restraints within American society, it is almost impossible to imagine a return to classical military rivalry and balancing between the US and the great powers. For the great powers to see the US as an enemy would require excesses of US behaviour well beyond anything so far seen or mooted, and would involve a massive breakdown of the existing institutional structure of international society. But for the great powers to reject the legitimacy of US leadership is much more imaginable, and opens up a range of possible actions by which they might seek to restrain or contain its behaviour.

The problem of a 'rogue' US poses many of the same problems that come up in the consideration of how the US and the great powers should deal with a rising China. Like China, a rogue US can be confronted with elements of containment where its policies threaten others and elements of engagement attempting to influence its domestic debates and political structure to evolve in a more benign direction. Both aim at influencing the domestic political debates within the US, containment indirectly by raising the costs of certain behaviours, engagement directly by participation in US domestic debates. Bandwagoning with the US almost regardless of what it does in the hope of retaining some influence over its policy (the Blair strategy) is a third option, interestingly never discussed in relation to dealing with China.

In terms of containment, and pressuring US policy from the outside, there are two ways in which the great powers can raise the costs of the US. It is absolutely clear that the American public are not unanimous in support of the Bush administration's policies. Significant support for multilateralism, and opposition to NMD, exists among large sections of the American public and elite. The 'war on terrorism' picks up a general legitimacy from the reactions to September 11, but this support is in the longer run conditional on considerations of cost and effect. The great powers, and indeed other states, can play into this political equation by increasing the economic and material costs to the US of its unilateralism, and/or by decreasing the international legitimacy of US actions. In both cases the specific, immediate aim would be to affect the particular policy concerned, and the general, longer term one to change the balance of debate within the US away from unilateralism and back towards multilateralism.

The main way to raise costs to the US for its political and military unilateralism is for other states to refuse to participate in or help pay for the more extreme instances of US foreign policy. The differences between the first and second US-led wars on Iraq demonstrate some of the potential here, with Japan, Germany and some of the Gulf Arab states largely covering the cost of the first war, and the US having largely to cover the cost of the second out of its own pocket. Another example is from trade policy, where, for example, the EU effectively threatened to target its WTO-sanctioned tariffs (in retaliation for illegal US tariffs on steel) against electorally sensitive constituencies. Given the pressure on US budgets from existing deficits, such action turns the screw on the domestic debates in the US. On a case-by-case basis, such refusal can be done within the context of existing alliance structures without bringing them into question. Even that most committed of US allies, Britain, did not support the US during the Vietnam War.

Legitimacy can be affected on a case-by-case basis by actions ranging from abstention or voting against in international forums, to public statements of disapproval. There is scope here both for governments and for peoples. If Britain, for example, had said that it would not participate in the second invasion of Iraq unless there was a new UNSC resolution specifically authorizing such action, it could have had a substantial impact in degrading the legitimacy of the operation. Instead, Tony Blair went the route of trying to get moderating influence by going along with US unilateralism, and the act of delegitimization was carried out by large public demonstrations. A refusal by Britain to join in would have made some, but not all that much, difference to US capabilities to perform the mission, but it would have had a much bigger impact on the perceived legitimacy of that mission within the US. It remains to be discovered just how much influence outside opinion can have on the internal debates about US foreign policy, but in order to have any chance it is essential to reconstitute the roles of loyal opposition and critical friend. Accepting

Bush's 'with us or against us' simply casts critics as enemies and closes the door to friendly but critical engagement with US foreign policy-making. Individuals and NGOs have responsibilities here too, either to oppose their governments (as in Britain and Spain over Iraq) or to support them (as in France and Germany). Germany, the EU and Japan have less room for manoeuvre as 'critical friends' than Britain because expectations of their participation are lower. Expectations of France are also low because, although it has some capability to join in, it has a long record of contrarian position-taking in relation to US policy. At some point, sustained disaffection would bring alliances into question: one cannot remain allied to a country when there is widespread and general disagreement about policy. The threat to terminate alliances is a big move, and one that affects both cost and legitimacy considerations. Termination of alliances would be the ultimate statement of illegitimacy. As argued in part II, if Europe and/or Japan broke their alliance ties to the US that would have a major impact not just on the legitimacy of particular US actions, but also in its overall capability, and most especially on its ability to claim standing as the sole superpower.

In terms of direct engagement, one obvious target for outsiders is to attempt to undo some of the effects of September 11 that have accelerated the US's turn towards offensive liberalism. Intensified and well-publicized international collaboration to reduce the threat from the linkage between al-Qaeda type terrorists and WMD would address this opportunity, and up to a point is being done through upgrading and coordinating intelligence and police counter-terrorist activities. Another way forward on this is to strengthen the international regimes that work against the spread of nuclear, chemical and biological weapons. But even this is not straightforward. One peculiar aspect of recent US unilateralism is that it has acted specifically to weaken the operation of regimes addressing chemical and biological weapons and trade in small arms, thus shutting off one avenue by which its insecurities might be collectively addressed. And as illustrated by the war against Iraq, a more general difficulty arises over deep differences of opinion both about the connections between so-called rogue states and terrorism, and about the distinction between al-Qaeda type terrorism and more localized struggles over political status and particular pieces of territory such as Israel/Palestine. To the extent that the US view of the 'war on terrorism' involves carte blanche rights of pre-emptive intervention and regime change, it expresses more the problem of US unilateralism, Manicheanism and hypersecuritization than the common ground of anti-terrorism. This is especially so where supposed anti-terrorist activities become entangled with other, more controversial US policy interests such as oil and Israel, as they do in much of the Middle East (Ortega 2003). Where this is the case, the 'war on terrorism' shifts from reflecting a shared interest between the US and the great powers to defining some of the key issues that put them at odds. The great powers can act here, but they need to keep extremely clear the distinction between their shared interest with the US and the issues where they oppose it. The shared interest is in dealing with nihilistic extremists who threaten the whole fabric of international society. The opposition is to unacceptable acts of US extremism whose main effect is to fill the recruiting offices of al-Qaeda, and to undermine the credibility of Western governments by exposing them as either liars or incompetents.

More generally, the great powers (and others) have some scope for trying to change the self-image of the US as the sole superpower. For the reasons already argued, this is not, and should not be, a question about supporting or opposing US leadership per se. US leadership is necessary and in many ways desirable, so the issue is about the form, style and substance of the leadership, not about the fact of it. This distinction needs to be prominent in the rhetoric of the great powers, and the frequent French practice of failing to make it needs to be relentlessly opposed. The great powers need to make clear their principled acceptance of US leadership at the same time as rejecting the project of the Bush administration to seek unfettered freedom of action for itself. They need to make clear that a US pursuit of dominance will be seen as threatening and responded to as such. They have to put on the table in explicit fashion that, while there are many deep values that they share with the US, they do not accept that the US is always and everywhere right, just, or in possession of the perfect model for the future of humankind. They need to confront the US both with the necessity and the desirability of its leadership, and with the fact that excesses of paranoia (hypersecuritization), crusading moralism (Manicheanism) and egotism (unilateralism) by the US threaten the good functioning and stability of international society. President Bush actually had the right idea with his initial talk about a humbler US foreign policy, but lost the plot in overreacting to September 11. The tone of this engagement needs to be friendly but firm, and the substance of it needs to be backed up with generous economic, military and political support for consensual projects and equally stiff imposition of material and political costs when the US itself becomes the problem.

A project along these lines might perhaps be helped from within by the probability that, as many American writers observe, the US will not be much good at being an imperial power. The practice of empire will expose the same contradictions with its domestic democracy for the US as it did earlier for Britain. Empire requires acceptance of unequal political and human status, an ability to use force ruthlessly against civilians in a sustained way, and a will to pay a heavy economic price for imperial prestige and splendour, none of which will sit easily with American values.

To the extent that the legitimacy of a new US imperialism is tied to the imposed democratization of foreign lands, that project is likely to fail. Except for the very special circumstances of Germany and Japan after the Second World War, the US record in exporting democracy is largely dismal, whether in Central America and the Caribbean, South America, the Middle East or Asia. Failure in the current round should help to undermine the legitimacy of the imperial project within the US.

In sum, the great powers are not helpless in the face of the US. They do have a range of options other than bandwagoning or balancing with which to respond. Some of these are fairly drastic and long-term, but there are also substantial things in the middle range. They might, in particular, be able to influence the evolution of policy debates within the US by adopting a conscious policy of rejecting US leadership from the front where they disagree with the action being taken, and in so doing raise the costs of unilateralism to Washington both in material and in political terms. It remains to be seen whether widening opposition abroad will have any impact on the strongly embedded self-belief within the US about its own essential virtue. As Daalder and Lindsay (2003: 80, 194) argue, the Bush administration used September 11 to reinforce their view of the US as 'a uniquely just and beneficent great power', and reacted with incomprehension to the idea that peoples and countries abroad could hate or fear it. Only friends have any hope of influencing that belief, which puts a particular burden on Britain. I believe that US leadership in the half-century up to 2000, even with all of its faults and mistakes taken into account, had a broadly benign effect on the development of international society unprecedented in the annals of history. Those who share this belief have a powerful moral obligation to oppose the current turn in US policy which threatens to undo this legacy. Perhaps the best way to do that is to get some purchase on the domestic debates within the US by making plain the degree to which its current policies undermine its vision of itself as the future of humankind. The price for this in the short term might be a variety of punishments from the US of the kind mooted for France and Germany after their opposition to the second invasion of Iraq. But only if there is a willingness to accept the short-term risks of such costs will there be much hope of eventually deflecting the US from the path of unilateralism, Manicheanism and hypersecuritization down which unipolarity and September 11 have driven it.

The great powers do matter in twenty-first century world politics. There is a big difference between a world with one superpower and then only regional powers and one with several great powers alongside the superpower. In terms of capabilities, the great powers play a major role in shaping both the present power structure and the alternatives to it. In terms of identity, the great powers make an important input into whether the social structure is one of enemies, rivals or friends, and therefore into the character of international society. On both of these counts, the great powers have choices about whether to pull the props from US super-powerdom or work to keep them in place. We are not, therefore, in a unipolar world in the simple sense in which some neorealists and many politicians and political pundits would have us believe. We are in a more complicated world than that, and the existence of great powers alongside the superpower creates both opportunities and responsibilities to shape the direction in which world politics unfolds in the coming decades.

References

Adler, Emanuel, and Michael N. Barnett (eds) (1998) *Security Communities*. Cambridge: Cambridge University Press.

Ambrosio, Thomas (2001) 'Russia's Quest for Multipolarity: A Response to US Foreign Policy in the Post-Cold War Era'. *European Security*, 10 (1), 45–67.

Anderson, Benedict (1983) *Imagined Communities: Reflections on the Origin and Spread of Nationalism*. London: Verso.

Arrighi, Giovanni, and Beverly J. Silver (2001) 'Capitalism and World (Dis)order'. In Michael Cox, Tim Dunne and Ken Booth (eds), *Empires, Systems and States: Great Transformations in International Politics*. Cambridge: Cambridge University Press, 257–79.

Ash, Timothy Garton (2002) 'The Peril of Too Much Power'. *New York Times*, 9 April.

Bacevich, Andrew J. (2002) *American Empire: The Realities and Consequences of U.S. Diplomacy*. Cambridge, MA: Harvard University Press.

Bender, Peter (2003) 'America: The New Roman Empire?'. *Orbis*, Winter, 145–59.

Berger, Thomas U. (1993) 'From Sword to Chrysanthemum: Japan's Culture of Anti-Militarism'. *International Security*, 17 (4), 119–50.

Bobrow, Davis B. (2001) 'Visions of (In)Security and American Strategic Style'. *International Studies Perspectives*, 2 (1), 1–12.

Bolton, John R. (2000) 'Unilateralism is Not Isolationism'. In Gwyn Prins (ed.), *Understanding Unilateralism in American Foreign Relations*. London: RIIA, 50–82.

Bracken, Paul (1994) 'The Military Crisis of the Nation State: Will Asia be Different from Europe?'. *Political Studies*, 42 (Special Issue), 97–114.

Brown, Bartram S. (2002) 'Unilateralism, Multilateralism and the International Criminal Court'. In Stewart Patrick and Shepard Forman (eds), *Multilateralism in U.S. Foreign Policy*. Boulder, CO: Lynne Rienner, 323–44.

Brown, Chris (1995) 'International Political Theory and the Idea of World Community'. In Ken Booth and Steve Smith (eds), *International Political Theory Today*. Cambridge: Cambridge University Press, 90–109.

Buchan, David (1993) *Europe: The Strange Superpower*. Aldershot: Dartmouth.

Bueno de Mesquita, Bruce (1975) 'Measuring Systemic Polarity'. *Journal of Conflict Resolution*, 19 (1), 187–216.

Bull, Hedley (1977) *The Anarchical Society*. London: Macmillan.

Bull, Hedley (1984) *Justice in International Relations*. Waterloo, Ontario: University of Waterloo [Hagey Lectures].

Bull, Hedley, and Adam Watson (eds) (1984) *The Expansion of International Society*. Oxford: Oxford University Press.

Bush, George W. (2001) 'Remarks by the President to Students and Faculty at National Defence University'. Washington, DC: White House, Office of the Press Secretary, 1 May.

Bush, George W. (2002) *The National Security Strategy of the United States of America*. Washington, DC: White House, September.

Buzan, Barry (1984) 'Economic Structure and International Security: The Limits of the Liberal Case'. *International Organization*, 38 (4), 597–624.

Buzan, Barry (1987) *An Introduction to Strategic Studies*. London: Macmillan.

Buzan, Barry (1988) 'Japan's Future: Old History versus New Roles'. *International Affairs*, 64 (4), 557–73.

Buzan, Barry ([1983] 1991a) *People, States and Fear: An Agenda for International Security Studies in the Post-Cold War Era*. 2nd edn, Hemel Hempstead: Harvester Wheatsheaf.

Buzan, Barry (1991b) 'New Patterns of Global Security in the Twenty-First Century'. *International Affairs*, 67 (3), 431–51.

Buzan, Barry (1996) 'International Security in East Asia in the 21st Century: Options for Japan'. *Dokkyo International Review*, 9, 281–314.

Buzan, Barry (1998) 'The Asia Pacific: What Sort of Region in What Sort of World?'. In Anthony McGrew and Christopher Brook (eds), *Asia-Pacific in the New World Order*. London: Routledge, 68–87.

Buzan, Barry (2002) 'South Asia Moving Towards Transformation: Emergence of India as a Great Power'. *International Studies*, 39 (1), 1–24.

Buzan, Barry (2004a) *From International to World Society: English School Theory and the Social Structure of Globalisation*. Cambridge: Cambridge University Press.

Buzan, Barry (forthcoming 2004b) 'The Security Dynamics of a 1 + 4 World'. In Ersel Aydinli and James N. Rosenau (eds), *Paradigms in Transition: Globalization, Security and the Nation State*. New York: SUNY Press.

Buzan, Barry (2004c) 'Conclusions: How and to Whom Does China Matter?'. In Barry Buzan and Rosemary Foot (eds), *Does China Matter?* London: Routledge, chap. 10.

Buzan, Barry, and Rosemary Foot (eds) (2004) *Does China Matter?* London: Routledge.

Buzan, Barry, and Richard Little (2000) *International Systems in World History: Remaking the Study of International Relations*. Oxford: Oxford University Press.

Buzan, Barry, and Gerald Segal (1994) 'Rethinking East Asian Security'. *Survival*, 36 (2), 3–21.

Buzan, Barry, and Ole Wæver (2003) *Regions and Powers: The Structure of International Security*. Cambridge: Cambridge University Press.

Buzan, Barry, Charles Jones and Richard Little (1993) *The Logic of Anarchy*. New York: Columbia University Press.

Buzan, Barry, Ole Wæver and Jaap de Wilde (1998) *Security: A New Framework for Analysis*. Boulder, CO: Lynne Rienner.

Calleo, David (1996) 'Restarting the Marxist Clock? The Economic Fragility of the West'. *World Policy Journal*, 13 (2), 57–64.

Calleo, David (1999) 'The United States and the Great Powers'. *World Policy Journal*, 16 (3), 11–19.

Campbell, David (1992) *Writing Security: United States Foreign Policy and the Politics of Identity*. Manchester: Manchester University Press.

Carpenter, Ted Galen (1991) 'The New World Disorder'. *Foreign Policy*, 84, 24–39.

Cederman, Lars-Erik (1994) 'Emergent Polarity: Analyzing State-Formation and Power Politics'. *International Studies Quarterly*, 38 (4), 501–33.

Cerny, Philip (1995) 'Globalization and the Changing Logic of Collective Action'. *International Organization*, 49 (4), 595–625.

Cerny, Phil (2000) 'The New Security Dilemma: Divisibility, Defection and Disorder in the Global Arena'. *Review of International Studies*, 26 (4), 623–46.

Chace, James (2003) 'Present at the Destruction: The Death of American Internationalism'. *World Policy Journal*, Spring, 1–5.

Chan, Steve (1997) 'In Search of Democratic Peace: Problems and Promise'. *Mershon International Studies Review*, 41 (1), 59–91.

Clark, Ian (1999) *Globalization and International Relations Theory*. Oxford: Oxford University Press.

Cochran, Molly (1999) *Normative Theory in International Relations: A Pragmatic Approach*. Cambridge: Cambridge University Press.

Cohen, Raymond (1994) 'Pacific Unions: A Reappraisal of the Theory that Democracies Do not Go to War with Each Other'. *Review of International Studies*, 20 (3), 207–23.

Cohen, Raymond (1995a) 'In the Beginning: Diplomatic Negotiation in the Ancient Near East'. Paper presented to the ECPR-SGIR Conference, Paris, September [37pp].

Cohen, Raymond (1995b) 'Diplomacy 2000 BC–2000 AD'. Paper presented to British International Studies Association Conference, Southampton, December [16pp].

Cohen, Raymond (1998) 'The Great Tradition: The Spread of Diplomacy in the Ancient World'. Paper presented at the Hebrew University, Jerusalem, July [17pp].

Cooper, Robert (1996) *The Postmodern State and the World Order*. London: Demos [Paper no. 19].

Cox, Michael (2003) 'Commentary: Martians and Venutians in the New World Order'. *International Affairs*, 79 (3), 523–32.

Cronin, Bruce (1999) *Community Under Anarchy: Transnational Identity and the Evolution of Cooperation*. New York: Columbia University Press.

Crossette, Barbara (2002) 'Killing One's Progeny: America and the United Nations'. *World Policy Journal*, Fall, 54–9.

Daalder, Ivo H., and James M. Lindsay (2003) *America Unbound: The Bush Revolution in Foreign Policy*. Washington, DC: Brookings Institution Press.

Deudney, Daniel (1995) 'The Philadelphia System: Sovereignty, Arms Control, and Balance of Power in American States Union, circa 1789–1861'. *International Organization*, 49 (2), 191–229.

Deutsch, Karl W., and J. David Singer (1964) 'Multipolar Systems and International Stability'. *World Politics*, 16, 390–406.

Deutsch, Karl W., Sidney A. Burrell, Robert A. Kann, Maurice Lee Jr., Martin Lichterman, Raymond E. Lindgren, Francis L. Loewenheim and Richard W. van Wagenen (1957) *Political Community and the North Atlantic Area: International Organization in the Light of Historical Experience*. Princeton, NJ: Princeton University Press.

Dibb, Paul (1988) *The Soviet Union: The Incomplete Superpower*. Basingstoke: Macmillan.

Doyle, Michael (1986) 'Liberalism and World Politics'. *American Political Science Review*, 80 (4), 1151–69.

Drifte, Reinhard (2000) 'US Impact on Japanese–Chinese Security Relations'. *Security Dialogue*, 31 (4), 449–62.

Dunne, Tim (2003) 'Society and Hierarchy in International Relations'. *International Relations*, 17 (3), 303–20.

Dunne, Tim, and Nicholas Wheeler (1996) 'Hedley Bull's Pluralism of the Intellect and Solidarism of the Will'. *International Affairs*, 72 (1), 91–107.

Elliott, Kimberly Ann, and Gary Clyde Hufbauer (2002) 'Ambivalent Multilateralism and the Emerging Backlash: The IMF and WTO'. In Stewart Patrick and Shepard Forman (eds), *Multilateralism in U.S. Foreign Policy*. Boulder, CO: Lynne Rienner, 377–413.

Fairbank, John King (1968) *The Chinese World Order: Traditional China's Foreign Relations*. Cambridge, MA: Harvard University Press.

Foot, Rosemary (2001) 'Chinese Power and the Idea of a Responsible State'. *China Journal*, 45, 1–19.

Forman, Shepard (2002) 'Multilateralism as a Matter of Fact: U.S. Leadership and the Management of the International Public Sector'. In Stewart Patrick and Shepard Forman (eds), *Multilateralism in U.S. Foreign Policy*. Boulder, CO: Lynne Rienner, 437–60.

Freedman, Lawrence (1999) 'The New Great Power Politics'. In Alexei G. Arbatov, Karl Kaiser and Robert Legvold (eds), *Russia and the West: The 21st Century Security Environment*. Armonk, NY: East–West Institute, 21–43.

Friedberg, Aaron L. (1993) 'Ripe for Rivalry: Prospects for Peace in a Multipolar Asia'. *International Security*, 18 (3), 5–33.

Gaddis, John Lewis (1992–3) 'International Relations Theory and the End of the Cold War'. *International Security*, 17 (3), 5–58.

Galtung, Johan (1973) *European Community: A Superpower in the Making*. London: Allen & Unwin.

Gerson, Allan (2000) 'Multilateralism a la Carte: The Consequences of Unilateral "Pick and Pay" Approaches'. *European Journal of International Law*, 11 (1), 61–6.

Gilpin, Robert (1981) *War and Change in World Politics*. Cambridge: Cambridge University Press.

Gilpin, Robert (1987) *The Political Economy of International Relations*. Princeton, NJ: Princeton University Press.

Gnesotto, Nicole (2003a) 'After Copenhagen: Abandoning the Fiction'. *European Union Institute for Security Studies Newsletter*, 5, January, 1, 4.

Gnesotto, Nicole (2003b) 'EU, US: Visions of the World, Visions of the Other'. In Gustav Lindstrom (ed.), *Shift or Rift: Assessing US–EU Relations After Iraq*. Paris: European Union Institute for Security Studies, 21–42.

Goldgeier, James M., and Michael, McFaul (1992) 'A Tale of Two Worlds: Core and Periphery in the Post-Cold War Era'. *International Organization*, 46 (2), 467–91.

Gompert, David C. (2003) 'What Does America Want of Europe?'. In Gustav Lindstrom (ed.), *Shift or Rift: Assessing US–EU Relations After Iraq*. Paris: European Union Institute for Security Studies, 43–75.

Graham, Thomas Jr., and Damien La Vera (2002) 'Nuclear Weapons: The Comprehensive Test Ban Treaty and National Missile Defense'. In Stewart Patrick and Shepard Forman (eds), *Multilateralism in U.S. Foreign Policy*. Boulder, CO: Lynne Rienner, 225–45.

Guttman, Robert J. (ed.) (2001) *Europe in the New Century: Visions of an Emerging Superpower*. Boulder, CO: Lynne Rienner.

Guzzini, Stefano (1993) 'Structural Power: The Limits of Neorealist Analysis'. *International Organization*, 47 (3), 443–78.

Guzzini, Stefano (1998) *Realism in International Relations and International Political Economy: The Continuing Story of a Death Foretold*. London: Routledge.

Guzzini, Stefano (2002) 'Foreign Policy Without Diplomacy: The Bush Administration at a Crossroads'. *International Relations*, 16 (2), 291–7.

Haas, Michael (1970) 'International Sub-Systems: Stability and Polarity'. *American Political Science Review*, 64 (1), 98–123.

Haass, Richard N. (1999) 'What to Do with American Primacy'. *Foreign Affairs*, Sept./Oct. <http://uwadmnweb.uwyo.edu/Pols/online/Schenker/200001/HaassAmericanPrimacy.html>.

Hansen, Birthe (2000) *Unipolarity and the Middle East*. Richmond, Surrey: Curzon Press.

Hassner, Pierre (2002) *The United States: The Empire of Force or the Force of Empire?* Paris: European Union Institute for Security Studies [Chaillot Papers no. 54].

Held, David, Anthony McGrew, David Goldblatt and Jonathan Perraton (1999) *Global Transformation: Politics, Economics and Culture*. Cambridge: Polity.

Hendrickson, David C. (2002) 'Towards Universal Empire: The Dangerous Quest for Absolute Security'. *World Policy Journal*, Fall, 1–10.

Herz, John (1969) 'The Territorial State Revisited'. In James N. Rosenau (ed.), *International Politics and Foreign Policy*. New York: Free Press, 76–89.

Hinton, Harold C. (1975) *Three and a Half Powers: The New Balance in Asia*. Bloomington: Indiana University Press.

Hirst, Paul, and Grahame Thompson (1996) *Globalization in Question: The International Economy and the Possibilities of Governance*. Cambridge: Polity.

Hodge, Carl Cavanagh (1998–9) 'Europe as a Great Power: A Work in Progress?'. *International Journal*, 53 (3), 487–504.

Hoffmann, Stanley (1981) 'Security in an Age of Turbulence: Means of Response'. In *Adelphi Paper 167, Third World Conflict and International Security*, part II. London: IISS, 1–18.

Hoffmann, Stanley (2003) 'The Crisis in Transatlantic Relations'. In Gustav Lindstrom (ed.), *Shift or Rift: Assessing US–EU Relations After Iraq*. Paris: European Union Institute for Security Studies, 13–20.

Hollis, Martin, and Steve Smith (1990) *Explaining and Understanding International Relations*. Oxford: Oxford University Press.

Holsti, Kalevi J. (2002) 'The Institutions of International Politics: Continuity, Change, and Transformation'. Paper presented at the ISA Convention, New Orleans, March [62pp].

Hopf, Ted (1991) 'Polarity, the Offense–Defense Balance, and War'. *American Political Science Review*, 85 (2), 475–93.

Howes, Dustin Ellis (2003) 'When States Choose to Die: Reassessing Assumptions About What States Want'. *International Studies Quarterly*, 47 (4), 669–92.

Huntington, Samuel P. (1991) 'America's Changing Strategic Interests'. *Survival*, 33 (1), 35–6.

Huntington, Samuel P. (1993) 'Why International Primacy Matters'. *International Security*, 17 (4), 68–83.

Huntington, Samuel P. (1996) *The Clash of Civilizations and the Remaking of World Order*. New York: Simon & Schuster.

Huntington, Samuel P. (1999) 'The Lonely Superpower'. *Foreign Affairs*, 78 (2), 35–49.

Hurd, Ian (1999) 'Legitimacy and Authority in International Politics'. *International Organization*, 53 (2), 379–408.

IISS (2002) *The Military Balance 2002–2003*. London: International Institute for Strategic Studies.

Ikenberry, G. John (2001) *After Victory: Institutions, Strategic Restraint and the Rebuilding of Order After Major Wars*. Princeton, NJ: Princeton University Press.

Ikenberry, G. John (2002a) 'Multilateralism and U.S. Grand Strategy'. In Stewart Patrick and Shepard Forman (eds), *Multilateralism in U.S. Foreign Policy*. Boulder, CO: Lynne Rienner, 121–40.

Ikenberry, G. John (2002b) 'Introduction' and 'Conclusion'. In G. John Ikenberry (ed.), *America Unrivalled: The Future of the Balance of Power*. Ithaca, NY: Cornell University Press, 1–26, 284–310.

Ikenberry, G. John (2003) 'Strategic Reactions to American Preeminence: Great Power Politics in the Age of Unipolarity'. <www.odci.gov/nic/pubs/conference_reports/Ikenberry.htm>.

Jackson, Robert (2000) *The Global Covenant: Human Conduct in a World of States*. Oxford: Oxford University Press.

Jacobson, Harold K. (2002) 'Climate Change: Unilateralism, Realism, and Two-Level Games'. In Stewart Patrick and Shepard Forman (eds), *Multilateralism in U.S. Foreign Policy*. Boulder, CO: Lynne Rienner, 415–34.

James, Patrick, and Michael Brecher (1988) 'Stability and Polarity: New Paths for Enquiry'. *Journal of Peace Research*, 25 (1), 31–42.

Jervis, Robert (1993) 'International Primacy: Is the Game Worth the Candle?'. *International Security*, 17 (4), 52–67.

Job, Brian L. (1999) 'Managing Rising and Declining Powers'. Paper presented at the workshop on Security Order in the Asia-Pacific, East-West Center, Honolulu.

Joffe, Josef (2001) 'Clinton's World: Purpose, Policy and Weltanschauung'. *Washington Quarterly*, 24 (1), 141–54.

Joffe, Josef (2002) 'Defying History and Theory: The United States as the "Last Remaining Superpower"'. In G. John Ikenberry (ed.), *America Unrivalled: The Future of the Balance of Power*. Ithaca, NY: Cornell University Press, 155–80.

Johnston, Alastair Iain (2003) 'Is China a Status Quo Power?'. *International Security*, 27 (4), 5–56.

Kagan, Donald, Gary Schmitt and Thomas Donnelly (2000) *Rebuilding America's Defenses: Strategy, Forces and Resources for a New Century*. Washington, DC: Project for the New American Century.

Kagan, Robert (2002) 'Power and Weakness'. *Policy Review*, 113, 1–29.

Kagan, Robert (2003) *Paradise and Power: America and Europe in the New World Order*. London: Atlantic Books.

Kaldor, Mary (1990) *The Imaginary War: Understanding the East–West Conflict*. Oxford: Blackwell.

Kang, Dave (1995) 'The Middle Road: Security and Cooperation in Northeast Asia'. Unpublished MS, Dartmouth College, Hanover, NH, July 6.

Kang, Dave (2000) 'Culture, Hierarchy and Stability in Asian International Relations'. Unpublished MS, Dartmouth College, Hanover, NH [42pp].

Kang, Dave (2003) 'Getting Asia Wrong: The Need for New Analytical Frameworks'. *International Security*, 27 (4), 57–85.

Kaplan, Morton (1957) *System and Process in International Politics*. New York: John Wiley.

Kapstein, Ethan B. (1999) 'Does Unipolarity Have a Future?'. In Ethan B. Kapstein and Michael Mastanduno (eds), *Unipolar Politics: Realism and State Strategies After the Cold War*. New York: Columbia University Press, 464–90.

Kapstein, Ethan B., and Michael Mastanduno (eds) (1999) *Unipolar Politics: Realism and State Strategies After the Cold War*. New York: Columbia University Press.

Karns, Margaret P., and Karen A. Mingst (2002) 'The United States as "Deadbeat"? U.S. Policy and the UN Financial Crisis'. In Stewart Patrick and Shepard Forman (eds), *Multilateralism in U.S. Foreign Policy*. Boulder, CO: Lynne Rienner, 267–94.

Katzenstein, Peter J. (1996) 'Introduction: Alternate Perspectives on National Security'. In Peter J. Katzenstein (ed.), *The Culture of National Security: Norms and Identity in World Politics*. New York: Columbia University Press, 1–32.

Katzenstein, Peter J., and Nobou Okawara (1993) 'Japan's National Security: Structures, Norms, Policies'. *International Security*, 17 (4), 84–118.

Keene, Edward (2002) *Beyond the Anarchical Society: Grotius, Colonialism and Order in World Politics*. Cambridge: Cambridge University Press.

Kegley, Charles W., and Gregory Raymond (1992) 'Must We Fear a Post-Cold War Multipolar System?'. *Journal of Conflict Resolution*, 36 (3), 573–85.

Kegley, Charles W., and Gregory Raymond (1994) *A Multipolar Peace? Great Power Politics in the 21st Century*. New York: St Martin's Press.

Kennedy, Paul (1989) *The Rise and Fall of the Great Powers*. London: Fontana.

Keohane, Robert O. (1984) *After Hegemony: Cooperation and Discord in the World Political Economy*. Princeton, NJ: Princeton University Press.

Keohane, Robert O. (ed.) (1986) *Neorealism and its Critics*. New York: Columbia University Press.

Keohane, Robert O. (1988) 'International Institutions: Two Approaches'. *International Studies Quarterly*, 32 (4), 379–96.

Keohane, Robert O. (1995) 'Hobbes' Dilemma and Institutional Change in World Politics: Sovereignty in International Society'. In Hans-Henrik Holm and Georg Sørensen (eds), *Whose World Order*. Boulder, CO: Westview Press, 165–86.

Keohane, Robert O., and Joseph S. Nye (1977) *Power and Interdependence*. Boston: Little, Brown.

Kindleberger, Charles P. (1973) *The World in Depression 1929–39*. London: Allen Lane.

Kindleberger, Charles P. (1981) 'Dominance and Leadership in the International Economy'. *International Studies Quarterly*, 25 (2/3), 242–54.

Kokaz, Nancy (2001) 'Between Anarchy and Tyranny: Excellence and the Pursuit of Power and Peace in Ancient Greece'. In Michael Cox, Tim Dunne and Ken Booth (eds), *Empires, Systems and States: Great Transformations in International Politics*. Cambridge: Cambridge University Press, 91–118.

Krasner, Stephen D. (1995) 'Power Politics, Institutions and Transnational Relations'. In Thomas Risse-Kappen (ed.), *Bringing Transnational Relations Back In*. Cambridge: Cambridge University Press, 257–79.

Kratochwil, Friedrich (1989) *Rules, Norms and Decisions: On the Conditions of Practical and Legal Reasoning in International Relations and Domestic Affairs*. Cambridge: Cambridge University Press.

Krauthammer, Charles (2001) 'Unilateralism is the Key to our Success'. *Guardian Weekly*, 22 December.

Kull, Steven (2002) 'Public Attitudes Towards Multilateralism'. In Stewart Patrick and Shepard Forman (eds), *Multilateralism in U.S. Foreign Policy*. Boulder, CO: Lynne Rienner, 99–120.

Kupchan, Charles A. (1998) 'After Pax Americana: Benign Power, Regional Integration, and the Sources of Stable Multipolarity'. *International Security*, 23 (2), 40–79.

Kupchan, Charles A. (2002) *The End of the American Era: US Foreign Policy and the Geopolitics of the Twenty-First Century*. New York: Alfred Knopf.

Lake, David A. (1999) 'Ulysses's Triumph: American Power and the New World Order'. *Security Studies*, 8 (4), 44–78.

Lake, David A., and Patrick M. Morgan (eds) (1997) *Regional Orders: Building Security in a New World*. University Park: Pennsylvania State University Press.

Layne, Christopher (1993) 'The Unipolar Illusion: Why Other Great Powers Will Rise'. *International Security*, 17 (4), 5–51.

Layne, Christopher (1997) 'From Preponderance to Offshore Balancing: America's Future Grand Strategy'. *International Security*, 22 (1), 86–124.

Leffler, Melvyn P. (2003) '9/11 and the Past and Future of American Foreign Policy'. *International Affairs*, 79 (5), 1045–63.

Legro, Jeffrey W. (2000) 'Whence American Internationalism'. *International Organization*, 54 (2), 253–89.

Lepgold, Joseph, and Timothy McKeown (1995) 'Is American Foreign Policy Exceptional? An Empirical Analysis'. *Political Science Quarterly*, 110 (3), 369–84.

Lindley-French, Julian (2002) *Terms of Engagement: The Paradox of American Power and the Transatlantic Dilemma Post-11 September*. Paris: European Union Institute for Security Studies [Chaillot Papers no. 52].

Lipschutz, Ronnie D. (2002) 'The Clash of Governmentalities: The Fall of the UN Republic and America's Reach for Imperium'. Unpublished MS, University of California, Santa Cruz, September 29.

Lipset, Seymour Martin (1996) *American Exceptionalism: A Double-Edged Sword*. New York: W.W. Norton.

Lyman, Princeton N. (2002) 'The Growing Influence of Domestic Factors'. In Stewart Patrick and Shepard Forman (eds), *Multilateralism in U.S. Foreign Policy*. Boulder, CO: Lynne Rienner, 75–97.

Mahbubani, Kishore (1995) 'The Pacific Impulse'. *Survival*, 37 (1), 105–20.

Mansfield, Edward D. (1993) 'Concentration, Polarity, and the Distribution of Power'. *International Studies Quarterly*, 37 (1), 105–28.

March, James G., and Johan P. Olsen (1998) 'The Institutional Dynamics of International Political Orders'. *International Organization*, 52 (4), 943–69.

Mastanduno, Michael (1997) 'Preserving the Unipolar Moment: Realist Theories and US Grand Strategy After the Cold War'. *International Security*, 21 (4), 51–2.

Mastanduno, Michael (2002) 'Extraterritorial Sanctions: Managing "Hyper-Unilateralism" in U.S. Foreign Policy'. In Stewart Patrick and Shepard Forman (eds), *Multilateralism in U.S. Foreign Policy*. Boulder, CO: Lynne Rienner, 295–322.

Mastanduno, Michael, and Ethan B. Kapstein (1999) 'Realism and State Strategies After the Cold War'. In Ethan B. Kapstein and Michael Mastanduno (eds), *Unipolar Politics: Realism and State Strategies After the Cold War*. New York: Columbia University Press, 1–27.

Maull, Hanns W. (1990–1) 'Germany and Japan: The New Civilian Powers'. *Foreign Affairs*, 69 (5), 91–106.

Mayall, James (1990) *Nationalism and International Society*. Cambridge: Cambridge University Press.

Mayall, James (2000) *World Politics: Progress and its Limits*. Cambridge: Polity.

Mearsheimer, John J. (1990) 'Back to the Future: Instability in Europe after the Cold War'. *International Security*, 15 (1), 5–56.

Midlarsky, Manus, and Ted Hopf (1993) 'Polarity and International Stability'. *American Political Science Review*, 87 (1), 173–80.

Moravscik, Andrew (2002) 'Why Is U.S. Human Rights Policy So Unilateralist?'. In Stewart Patrick and Shepard Forman (eds), *Multilateralism in U.S. Foreign Policy*. Boulder, CO: Lynne Rienner, 345–76.

Morgenthau, Hans (1978) *Politics Among Nations*. New York: Alfred Knopf.

Mouritzen, Hans (1980) 'Selecting Explanatory Levels in International Politics: Evaluating a Set of Criteria'. *Cooperation and Conflict*, 15, 169–82.

Mouritzen, Hans (1997) 'Kenneth Waltz: A Critical Rationalist between International Politics and Foreign Policy'. In Iver B. Neumann and Ole Wæver (eds), *The Future of International Relations: Masters in the Making?* London: Routledge, 66–89.

Mouritzen, Hans (1998) *Theory and Reality of International Politics*. Aldershot: Ashgate.

Nau, Henry (2001) 'Why "The Rise and Fall of the Great Powers" Was Wrong'. *Review of International Studies*, 27 (4), 579–92.

Nau, Henry (2002) 'Alliance at Risk'. *The World Today*, May, 17–18.

Nogee, Joseph L. (1974) 'Polarity: An Ambiguous Concept'. *Orbis*, 18 (4), 1193–224.

Nye, Joseph S. (1992) 'What New World Order?'. *Foreign Affairs*, 71 (2), 83–96.

Nye, Joseph S. (2002) *The Paradox of American Power: Why the World's Only Superpower Can't Go It Alone*. Oxford: Oxford University Press.

Nye, Joseph S. (2002–3) 'Limits of American Power'. *Political Science Quarterly*, 117 (4), 545–59.

OECD (1998) *Open Markets Matter: The Benefits of Trade and Investment Liberalisation*. Paris: OECD.

O'Hanlon, Michael E., Susa E. Rice and James B. Steinberg (2002) 'The New National Security Strategy of Preemption'. *Policy Brief no. 113*. Washington, DC: Brookings Institution [8pp].

Olsen, Edward (2002) *US National Defense for the Twenty-First Century*. London: Frank Cass.

Oneal, John R., and Bruce Russett (1999) 'The Kantian Peace: The Pacific Benefits of Democracy, Interdependence and International Organizations, 1885–1992'. *World Politics*, 52 (1), 1–37.

Ortega, Martin (2003) 'The Achilles Heel of Transatlantic Relations'. In Gustav Lindstrom (ed.), *Shift or Rift: Assessing US–EU Relations After Iraq*. Paris: European Union Institute for Security Studies, 147–67.

Patrick, Stewart (2002) 'Multilateralism and its Discontents: The Causes and Consequences of U.S. Ambivalence'. In Stewart Patrick and Shepard Forman (eds), *Multilateralism in U.S. Foreign Policy*. Boulder, CO: Lynne Rienner, 1–44.

Posen, Barry R., and Andrew L. Ross (1996–7) 'Competing Visions for US Grand Strategy'. *International Security*, 21 (3), 5–53.

Prestowitz, Clyde P. (2003) *Rogue Nation: American Unilateralism and the Failure of Good Intentions*. New York: Basic Books.

Rabkin, Jeremy (2000) 'When Can America be Bound by International Law?'. In Gwyn Prins (ed.), *Understanding Unilateralism in American Foreign Relations*. London: RIIA, 106–25.

Ralph, Jason (2002) 'Good International Citizenship? An English School Analysis of American Policy Towards the International Criminal Court'. Paper presented to the BISA Conference, London, 16–18 December [21pp].

Reisman, W. Michael (1999–2000) 'The United States and International Institutions'. *Survival*, 41 (4), 62–80.

Rengger, Nicholas (1992) 'A City Which Sustains All Things? Communitarianism and International Society'. *Millennium*, 21 (3), 353–69.

Rengger, N. J. (2000) *International Relations, Political Theory and the Problem of Order*. London: Routledge.

Riker, William H. (1962) *The Theory of Political Coalitions*. New Haven, CT: Yale University Press.

Rosecrance, Richard N. (1969) 'Bipolarity, Multipolarity, and the Future'. In James N. Rosenau (ed.), *International Politics and Foreign Policy*. New York: Free Press, 324–35.

Rosecrance, Richard N. (1973) *International Relations: Peace or War*. New York: McGraw-Hill.

Rosecrance, Richard N. (1992) 'A New Concert of Powers'. *Foreign Affairs*, 71 (2), 64–82.

Rosecrance, Richard N., and Chih-Cheng Lo (1996) 'Balancing, Stability and War: The Mysterious Case of the Napoleonic International System'. *International Studies Quarterly*, 40 (4), 479–500.

Rosenau, James N. (1966): 'Pre-Theories and Theories of Foreign Policy'. In R. Barry Farrell (ed.), *Approaches to Comparative and International Politics*. Evanston, IL: Northwestern University Press, 27–92.

Ross, Robert S. (1999) 'The Geography of the Peace: East Asia in the Twenty-First Century'. *International Security*, 23 (4), 81–118.

Roy, Denny (1994) 'Hegemon on the Horizon? China's Threat to East Asian Security'. *International Security*, 19 (1), 149–68.

Ruggie, John Gerard (2003) 'American Exceptionalism, Exemptionalism and Global Governance'. In Michael Ignatieff (ed.), *American Exceptionalism and Human Rights*. Princeton, NJ: Princeton University Press.

Sabrosky, Alan Ned (ed.) (1985) *Polarity and War*. Boulder, CO: Westview Press.

Salter, Mark (2002) *Barbarians and Civilization in International Relations*. London: Pluto Press.

Schlesinger, Arthur M., Jr. (2000) 'Unilateralism in Historical Perspective'. In Gwyn Prins (ed.), *Understanding Unilateralism in American Foreign Relations*. London: RIIA, 18–29.

Scholte, Jan Aart (2000) *Globalization: A Critical Introduction*. Basingstoke: Macmillan.

Schweller, Randall L. (1993) 'Tripolarity and the Second World War'. *International Studies Quarterly*, 37 (1), 73–103.

Schweller, Randall L., and William C. Wohlforth (2000) 'Power Test: Evaluating Realism in Response to the End of the Cold War'. *Security Studies*, 9 (3), 60–107.

Segal, Gerald (1982) *The Great Power Triangle*. London: Macmillan.

Segal, Gerald (1988) 'As China Grows Strong'. *International Affairs*, 64 (2), 218–31.

Segal, Gerald (1999) 'Does China Matter?'. *Foreign Affairs*, 78 (5), 24–36.

Sen Gupta, Bhabani (1997) 'India in the Twenty-First Century'. *International Affairs*, 73 (2), 297–314.

Shambaugh, David (1994) 'Growing Strong: China's Challenge to Asian Security'. *Survival*, 36 (2), 43–59.

Sick, Gary (2002) 'Imperial Moment'. *The World Today*, 58 (12), 4–6.

Simon, Sheldon W. (1994) 'East Asian Security: The Playing Field has Changed'. *Asian Survey*, 34 (12), 1047–63.

Singer, J. David, Stuart Bremer and John Stuckey (1972) 'Capability Distribution, Uncertainty and Major Power War, 1820–1965'. In Bruce M. Russett (ed.), *Peace, War, and Numbers*. Beverly Hills, CA: Sage, 19–48.

Singer, Max, and Aaron Wildavsky (1993) *The Real World Order: Zones of Peace/ Zones of Turmoil*. Chatham, NJ: Chatham House Publishers.

Smith, Anthony D. (1991) *National Identity*. Harmondsworth: Penguin.

Smith, Steve (2002) 'The United States and the Discipline of International Relations: Hegemonic Country, Hegemonic Discipline'. *International Studies Review*, 4 (2), 67–85.

Smith, Steve, Ken Booth and Marysia Zalewski (eds) (1996) *International Theory: Positivism and Beyond*. Cambridge: Cambridge University Press.

Smithson, Amy E. (2002) 'The Chemical Weapons Convention'. In Stewart Patrick and Shepard Forman (eds), *Multilateralism in U.S. Foreign Policy*. Boulder, CO: Lynne Rienner, 247–65.

Soeya, Yoshihide (1998) 'Japan: Normative Constraints Versus Structural Imperatives'. In Muthiah Alagappa (ed.), *Asian Security Practice*. Stanford, CA: Stanford University Press, 198–233.

Sofka, James R. (2001) 'The Eighteenth Century International System: Parity or Primacy'. In Michael Cox, Tim Dunne and Ken Booth (eds), *Empires, Systems and States: Great Transformations in International Politics*. Cambridge: Cambridge University Press, 147–63.

Spiro, Peter J. (2000) 'The New Sovereigntists: American Exceptionalism and its False Prophets'. *Foreign Affairs*, 79 (6), 9–15.

Spruyt, Hendrik (1998) 'A New Architecture for Peace? Reconfiguring Japan among the Great Powers'. *Pacific Review*, 11 (3), 364–88.

Stokes, Bruce (1996) 'Divergent Paths: US–Japan Relations towards the Twenty-First Century'. *International Affairs*, 72 (2), 281–91.

Sutter, Robert (2002) 'China's Recent Approach to Asia: Seeking Long-Term Gains'. PacNet Newsletter, 23 (7 June). <http://www.csis.org/pacfor/pac0223.htm>.

Thomas, Raju C. G. (ed.) (1983) *The Great Power Triangle and Asian Security*. Lexington, MA: Lexington Books.

To, Lee Lai (1997) 'East Asian Assessments of China's Security Policy'. *International Affairs*, 73 (2), 251–63.

Twomey, Christopher P. (2000) 'Japan: A Circumscribed Balancer'. *Security Studies*, 9 (4), 167–205.

Van Ness, Peter (2002) 'Hegemony, Not Anarchy: Why China and Japan are Not Balancing US Unipolar Power'. *International Relations of the Asia-Pacific*, 2 (1), 131–50.

van Wolferen, Karel (1989) *The Enigma of Japanese Power*. London: Macmillan.

Wæver, Ole (1995) 'Securitization and Desecuritization'. In Ronnie D. Lipschutz (ed.), *On Security*. New York: Columbia University Press, 46–86.

Wæver, Ole (1996a) 'Europe's Three Empires: A Watsonian Interpretation of Post-Wall European Security'. In Rick Fawn and Jeremy Larkins (eds), *International Society After the Cold War: Anarchy and Order Reconsidered*. London: Macmillan & Millennium, 220–60.

Wæver, Ole (1996b) 'European Security Identities'. *Journal of Common Market Studies*, 34 (1), 103–32.

Wæver, Ole (1997) 'Imperial Metaphors: Emerging European Analogies to Pre-Nation State Imperial Systems'. In Ola Tunander, Pavel Baev and Victoria Ingrid Einagel (eds), *Geopolitics in Post-Wall Europe: Security, Territory, and Identity*. London: Sage, 59–93.

Wæver, Ole (1998) 'Security, Insecurity, and Asecurity in the West European Non-War Community'. In Emmanuel Adler and Michael Barnett (eds), *Security Communities*. Cambridge: Cambridge University Press, 69–118.

Wæver, Ole (2000) 'The EU as a Security Actor: Reflections from a Pessimistic Constructivist on Post-Sovereign Security Orders'. In Morten Kelstrup and Michael C. Williams (eds), *International Relations Theory and the Politics of European Integration: Power, Security and Community*. London: Routledge, 250–94.

Wagner, R. Harrison (1993) 'What was Bipolarity?'. *International Organization*, 47 (1), 77–106.

Walker, Martin (2000) 'Europe: Superstate or Superpower?'. *World Policy Journal*, 27 (4), 7–16.

Walt, Stephen M. (1987) *The Origins of Alliances*. Ithaca, NY: Cornell University Press.

Walton, C. Dale (1997) 'Europe United: The Rise of a Second Superpower and its Effect on World Order'. *European Security*, 6 (4), 44–54.

Waltz, Kenneth N. (1959) *Man, The State and War*. New York: Columbia University Press.

Waltz, Kenneth N. (1964) 'The Stability of a Bipolar World'. *Daedalus*, 93 (3), 881–909.

Waltz, Kenneth N. (1969) 'International Structure, National Force, and the Balance of World Power'. In James N. Rosenau (ed.), *International Politics and Foreign Policy*. New York: Free Press, 304–14.

Waltz, Kenneth N. (1979) *Theory of International Politics*. Reading, MA: Addison-Wesley.

Waltz, Kenneth N. (1986) 'Reflections on Theory of International Politics: A Response to my Critics'. In Robert O. Keohane (ed.), *Neorealism and its Critics*. New York: Columbia University Press, 322–45.

Waltz, Kenneth N. (1990) 'Realist Thought and Neorealist Theory'. *Journal of International Affairs*, 44 (1), 21–37.

Waltz, Kenneth N. (1993a) 'The Emerging Structure of International Politics'. *International Security*, 18 (2), 44–79.

Waltz, Kenneth N. (1993b) 'The New World Order'. *Millennium*, 22 (2), 187–95.

Waltz, Kenneth N. (2000) 'Structural Realism After the Cold War'. *International Security*, 25 (1), 5–41.

Watson, Adam (1992) *The Evolution of International Society*. London: Routledge.

Wayman, Frank W. (1984) 'Bipolarity and War: The Role of Capability Concentration and Alliance Patterns among Major Powers 1816–1965'. *Journal of Peace Research*, 21 (1), 61–78.

Wedgwood, Ruth (2002) 'Unilateral Action in a Multilateral World'. In Stewart Patrick and Shepard Forman (eds), *Multilateralism in U.S. Foreign Policy*. Boulder, CO: Lynne Rienner, 1–44.

Weller, Marc (2002) 'Undoing the Global Constitution: UN Security Council Action on the International Criminal Court'. *International Affairs*, 78 (4), 693–712.

Wendt, Alexander (1992) 'Anarchy is What States Make of it: The Social Construction of Power Politics'. *International Organization*, 46 (2), 391–425.

Wendt, Alexander (1999) *Social Theory of International Politics*. Cambridge: Cambridge University Press.

Wight, Martin (1977) *Systems of States*. Leicester: Leicester University Press.

Wight, Martin (1979) *Power Politics*. Harmondsworth: Penguin.

Wilkinson, David (1999) 'Unipolarity without Hegemony'. *International Studies Review*, 1 (2), 141–72.

Wohlforth, William C. (1999) 'The Stability of a Unipolar World'. *International Security*, 24 (1), 5–41.

Woods, Ngaire (ed.) (2000) *The Political Economy of Globalization*. Basingstoke: Macmillan.

WSRG [World Society Research Group] (2000) 'Introduction: World Society'. In Mathias Albert, Lothar Brock and Klaus Dieter Wolf (eds), *Civilizing World Politics: Society and Community Beyond the State*. Lanham, MD: Rowman & Littlefield, 1–17.

Wyatt-Walter, Andrew (1995) 'Regionalism, Globalism, and World Economic Order'. In Louise Fawcett and Andrew Hurrell (eds), *Regionalism in World Politics*. Oxford: Oxford University Press, 74–121.

Yahuda, Michael (2002) 'The Limits of Economic Interdependence: Sino-Japanese Relations'. Unpublished MS, LSE [13pp].

Zacher, Mark (1992) 'The Decaying Pillars of the Westphalian Temple'. In J. N. Rosenau and E.-O. Czempiel (eds), *Governance without Government: Order and Change in World Politics.* Cambridge: Cambridge University Press, 58–102.

Zhang, Yongjin (1998) *China in International Society Since 1949: Alienation and Beyond.* Basingstoke: Macmillan.

Zhang, Yongjin (2001) 'System, Empire and State in Chinese International Relations'. In Michael Cox, Tim Dunne and Ken Booth (eds), *Empires, Systems and States: Great Transformations in International Politics.* Cambridge: Cambridge University Press, 43–63.

Index